SPECTACULAR GIRLS

Spectacular Girls

Media Fascination and Celebrity Culture

Sarah Projansky

NEW YORK UNIVERSITY PRESS
New York and London

NEW YORK UNIVERSITY PRESS
New York and London
www.nyupress.org

References to Internet websites (URLs) were accurate at the time of writing.
Neither the author nor New York University Press is responsible for URLs that
may have expired or changed since the manuscript was prepared.

LIBRARY OF CONGRESS CATALOGING-IN-PUBLICATION DATA
Projansky, Sarah, 1965-
Spectacular girls : media fascination and celebrity culture / Sarah Projansky.
pages cm
Includes bibliographical references and index.
ISBN 978-0-8147-7021-4 (cl: alk. paper)
ISBN 978-0-8147-2481-1 (pbk : alk. paper)
1. Women in mass media. 2. Celebrities in mass media. 3. Mass media and girls. I. Title.
P96.W6P88 2014
302.230835'2—dc23
                          2013034205

New York University Press books are printed on acid-free paper,
and their binding materials are chosen for strength and durability.
We strive to use environmentally responsible suppliers and materials
to the greatest extent possible in publishing our books.

Manufactured in the United States of America

10 9 8 7 6 5 4 3 2 1

Also available as an ebook

In memory of Leah R. Vande Berg
mentor, scholar, friend

For Mina and Daniel

CONTENTS

ILLUSTRATIONS

ACKNOWLEDGMENTS

I have been working and publishing on the topic of girls and media culture for more than a decade; hence, I want to thank many more people than I have space to name here in these acknowledgments. The mentors, colleagues, research assistants, students, and conference and public talk audiences I have encountered over the years have been invaluable to me as I have explored this topic and figured out the shape this book would take.

I want to mention the early support Judith Newton and Rosa Linda Fregoso gave me as I navigated the path toward becoming a Women's and Gender Studies scholar and teacher committed to interdisciplinary and socially relevant work. I do not know if I would have pursued this topic without their encouragement and steadfast belief in me. Also early on, the late Leah R. Vande Berg shaped me as a teacher and a scholar. I will never forget the day I met her: she showed up for our meeting in a fabulous purple hat, embraced me without hesitation, and became an instant friend and mentor and later collaborator. Her unwavering faith in me made this book possible. At the University of Illinois, Angharad Valdivia, C. L. Cole, and Leslie Reagan proved equally supportive as friends, mentors, and collaborators. Anghy's insights about girls' studies both in print and in conversation have deeply shaped this book. Cole's energy and readiness to try something new have both inspired me and pushed me forward. Leslie's fierce feminist scholarship and practical life advice kept me going and fed my soul. Also at Illinois, Ruth Nicole Brown and Eric McDuffie were two of the best colleagues anyone could ever hope to have. Their generosity and critical acumen inspired and supported me during the years we worked together. Additionally, Joan Chan—first my student, then my research assistant, and now a lifelong friend—has influenced this book deeply, not only because she helped uncover innumerable resources over the years, but also because she always looked me in the eye and asked just the right question to make me understand a problem from a new perspective. In addition, Crystal Dinwiddie, Amy Hasinoff, Adam Mann, and Amber Buck served as research assistants at key stages of the project; I could not have finished without their impeccable research skills. I also want to thank my new Film and Media Arts, Gender Studies, and Communication colleagues at the University of Utah, all of whom have been supportive and welcoming.

While I cannot name her here (in order to protect anonymity) I want to thank the public school teacher who opened her classroom to me and worked with me to develop the media project I discuss in chapter 6. She is one of the absolute best teachers I have ever known, and I am incredibly lucky to have learned from her. As well, the students in her classroom gave enthusiastically of their time and energy. I want to thank each and every one of them for sharing their insights about media with me.

This book has been supported by generous grants from the University of Illinois Research Board and the Illinois Program for Research in the Humanities, for which I am grateful. At New York University Press, Eric Zinner, Ciara McLaughlin, Alicia Nadkarni, Dorothea Halliday, and Nicholas Taylor have been hugely helpful and supportive. I very much appreciate their ability to combine high standards with kind patience. I also want to thank Yoshitomo Nara for sharing his striking artwork, which appears on the cover of this book. As well, the anonymous reviewers provided insightful and detailed suggestions for revision. Because they were anonymous, I cannot thank them by name, but I want them to know just how much they helped me think through my ideas, develop my argument, and sharpen my thinking while writing the book. As a result of their efforts, the book is much better than it would have been, and I thank them for that.

Many girls' studies and media studies scholars have inspired me, many of whom I cite in this book. In particular, I would like to thank Sarah Banet-Weiser, Ruth Nicole Brown, Peter X. Feng, Derek Johnson, Mary Celeste Kearney, Angela McRobbie, Diane Negra, Hilary Radner, Timothy Shary, Yvonne Tasker, and Paula Treichler for their outstanding and inspirational scholarship and for their support of me and my work.

My family has been a constant source of strength. My parents (Joette Warren, Arnold Projansky, and Dolores Projansky), my siblings and their partners (Anita, Harvey, Daniel, Diana, Rachel, Ben, and Lori), and my nieces and nephew (Leila, Josh, Nora, Sonia, and Nikita) have all tolerated what I know seemed to them to be endless work on my book.

In addition, my sister Rachel, a public school teacher, generously read a draft of chapter 6, challenging me to think carefully about my claims and the meaning and purpose of elementary school education. My brother Daniel and sister-in-law Diana, through conversations about their approaches to working in children's media, helped me think more carefully about the complexity of the media industry. And at the very end, my mother took time out of her vacation and her busy life to read every word of the book twice, making sure everything was just right. I am sure any typos that slipped through were inserted after she read the manuscript. I thank all of my family for their unwavering love and support.

There is no way I can fully express my deep appreciation for my life partner, Kent Ono. An intellectual sounding board, careful editor, inspirational scholar, and loving partner and co-parent, he has been only patient and supportive through the entire process of writing this book, whether he was reading drafts, talking through my ideas, caring for our children while I worked, encouraging me to take a nap, or cooking dinner. He and I research and publish very differently, and yet he has only ever supported me in my own endeavors. To have a loving life partner who is also a supportive and challenging intellectual partner is a gift I am grateful for every day of my life. Finally, my children, Mina and Daniel, have been patient even when they did not want to be, have loved me even when I was not around enough, and have taken seriously my commitment to finishing this project. Through the example of how they live their lives, they have each challenged me to think carefully and more fully about the complexity of the intersection of youth and gender. This book is for them.

Introduction

Finding Alternative Girlhoods

> As the 21st century picks up speed and settles into place,
> childhood has become a spectacle—a site of accumulation
> and commodification—in whose name much is done.
> —Cindi Katz, "Childhood as Spectacle"

All girls are spectacular. I take this as a given. I consider it to be a feminist claim. Nevertheless, contemporary U.S. media tell us otherwise. Hence, I start with this assertion to remind myself and my readers that it is possible to believe this to be true. In media, some girls are fabulous, others are not; some girls' stories are worth telling over and over again; others warrant telling only in passing or not at all. Girls who are large, differently abled, queer, of color, and/or poor; make "bad" or "dangerous" choices; feel depressed; or even just act silly (1) simply do not exist in media culture; or (2) appear in marginalized representations, on the periphery, with sidekick status; or (3) populate ubiquitous disparaging, disdainful, anxious, and/or protectionist depictions that shore up a narrow version of acceptable girlhood: the impossibly high-achieving heterosexual white girl who plays sports, loves science, is gorgeous but not hyper-sexual, is fit but not too thin, learns from her (minor) mistakes, and certainly will change the world someday.

This book is, in part, about the ways in which media produce some girls as spectacular while belittling others. Its primary investment, however, is in paying sustained analytical attention to the many girls who fall outside a narrow definition of conventional girlhood. Working as a feminist media scholar committed to fighting racism and affirming queerness and LGBTQ identities, in this book I rethink what "spectacular" means and redefine which girls count in that context. Thus this book is about high-profile girls who may illustrate the media's process of marginalization, but who also open up multiple, complex, multilayered, and/or contradictory versions of girlhood, right at the heart of media culture. These alternative girls, too, are spectacular.

Since approximately 1990, girls have appeared often and everywhere in U.S. media culture. Girl celebrities, characters, and products abound in film, television, print, sports, and music and on the Internet, appearing repeatedly in the mediascape. These girls and products include a dizzying number of examples: Selena Gomez, Raven-Symoné, Bratz, Amélie Mauresmo, Dominique Dawes, *Whale Rider* (2002), Kai-Lan, Miley Cyrus, Hannah Montana, Mary-Kate and Ashley Olsen, Michelle Wie, Jackie Evancho, Lindsay Lohan, Britney Spears, *Pretty Little Liars* (2010–present), Bella, Dora, Lizzie McGuire, Katniss, Tia and Tamera Mowry, Miranda Cosgrove, China Anne McClain, Buffy, Willow, Sabrina, Kim Possible, Brenda Song, Bristol Palin, Hermione, *Teen Vogue*, Lilo, "I Kissed a Girl," Taylor Swift, and Gabby Douglas, to name a few. Concomitantly, media are fascinated with everyday girls, both girls who achieve temporary and "accidental"[1] celebrity status (i.e., "fifteen minutes of fame") and generic categories of girls. These many girls include Caylee Anthony, JonBenét Ramsey, Jessica Dubroff, Honey Boo Boo/Alana Thompson, mean girls, gamma girls, Ophelias, AMBER Alerts, Girls Gone Mild, teen moms, Lolitas, Nike "If You Let Me Play" girls, tween girls, Jamie Keiles of the Seventeen Magazine Project, Tavi Gevinson of TheStyleRookie.com, and Gaby Rodriguez of the Pregnancy Project (again, to name only a few).

Anita Harris argues two types of girls dominate in contemporary media and political culture: the can-do girl who is "confident, resilient, and empowered," and the at-risk girl who "lack[s] self esteem"[2] and/or engages in risky behavior. The can-do girl is a successful athlete. The at-risk girl is a pregnant teen. The can-do girl is independent and confident. The at-risk girl is depressed. The can-do girl is beautiful and fit. The at-risk girl is hyper-sexualized at too young an age. The can-do girl is smart. The at-risk girl uses drugs and has unprotected sex. The can-do girl has girl power. The at-risk girl lacks resources. The can-do girl reads *The Sisterhood of the Traveling Pants* and *The Hunger Games*.

Figure I.1. Gabby Douglas appears on the cover of *Time* in celebration of the 2012 Summer Olympics, July 30, 2012.

The at-risk girl sexts. In short, the can-do girl has the world at her feet, while the at-risk girl "loses her voice."[3]

As Marnina Gonick argues, these two narratives circulate simultaneously in contemporary media culture, and in fact support each other. Specifically, the at-risk narrative "acts as a warning to all young women that failure is an ever-lurking possibility that must be staved off through sustained application."[4] The can-do girl must be vigilant, lest she become at-risk. Harris illustrates that this vigilance includes a neoliberal approach to work/career (emphasizing flexibility and personal responsibility), as well as an investment in consumer culture designed to incessantly groom the ideal can-do body and personality. When thinking about high-profile girl celebrities in the media, perhaps the best example of the interaction of the can-do and at-risk narratives is what others call the "trainwreck" female celebrity[5] or the "celebrity meltdown,"[6] and I call the "crash-and-burn" girl: the can-do girl who has it all, but who—through weakness and/or the inability to live with the pressure of celebrity during the process of growing up—makes a mistake and therefore faces a spectacular descent into at-risk status. Jennifer Capriati, Britney Spears, Lindsay Lohan, Keisha Castle-Hughes, Jamie Lynn Spears, and Demi Lovato come to mind.[7] Both the can-do/at-risk dichotomy and the media obsession with the crash-and-burn girl celebrity illustrate a concomitant love *and* contempt for girls. These are representations I call ambivalent, following Homi Bhabha, because of their anxious repetition of both fetishistic desire and phobic derision.[8]

This conjoined ambivalent can-do/at-risk narrative authorizes the surveillance and discipline not only of high-profile celebrities, but also of everyday girls.[9] One form of surveillance is protectionist, coalescing in a moral panic about the threat to all girls of at-risk status, epitomized by Mary Pipher's 1994 *Reviving Ophelia: Saving the Selves of Adolescent Girls* and continuing to the present day in newspaper articles such as "Little Girls Are Made of Sugar—Not Spice: Parents Decry Marketers Who Push Sexuality";[10] the most recently released save-your-daughter-from-the-media mass-market books, *Cinderella Ate My Daughter*[11] and *Princess Recovery*;[12] and the 2012 documentary *Sexy Baby*.[13] As is typical of moral panics, this one—spread in large part through media—holds media themselves responsible for the threat to girls.[14] Here, what I call the "Ophelia Thesis" (chapter 6) assumes that media depictions of hyper-sexualized girls lead to decreased self-esteem and potentially poor choices to put one's own body on display or engage in early sexual activity. Yet, in the process of "reporting" on and worrying about this, media further perpetuate the at-risk narrative, reproducing and reifying images of girls as hyper-sexualized and miserable. In short, media contribute to the creation of the at-risk narrative, produce a moral panic about the girl figure at the center of that narrative, and then—through the process of worrying—perpetuate the very depictions of girls about which they worry. Analogous to Michel Foucault's "repressive hypothesis" about Victorian sexuality,[15] the contemporary moral panic about the at-risk girl perpetuates—rather than helps to overcome—the discursive condition of her existence. As Angela McRobbie and Sarah Thonton put it, "Moral panics seem to have become a goal."[16]

While this moral panic about the at-risk girl is strong in turn-of-the-twenty-first-century media culture,[17] celebration of the can-do girl is equally common. This version of girlhood is a fantasy promise that if girls work hard, not only can they avoid becoming at-risk, but they can achieve anything. Particularly in neoliberal consumer culture, this narrative promises unbelievable happiness and achievement—girl power—for the girl who embodies can-do status through career, fashion, and lifestyle choices. While the moral panic depictions of the at-risk girl are paradoxical (in that they contribute to the production of the very thing about which they worry), the girl power depictions of the can-do girl are more straightforward: they provide superhuman television heroes such as True Jackson (who is skilled enough as a teenager to help run a major fashion magazine) and Buffy (who slays vampires and eventually saves the world for the Buffy in every girl), and they market products by suggesting that girls can express and maintain their can-do status through consumer choices.

In this book, I argue that collectively these media depictions illustrate the spectacularization of girls in turn-of-the-twenty-first-century media culture. By this, I mean several things. First, media incessantly look at and invite us to look at girls. Girls are objects at which we gaze, whether we want to or not. They are everywhere in our mediascapes. As such, media turn girls into spectacles—*visual objects on display*.[18] Second, some mediated girls are also spectacular, as in *fabulous*. The can-do girls' achievements, athletic abilities, intelligence, and self-confidence dazzle. Third, some girls are spectacles, or *scandals*. Media wait with bated breath—paparazzi seek out and produce—the moment of a celebrity girl's fall.[19] Politicians and pundits worry about teen pregnancy, sexting, and online pedophiles. Sociologists and psychologists identify problems supposedly particular to girls, such as eating disorders, lack of self-esteem, and mean girl behavior. Journalists and parents worry about the hyper-sexualization of girls in media depictions and fashion trends. All this is part of the spectacularization of girlhood in turn-of-the-twenty-first-century media culture: the discursive production and social regulation of the girl as a fabulous and/or scandalous object on display.

The spectacularization of girlhood, I argue, takes place within celebrity culture. Of course, the fact of celebrity is not new: scholars trace celebrity back not by decades but by centuries.[20] Nevertheless, the recent growth of celebrity studies as a field, perhaps best illustrated by the new journal *Celebrity Studies* (2010–present), makes clear that "in the current environment where images and clips circulate freely, repetitively, and non-sequentially" there is an "intensification" of celebrity.[21] As Graeme Turner argues, "It is the pervasiveness of celebrity culture that marks out the contemporary version."[22] Given that media's fascination with celebrities and girls is intensifying simultaneously, and given that discourses of girlhood and celebrity are both about individualism and identity,[23] it is crucial that we explore how celebrity and girlhood depend on and affect each other. If, as Su Holmes and Sean Redmond argue, celebrity "characterizes the dominant way in which people are made legible in the public sphere,"[24] then it follows that media depictions of all girls (not just "actual" celebrities) are made legible through discourses of celebrity, including the spectacularization of identity. And, if as Turner argues, "in a highly convergent media environment, where cross-media and cross-platform content and promotion has become increasingly the norm, the manufacture of and trade in celebrity has become a commercial strategy for media organizations of all kinds,"[25] it follows that the girl celebrity plays a key role in the marketing of, for example, magazines (chapter 2), films (chapter 3), sports (chapter 4), and Disney and Nickelodeon as both cable channels and brands (see below).

Despite the link I draw here between spectacular girls and celebrity culture, I do not use "spectacle" and "celebrity" as synonyms. Rather, I argue that spectacularization is a discursive and economic strategy of turn-of-the-twenty-first-century celebrity culture easily applied to girls.

To say that media spectacularize girls in celebrity culture is to emphasize the intense publicness of contemporary girlhood: the way in which girls are readily available to us, similar to the way every aspect of a celebrity's life is fair game for discussion, evaluation, and consumption. In thinking about girls in relation to celebrity culture, then, I am interested not only in individual girl celebrities, but also in how analysis of the spectacularization of girls can help us better understand how both celebrity culture and public girlhoods function. I begin this discussion in chapter 1, where I argue girl stars can be understood to epitomize the sexualized scandal at the heart of the star/celebrity system, and I continue to address it in relation to celebrities on magazine covers (chapter 2), girl stars in prominent films about girls (chapter 3), girl sports celebrities (chapter 4), the tragedy of a girl made famous by her death (chapter 5), and the complex perspective some everyday girls take on Selena Gomez as an ethnically ambiguous Disney girl celebrity (chapter 6). Each chapter, then, is in part a case study through which to explore the relationship between girls and celebrity, and the book as a whole illustrates how central girls are to celebrity culture.

While I argue that all girls are spectacularized within the context of celebrity culture, a central goal of this book is to insist that not all girls are spectacularized in the same way. Specifically, throughout the book I emphasize the varying racializations, genderings, and sexualities of spectacular girlhood. As many scholars have shown, the can-do girl is usually white, while the African American or Latina girl is usually at-risk. The everyday gamma girl is generally white, but the pregnant teen is almost always Latina or African American.[26] Exceptions prove the rule or imply "race-blindness": for example, Amy's status as a special white pregnant girl and then teen mom in *The Secret Life of the American Teenager* (2008–2013). And narratives in which can-do celebrity girls of color do appear rarely address racial specificity or racialization; thus they offer a color-blind ideology in children's culture that, as Sarah Turner argues, can reinscribe and reify whiteness: for example, China Anne McClain in *A.N.T. Farm* (2011–present).[27] Additionally, regardless of whether they are can-do or at-risk, the majority of girls in media culture simply are white. The celebrities who crash and burn are white. The central characters in most films and television shows about girls are white. As I explore in chapter 2, the girls who appear most often on the cover of mass-market magazines such as *Time, Newsweek,* and *People* are white. Girl gymnasts and figure skaters are white (the few girls of color—e.g., Michelle Kwan and Gabby Douglas—again, either prove the rule, promise race-blindness, or both). The "lost girl"—kidnapped or dead before her time—over whom media culture incessantly worries, is white.[28] As the African American girls whom Lisa Duke interviewed for her study of girls' use of teen magazines succinctly articulate, media offer a "blonde world."[29] Richard Dyer famously has written that whiteness is "everything and nothing": its "representational power" comes from its capacity to be everywhere but always remain unnamed.[30] Certainly, this property of whiteness operates in and through representations of girls in contemporary U.S. media culture. Just as certainly, though, girls of color do appear. A central project of this book, then, is to take seriously the complexity of their representation, to ask, as Rebecca Wanzo does about African American women, "Can this privileging of whiteness be circumvented? Under what conditions can a body of color become iconographic" or spectacular?[31]

Gender and sexuality, too, operate in and through representations of girls in media culture. Femininity and heteronormativity pervade the moral panic about girls sexualized too soon, just as they do many of the products marketed to the can-do girl in pursuit of both personal success and romance. Yet queer girls are present. Kathryn Stockton claims, "If you scratch a child, you will find a queer, in the sense of someone 'gay' or just plain strange."[32] For Stockton, the child is always queer because it is "'not-yet-straight,' since it . . . is not allowed to be sexual." In other words, if the child is not straight, it is queer. Drawing on Stockton, then, I would argue for the importance of "includ[ing] the 'normative' child" (or, for my purposes, the normative girl) as one of many possible "queer companions" of the more literal "gay child"/gay girl.[33] Hence I discuss explicit queer girlhood articulated through girls' own voices and/or actions, such as Amélie Mauresmo's (chapter 4) and Sakia Gunn's (chapter 5) self-presentation as LGBTQ; but I also address girls who emerge as queer through interpretive analytical practice. From this perspective, I read "mean girls" as queer because by definition they include an implicit critique of heteronormativity (chapter 3), and I read seven-year-old pilot Jessica Dubroff as queer (chapter 2). Appearing on the cover of both *Time* and *People* in a bomber jacket and baseball cap, Dubroff reads as what Judith Halberstam calls a "rogue tomboy," a tomboy who is not just (or even particularly) interested in being active ("like boys") and remaining a child just a little bit longer by resisting adulthood, but who more forcefully turns away from femininity and in fact toward an adult masculine persona: here, that of the pilot.[34]

In short, working as a feminist media scholar, I acknowledge the dominance of whiteness, femininity, heteronormativity, and their relationship to the can-do/at-risk dichotomy, but like Wanzo and Stockton I am uninterested in centering these girlhoods. Rather, this book spends the most time with girls who fall outside of or alter (sometimes ever so slightly) this dichotomy and/or who do not read as white and/ or heteronormative.[35] These girls include Tatum O'Neal, the least discussed but arguably queerest mega girl star from the 1970s (chapter 1); girls of color and queer girls who appear on the cover of mass magazines not as frequently as, but nevertheless alongside, the many can-do/ at-risk heteronormative white girls that populate these covers (chapter 2); the girl characters and stars from girl films of the last decade that led to sustained public debate over girls, including debate about the relationship between girls and feminism (*Mean Girls*/Lindsay Lohan, *Little Miss Sunshine*/Abigail Breslin, *Juno*/Ellen Page, and *Precious*/Gabourey Sidibe) (chapter 3); Venus Williams as a key teen tennis queen of the late 1990s who helped shift the meaning of "girl athlete" in racialized and politicized ways (chapter 4); Sakia Gunn, an African American lesbian/AG (aggressive) from Newark who was killed in a bias crime highly publicized not by the mainstream national press but by the local and alternative press (chapter 5); and, finally, ordinary and yet highly analytical third-grade girl media critics who were kind enough to work with me on a media project (chapter 6).

In each chapter, I engage various feminist media studies methodologies to seek out girls who do not simply perpetuate a can-do/at-risk dialectic. Whether I call these girls alternative, nonnormative, or—as other scholars have—"the body that was not [of concern],"[36] the "BBFF [black best friend forever],"[37] or "unloveable subjects,"[38] these girls are part of the contemporary mediascape of girlhood. To identify a dominant representation and then focus all one's analytical attention there—as much girls' media studies scholarship does[39]—is, at least in part, to reify that dominance. Instead, in this book I use my analysis and choice of topics and texts to refuse a monolithic definition of "dominant" or "mainstream." By paying attention to the variety of girlhoods available across many contemporary U.S. media forms, and by (as I call it in chapter 3) pushing back against the texts, I offer an optic that makes alternative versions of girlhood visible—when we choose to look for and toward them. Many scholars working in queer and/or Asian American media studies engage related methodologies. These scholars find resistant and pleasurable meanings in what they often acknowledge might otherwise be defined as racist and sexist texts[40] by focusing on stars (e.g., Nancy Kwan,[41] Marlene Dietrich and Greta Garbo,[42] Keanu Reeves[43]), or by "constructing an entirely separate narrative from scavenged bits and pieces of a film,"[44] or by refusing what Dyer calls the "climb-down [narrative] resolutions"[45] that deny the complexity and possibilities in the middle of the story. These are the kinds of reading practices Alexander Doty famously called "making things perfectly queer"[46] and Christine Geraghty recently argued can produce an "oh!" response when one pursues the "internally heterogeneous" nature of a text.[47] Sharing these scholars' critical investment in the politicized complexity of meaning making in and through media texts, in this book I use feminist analysis to shift the terrain, to rewrite who counts as spectacular in the mediascape of girlhood.

This book asks: What are the girlhoods in contemporary U.S. media culture that do not oscillate between can-do and at-risk, between cultural adoration and disdain? What other ways of understanding girlhood are possible in and through turn-of-the-twenty-first-century U.S. media culture? How can we use antiracist, queer, feminist girls' media criticism to upend—rather than to reify—the white heteronormativity that undergirds the can-do/at-risk dichotomy? And how can we use criticism to broaden and multiply the versions of girlhood visible in media culture? While I have already included many examples of queer girls and/or girls of color in this introduction, I know these are not necessarily the names that appear most frequently in public discussions of girls. For example, I know some of my readers may not recognize the name Brenda Song,[48] may not think of Raven-Symoné[49] as a key girl celebrity, and may not think of Willow along with Buffy as a version of girlhood offered by *Buffy the Vampire Slayer* (1997–2003). Yet I also assume (and hope) that some of my readers will have already noticed and appreciated that I include girls of color and/or queer girls in my initial overview of girls in contemporary media culture. By including these diverse girls in the very first pages of this book I mean to draw attention to and take seriously the presence of *alternative girls within the center*, to write the field of girlhood in a way that *sees their presence*. In short, this book offers a critical girls' media studies perspective and methodology in pursuit of alternative girls.

The Ubiquity of Girls, 1990–Present

Arguably, there are at least two reasons for the dramatic increase in U.S. media depictions of girls since the early 1990s. First, the mediated girl was already present and therefore easily available to address contemporary issues. As many scholars have shown, girls have appeared in U.S. media culture repeatedly over the past two centuries in ways that work through cultural anxieties about any number of social issues. For example, in the nineteenth and early twentieth century, black children, both girls and boys, appeared as "stereotypical . . . pickaninnies" in advertisements that worked to "portray blacks as happy and nonthreatening," and thereby helped to maintain racism as an institution and segregation as a system of enforced inequality.[50] In the early part of the twentieth century, public debates about age-of-consent laws and girls' sexual delinquency articulated anxiety about immigration and girls' and women's roles in the public sphere.[51] And in the 1950s the figure of the teenage bobby-soxer—a girl who wrought havoc at home yet strove toward heteronormative romance—appeared as incomprehensible, yet nevertheless fascinating, to adults. In particular, her engagement with consumer culture and the way she refigured the gendered structure of the family helped transform the postwar citizen–subject.[52]

Now, at the turn of the twenty-first century, the convenient figure of the girl—already adept at standing in for various social concerns—surfaces once again to work through contemporary social issues, such as, I would argue, neoliberalism and postfeminism.[53] Harris argues that the contemporary girl functions as an idealized citizen for the neoliberal global economy: a flexible, adaptable, pliant, enthusiastic, intelligent, and energetic participant in commodity consumption, personal responsibility, and mobile work. Hence, we can understand the current attention to girls as one way that media culture comes to terms with

neoliberalism. And, as I have argued elsewhere, contemporary spectacular girls are part of the evolution of postfeminism.[54] As the literal and
figurative daughter of postfeminists, the current girl inherits the desire
to "have it all," while embracing (unlike her mother, with no angst)
both girl power independence and persistent commodity consumption
that puts her sexualized body and her self on display. Hence the current
fascination with the girl both produces a moderate transformation of
hugely successful postfeminist discourse and is a cultural tool to make
sense of contemporary gendered and neoliberal politics.

Second, the ubiquity of girls in turn-of-the-twenty-first-century
media culture can be explained by their strategic usefulness to media
industries seeking to adapt to and capitalize on rapid technological
change. In the early 1990s, after cable television was deregulated and the
industry engaged in a massive push to bring cable to all U.S. households,
Nickelodeon sought to find a niche, opening its own studio in 1990. As
Sarah Banet-Weiser argues, through its hugely successful show *Clarissa
Explains It All* (1991–1994), the channel "discovered" that—contrary to
traditional industry assumptions—boys will watch shows about girls.[55]
The channel then became known as a champion of girl characters when
it followed *Clarissa* with *The Secret World of Alex Mack* (1994–1998),
The Mystery Files of Shelby Woo (1996–1998), *As Told by Ginger* (2000–
2009), *Dora the Explorer* (2000–present), *Taina* (2001–2002), *Zoey 101*
(2005–2008), *Just for Kicks* (2006), *Ni Hao, Kai-Lan* (2007–2009), *iCarly*
(2007–2012), *True Jackson, VP* (2008–2011), and *Victorious* (2010–2013).
Also in the early 1990s, Disney shifted from a premium pay channel
to a basic cable channel, and soon followed Nickelodeon's lead, pro-
gramming shows such as *Lizzie McGuire* (2001–2004), *Kim Possible*
(2002–2007), *That's So Raven* (2003–2007), *Hannah Montana* (2006–
2011), *Wizards of Waverly Place* (2007–2012), *Sonny with a Chance*
(2009–2011), *Good Luck Charlie* (2010–present), *Jesse* (2011–present),
and *A.N.T. Farm* (2011–present). It is important to point out that during
these decades both Nickelodeon and Disney aired many more shows
centering boys than those centering girls. Nevertheless, both conglomerates are known as supporters of girls and girl power, because many of
their most successful and well-known shows feature girls, and because
both produce multimedia girl celebrities. These celebrities exist well
beyond their shows, ensuring that even if someone does not watch

Hannah Montana or *Wizards of Waverly Place* or listen to Miley Cyrus's or Selena Gomez's music, they still know who these girls are.

Television, of course, was not the only media industry going through rapid change in the late twentieth century. The mass magazine industry shifted more and more toward market segmentation during this time, producing a number of magazines aimed at teen girls, including *Sassy* (1988–1996), *Cosmo Girl* (1999–2009), *Elle Girl* (2001–2006), and *Teen Vogue* (2003–present). And, as the Internet grew, many websites linked to the television shows and magazines I list here emerged, along with innumerable other sites that market products and/or empowerment to girls.[56] In short, developments in technology, related shifts in industry structure and targeted marketing,[57] and the proliferation of media platforms drew on and contributed to a growing cultural obsession with girls. Representations of girls, then, can be seen as playing a key role in cultural, social, economic, technological, and industrial shifts taking place at the turn of the twenty-first century.

Feminist Girls' Media Studies

Spectacular Girls fits within an area of thought at the intersection of feminist studies and media studies, what I call "feminist girls' media studies": feminist scholarship (however the author defines her/his feminism) that focuses on the relationship between girls and media. This research has been steadily increasing over the last two decades, so much so that beginning in 2007 overview essays within media studies began to appear in which authors define and tell the history of "girls' studies." Since 2007, at least ten of these overview essays have been published.[58] While each overview makes a unique contribution, here I briefly summarize the collective historical narrative they tell.

Most of these essays mention two 1970s/early-1980s foremothers of the field of girls' studies: Carol Gilligan and Angela McRobbie. Gilligan, working in the context of psychology and philosophy, gives us two central ideas: (1) girls have a "different voice," based in relationality rather than individuality, and (2) that voice faces the threat of loss as girls enter adulthood and are socialized as women.[59] This is an argument contemporary moral panic books often "misconstru[e]"[60] in order to build a case for the surveillance and protection of girls.[61] McRobbie, working in the context of both cultural studies and youth studies, challenges her fields for their lack of attention to girls and initiates a study of girls' complex relationships to media. Combining critical analysis of media representations with a nuanced understanding of girls' negotiations with media culture, McRobbie insists that girls and girl cultures matter; and she provides a model of scholarship that maintains a feminist investment in social justice and criticism of media industry structures, while also taking girls, their activities, and their pleasures seriously.[62]

Despite the influence of both Gilligan and McRobbie, the overview essays argue that in the 1980s feminist studies ignored girls, focusing instead on "equality" and explicitly distancing women from girls by criticizing the infantilization of women as girls. By the 1990s and into the twenty-first century, however, work on girls increased exponentially,[63] including multiple books, innumerable articles, special issues of journals,[64] the new *Journal of Girlhood Studies* (2008–present), onetime conferences,[65] professional associations,[66] and university certificates and minors.[67] There is now even a textbook.[68] This work comes out of many disciplines, including psychology, sociology, education, criminology, literary studies, history, communication, and media studies.

The overview essays argue that this increased scholarly attention to girls responds to the cultural moment of the early 1990s in which—as I spell out above—girls became a constant topic for discussion. In particular, the overviews mention anxiety texts that articulate at-risk girlhoods, such as Pipher's *Reviving Ophelia* and Roselind Wiseman's 2002 *Queen Bees and Wannabees: Helping Your Daughter Survive Cliques, Gossip, Boyfriends, and the New Realities of the Girl World*, as well as the rise in girl power figures, such as Rory of *Gilmore Girls* (2000–2007).[69] The essays claim girls' studies scholars working in psychology and sociology tend to follow Gilligan and emphasize the "girls in crisis" version of girlhood, producing reports such as the American Association of University Women's "How Schools Shortchange Girls" and the "Report of the APA Task Force on the Sexualization of Girls." Scholars working in communication, cultural, and media studies more often follow McRobbie and emphasize the girl power version of girlhood by (1) focusing on media representations of powerful girls (arguments either for resistant potential or against co-optation),[70] (2) listening to girls' voices (audience ethnographies),[71] or (3) defining girls as producers of culture (e.g., zines, video).[72]

After telling this girls' studies history, most of the overview essays make calls for future research: more listening to girls' voices, a greater attention to race and sexual diversity, an increased focus on political/economic/educational issues, less focus on "girls as victims," and more attention to "everyday girls." In other words, as I do here in this introduction, they call for a shift away from a focus on media culture's simultaneous adoration of and disdain for girls. Yet there is already a large body of work that goes beyond the can-do/at-risk dichotomy. In particular, there are two types of scholarship I include in my definition of feminist girls' media studies and draw on in this book, but which these overviews tend not to mention: ethnographies and public and social policy scholarship. Perhaps not coincidentally, this work also tends to center race and/or queer issues.

Ethnographies and work on everyday girls that address, at least in part, the role media play in girls' everyday lives (as opposed to girls' media production—an area well covered by the overviews), include *Not Our Kind of Girl: Unraveling the Myths of Black Teenage Motherhood*, in which Elaine Bell Kaplan addresses teen mothers' difficulties with the educational system and fraught relationships with men, made more difficult by media representations of teenage mothers as irresponsible and isolated from men and sexuality altogether. And Meenakshi Gigi Durham complicates our understanding of "girls' media" by asking how Indian American girls use mainstream, Indian, and diaspora media in different ways, and by paying attention to how the girls she interviews define the differences among their own, their parents', and their non-Indian friends' understandings of ideas about girls, gender, and sexuality in media.[73] This kind of ethnographic scholarship takes seriously the complex and varied roles media play in girls' everyday lives.

Girls' studies work on public and social policy can contribute to (re)definitions of girls and media as well. For example, in *Beyond Bad Girls: Gender, Violence, and Hype*, feminist criminologists Meda Chesney-Lind and Katherine Irwin look carefully at the interrelationship between (1) media images of violent girls (which tend to be "gang" girls of color in the late 1980s/early-1990s) and mean girls (which tend to be white middle-class girls in the late 1990s/early-2000s), and (2) the racial demographics in a recent increase in the criminalization and incarceration of girls. Through this comparison of media representations and criminal statistics, they find that the ideas of violent girls and mean girls, as well as highly publicized individual instances of school violence (e.g., Columbine), led to new school programs (e.g., "zero tolerance") that have the effect of regulating and punishing girls rather than supporting and protecting them—and, further, that these policies have a disproportional impact on girls of color. In *Black Girlhood Celebration: Toward a Hip-Hop Feminist Pedagogy*, Ruth Nicole Brown discusses her work to build a very specific and local space for black girls: SOLHOT (Saving Our Lives Hear Our Truths). In her book, Brown challenges the meaning of "girl" by pointing out that institutions, policies, after-school programs, and media culture all have narratives about the "black girl" that conflict with—but also deeply influence—black girls' everyday lived realities. For example, she points out that empowerment programs designed to give black girls "voice" contribute to (as much as respond to) media representations of black girls as endangered because the emphasis on empowerment means that the multiple ways in which black girls already speak (and the multiple things they already say) are defined as "loud" and "hyper-visible," but not as worth listening to, meaningful, or knowledgeable. SOLHOT and the theory Brown offers work against this representation of black girlhood by imagining a different space that centers girls, not as adults imagine they "should" be, but as they are.

By discussing this work in ethnography and public and social policy, my goal is to broaden the definition of feminist girls' media studies and to challenge the hegemony of moral panic/cultural obsession both in media culture and in some girls' studies work within media studies. My explicit method here is much like Angharad N. Valdivia's when she, in a few short pages, cites a great deal of recent scholarship on Latina girls and thereby illustrates the myopia of some girls' studies scholarship.[74] Citing work by Ruby Tapia, Rosa Linda Fregoso, Mary Beltrán, Cynthia Bejarano, and Vicki Mayer on teen pregnancy campaigns, representations of Latinas in gangs, the central Latina character in *Girlfight* (2000), and Latina girl audiences, respectively[75]—while also including her own analyses of America Ferrera, the Cheetah Girls, and Miranda (Lizzie McGuire's Latina best friend/sidekick)—Valdivia illustrates that, while many of these representations are fraught and problematic, not only are Latina girls very present in U.S. media culture, but a significant body of scholarship exists on the subject. Similarly, in *Queer Girls and Popular Culture:*

Reading, Resisting, and Creating Media, Susan Driver addresses the complexity and nuance of both media representations of queer girls and the ways in which queer girls interact with media. By taking queer girls as its subject, the book challenges media studies to think seriously about queer representations—not as ephemeral, marginal, or displaced (which Driver identifies as one typical critique of the representation of LGBTQ issues in popular media), but as an entire world with which queer girls engage on a regular, ongoing, and complex basis. In short, like Valdivia and Driver, in this book I argue that various alternative girls—often girls of color and/ or queer girls—are right there, right in front of us in the vast mediascape. The version of feminist girls' media studies on which I draw and to which I hope to contribute recognizes and grapples with this diverse, complex, and often contradictory field of representations of girls.

Overall, my definition of feminist girls' media studies centers work that addresses and engages much of the following: (1) complex, multiple, and multilayered media representations (not just dominant images and dominant media); (2) an intersectional perspective (especially in terms of race and sexuality); (3) historical specificity; (4) industry structure (including advertising, which incorporates niche marketing and the commodification of multiculturalism, postfeminism, and girl power); (5) public policy and activist work with girls; and (6) interdisciplinary ethnography. This kind of scholarship considers multiple approaches simultaneously and takes seriously a commitment to what Ella Shohat calls polycentric, multicultural feminism[76]—looking at multiple and diverse representations from many perspectives—regardless (or because) of the dominance of white, middle-class, heterosexual girls in the foreground of the cultural landscape. In this way, I hope not only to produce the kind of work the overviews of feminist girls' media studies call for, but also to see beyond or around the "mean girls" and the "Taylor Swifts" as we look at and for the many other girls who populate the contemporary mediascape.

A Note on Defining "Girl"

As I discuss in more detail in chapter 1, meanings of particular social categories—such as "child" and "girl"—vary considerably over time and across place,[77] and thus it is necessary for me to articulate explicitly how

I define "girl" in the context of turn-of-the-twenty-first-century U.S. media culture. In his influential book *Centuries of Childhood*, Philippe Ariès argues that prior to the sixteenth century younger people were understood as small adults, and that the concept of the child did not emerge until the sixteenth and seventeenth centuries, although other scholars have identified some evidence of earlier "stages of childhood."[78] Similarly, scholars have addressed the emergence of the concept of the "teenager" in the twentieth-century United States, some arguing that the term came to fruition after World War II, particularly as "a marketing term used by advertisers and manufacturers";[79] and some focusing on the earlier emergence of a girls' youth culture understood as "teenage" in the 1920s.[80] Perhaps the most recent shift in the definition of "girl" in the United States is the emergence in the early 1990s of the term "tween." At first "tween" was a marketing tool used in audience and consumer segmentation that was occurring in conjunction with technological changes and the simultaneous deregulation of the media and telecommunication industries.[81] Today, the term describes an actual life stage: the time between "child" and "teen" when children—or, as figure 2 makes clear, most often specifically girls—are approximately eight to twelve years old. Policy is written about the tween.[82] Psychologists and sociologists research tween behavior.[83] New stores emerge to produce and cater to tween tastes (e.g., Justice and American Girl Place). And, of course, advertisers try to reach tween dollars, while journalists and

Figure I.2. Toys"R"Us gendered marketing. The "Tween" sign is pink; the "True Heroes" sign is blue. Photo by the author.

pundits worry over tween behavior. Yet, twenty or so years ago, tweens did not exist, although of course there were people between the ages of eight and twelve.

In short, the very existence of human beings we understand to be "children," "teens," or "tweens" is discursively produced and historically and socially specific. Because of this, if the categories are to continue to exist, public discourse must return to the concepts again and again, producing, maintaining, and sometimes transforming them in the process. As Judith Butler argues, it is through "repetition" that discourse constitutes identities.[84] Like the meanings of "child," "teen," and "tween," the meaning of "girl" is discursively determined through repetition, yet also transformed through representational shifts in particular historical moments, including the turn of the twenty-first century, the focus of this book.

Scholars who focus on this time frame define girls in varying ways, implicitly drawing attention to the discursive versatility of "girl." Some girls' studies scholars define "girl" to include "young women" (usually college age).[85] Other girls' studies scholars are concerned with any cultural discussion of "girls," including, for example, middle-aged women who call themselves or are called "girls."[86] Relatedly, Diane Negra and Yvonne Tasker have pointed out that postfeminism depends on a consumerist "girling" of grown women.[87] And some African American scholars argue that because black girls are often denied girlhood, it is an important political move to claim girlhood for all black women.[88] While I draw on all of this work, for the purposes of this study I generally define a "girl" as someone under the age of eighteen. I choose this age both because it is a current legal category (the age of majority) and because it approximates a current common life-stage change—the time at which many girls leave formal schooling and/or their parents'/caregivers' home.

Most important, however, by defining eighteen as an admittedly arbitrary and historically specific dividing line between girl and woman, I make space to address the specificity of girls as teens, tweens, and children. This specificity includes not only these categories but also the ways in which many girls under the age of eighteen are not granted "girlhood status," particularly girls of color and girls who engage in public and/or queer sexuality, all of whom media and law often treat as adults. Alternatively, adult women who first rise to media visibility as children, tweens, or teens are rarely able to shake their status as girls, even when they are well into adulthood. Hence, in this book on girls and U.S. media culture, I insist on defining Venus Williams, Amélie Mauresmo, Sakia Gunn, and Precious as girls, I acknowledge that girlhood clings to now-adult celebrities such as Lindsay Lohan, Britney Spears, and Ellen Page, and—both to make space for these many girls and to resist postfeminist media culture's infantilization of women—I refuse to write about adults who are often called girls, such as Monica Lewinsky, Mia Hamm, the Spice Girls, Carrie and the *Sex and the City* gang, Lady Gaga, *The Girl with the Dragon Tattoo*, and Lena Dunham's *Girls*.

Chapters

Chapter 1 establishes two key concerns of the book: (1) the need to understand current representations of girls in relation to the past, and (2) how to theorize the girl star/celebrity. The chapter challenges contemporary "everything is new" and "it's worse than ever before" arguments about girls and the media by emphasizing continuities between the past and present. Specifically, I develop a girl-focused history of the Hollywood star system—ending with a close analysis of Tatum O'Neal's emergence as a star in the 1970s following the release of *Paper Moon* (1973)—to illustrate that girls have been important figures in media since at least the early twentieth century. In addition, the chapter argues that the girl has been more central to the formation and continued existence of the star and celebrity system than previous scholarship has acknowledged. The girl star in fact epitomizes the star system through both her hyper-whiteness and her status as, by definition, a scandal: an innocent and pure child paradoxically caught in the incessant and potentially corrupting sexualized gaze of celebrity culture. Hence, I argue anxious adoration of the girl star is about the scandal of putting the child on display.

Building on the star theory introduced in chapter 1, the second chapter covers the entire time frame of this book: 1990 to the present. Focusing on *Time*, *Newsweek*, and *People* magazine covers as one way to track the current ubiquity of girls in celebrity culture, I identify the dominance of both whiteness and the can-do/at-risk dichotomy. Having established this field of representation, however, the bulk of the chapter asks what other versions of girlhood can be found on these covers. Turning my attention to girls of color and/or girls who fall outside the can-do/at-risk dichotomy, I identify several alternative representations of girls, some only slightly challenging the dominance of the can-do white girl and others more transformative. Overall, the chapter argues that while all alternative girlhoods in U.S. media culture are not necessarily ideal from a feminist perspective, it is nevertheless crucial to use criticism to identify and pause over these girlhoods in order both to mark their existence and to pursue as much resistant potential as possible in their depictions.

Chapter 3 continues chapter 2's overview of contemporary representations of girls, focusing on the first decade of the twenty-first century and turning to a second media form/genre: girl films. The chapter identifies the four girl films from the last decade that elicited the most public discussion about girls in the national press, on national television/radio, and/or in the alternative/left press: *Mean Girls* (2004), *Little Miss Sunshine* (2006), *Juno* (2007), and *Precious* (2009). Once again, adoration/disdain and anxiety about the girl and the girl star appear; however, some of the debates about the films extend to discussions of their "feminism" and pedagogical usefulness for girls negotiating media culture. After examining these central themes, the chapter draws on a feminist media studies methodology in pursuit of optimistic anti-racist queer readings. I argue *Mean Girls* offers an implicit critique of heteronormativity, *Little Miss Sunshine* embraces girls' autoeroticism, *Juno* provides a character who incessantly makes her own choices and thereby drives the narrative, and *Precious* defines African American girlhood as both valuable and vibrant. The chapter does not offer these readings as "better" or "more accurate" than others; rather it insists that by understanding the films in multiple and even sometimes contradictory ways feminist media criticism can intervene in and broaden the public discussion of girlhood.

The fourth chapter is the first of two focused case studies of girls in turn-of-the-twenty-first-century media culture. Here, I examine tennis, a professional sport in which girl athletes often participate. In the late 1990s no fewer than fourteen high-profile teens were playing professional tennis, and first Venus Williams, Martina Hingis, and Anna Kournikova and then Amélie Mauresmo and Serena Williams, in particular, repeatedly made headlines in both the tennis world and non-sports media. I focus on Venus Williams in this context, engaging two methods of analysis: (1) comparison between coverage of Venus and of other girl players, and (2) a focus on live/near-live television coverage of her matches. Throughout, I both emphasize the specific racialization of her persona and draw attention to several instances in which I read Venus as challenging racism in both the media coverage and the tennis world. Thus, both in problematically racialized ways and in potentially resistant antiracist ways, depictions of Venus produce a specifically African American girlhood that brings change to the whiteness of tennis and by extension to the whiteness of contemporary definitions of girls.

Chapter 5 shifts media type again, centering local and alternative coverage of Sakia Gunn, a fifteen-year-old African American lesbian/ AG who was murdered in Newark, New Jersey, in a 2003 bias crime. Gunn both is and is not a high-profile mediated girl like the girls I discuss in the previous chapters. She made the cover of newspapers; her death led to sustained and continuing (as of this writing) public discussion in multiple media; her murder sparked public debate and scandal; and she was posthumously adored, mourned, and celebrated. Yet none of this attention happened in a sustained way in mass-market mainstream media sources. Thus she is a spectacular girl, but in alternative locations. As an explicitly queer African American girl, she is relatively atypical in the media, yet the argument of this chapter is that she is a spectacular girl nevertheless, that one can find and see her if one looks to media texts other than grocery store magazines, girl films and girl celebrities, and world-class athletes.

In the last chapter, I bring media analysis into a third-grade public school classroom. Moral panic discourse tells us that media damage girls; media literacy scholarship tells us that girls and boys need skills to make sense of and resist media; and after-school and empowerment programs tell us that producing media is good for girls. All of these assumptions at least in part subscribe to the Ophelia Thesis assumption that girls are vulnerable, that media exploit that vulnerability, and that we must therefore build protective structures around girls. In this chapter, I turn away from the Ophelia Thesis and toward the thinking girl, asking what analytical approaches girls take toward media. By working with a group of children over several weeks in their classroom, I identify four key ways in which girls (and boys) engage with media analytically: they focus on minute details; they ask endless questions; they reflect on media structures through creative production; and they pay a great deal of attention to the cultural production of gender. While they do not do all of these things all of the time, while they do struggle at times to separate themselves from the Ophelia Thesis, and while they do not have as developed an understanding of the cultural production of race and class as they do of the cultural production of gender, nevertheless they are quite analytical of media. In short, by defining girls as media critics this final chapter takes one more step away from dominant white can-do/at-risk representations of girls and one more step toward taking seriously the presence of alternative girls in U.S. media culture and social life: the two central goals of this book.

1

Pint-Sized and Precocious

The Girl Star in Film History

I was one of the last human beings to meet Tatum O'Neal as
a little girl. She wasn't a completely happy little girl. But she
hadn't yet known, as her father put it, "the recognition . . .
the notoriety." People still mistook her for a little boy. . . .
Now she is a movie star. . . . I hope she's a happy movie star,
but I don't know that movie stars are happier than little girls.
—Sam Blum, "The Real Love Story"

When my daughter was five years old, she frequently wore sunglasses.
When she did, teachers, friends' parents, and even strangers often
commented, "You look like a movie star." At the time, I was struck by
how readily everyday girls such as my daughter could signify some of
the meanings generated by and through the term "star": glamour, to-
be-looked-at-ness, performance, self-possession, independence, and
(paradoxically) adultness. I was also struck by how commonplace the
notion of a "girl star" is, so much so that the link between a five-year-
old, sunglasses, and stardom appears perfectly transparent, yet also fascinating enough to remark on to perfect strangers.

This chapter seeks to unpack this presumed transparency and high
visibility by theorizing the girl star in the context of both star studies
and girls' studies. I ask two interrelated questions: What role has the girl
played in the history of the star system? And, can the lens of star theory
help explain the role that representations of girls play in U.S. media culture? In order to explore the connection between girls and stars, it is
instructive to consider a key girl star of the 1970s: Tatum O'Neal. In
the context of the book's emphasis on turn-of-the-twenty-first-century media representations of girls, this first chapter's look back to the
1970s sets up a historical context for subsequent chapters, one that can

illuminate both continuities and discontinuities in the history of U.S. conceptions of girlhood, as well as contextualize the current relationship between "girl" and "star/celebrity."

A recurring theme in contemporary media is that "now, more than ever," girls are in the public eye. Yet, as a large body of historical scholarship demonstrates, this claim is not exactly accurate.[1] As I discuss in detail in the next chapter, it is true that an enormous amount of attention has been paid to girls since the early 1990s.[2] In fact, the abundance of such discourse is, at least in part, why I wrote this book. Yet, the "more than ever" part of this claim masks important earlier eruptions of public discourse about girls, including—to name only a few examples— attention to age-of-consent laws in the early 1900s,[3] anxiety about girl babysitters as laborers and nurturers,[4] and the mid-twentieth-century trope of the girl on the phone as a symbol of ambivalence about post– World War II femininity and domesticity.[5] As scholars researching these (and many other) issues have shown, throughout the twentieth century both media culture and public policy used the figure of the girl to work through various social anxieties, and in the process have shaped shifting meanings of girl itself.[6] Tatum O'Neal in the 1970s, then, is simply one of any number of case studies I could have chosen to provide a historical context for the turn-of-the-twenty-first-century depictions of girls I emphasize in the remainder of this book.

Nevertheless, I choose (1) a film star, (2) the 1970s, and (3) Tatum O'Neal in particular for several reasons. First, by discussing film, an industry that emerged just as the nineteenth century ended, I can offer a focused overview of the history of girls in twentieth-century media culture. This overview is not meant to be comprehensive; film stars simply offer one way to address the span of the last century. Second, while I include a discussion of girl stars throughout the twentieth century, I develop a fuller analysis of a 1970s girl star in particular because she is recent enough to raise questions about feminism, sexuality, gender, and race in ways that resonate with similar issues in current media, while also being distant enough from the present to emphasize the specificity of historical context. Finally, I choose Tatum O'Neal—rather than the more often-discussed 1970s girl film stars, Jodie Foster and Brooke Shields—in order to initiate a key goal of this book (one that I enact in each chapter): to explore marginalized figures who nevertheless are still spectacularized.[7] While Foster and Shields went on to more successful Hollywood careers than did O'Neal and have come to define 1970s girl stardom,[8] in the 1970s O'Neal was just as much a spectacular girl star as were Foster and Shields. It is not that O'Neal raises more important issues than do Foster or Shields, but rather that as an under-researched figure in the history of girls in U.S. media culture she not only deserves our attention but also provides an opportunity to complicate that history.

In short, this chapter tells part of the history of girls in U.S. media culture, in this case in U.S. film, and helps explain how girls can be understood through codes of stardom, one aspect of celebrity culture. Celebrity studies scholars argue persuasively that there are important differences among, for example, film stars, accidental celebrities, and television personalities:[9] "What constitutes celebrity in one cultural domain may be quite different in another."[10] Yet, as scholars also point out that the "pervasive circulation of contemporary media fame . . . does not respect media borders."[11] However we define various types of fame, then, they all are related to the ideas of "well-knownness,"[12] "commodity,"[13] and "emulation or . . . contempt"[14] that define celebrity. Thus this chapter both pays attention to the specificity of the history of the girl film star and defines her as an aspect of celebrity culture. Further, the chapter forges connections between star studies and girls' studies to argue for the importance of star and celebrity culture in understanding the mediation of girlhood and the importance of an attention to girls in the history and theory of the star system. And it insists that attention be paid not only to a marginalized spectacular girl, but also to the ways that anxiety and tensions surrounding gender, race, and sexuality are part of the complex and fraught (both adored and abhorred) version of girlhood she represents. In all these ways, the chapter provides a context for and initiates many of the overarching concerns of this book.

The chapter begins with an analysis of the place of the girl star in previous (primarily feminist) film studies scholarship on stars and the star system. Here, I tell a brief history of the girl star and argue that, although she has been under-examined in film studies, this scholarship inadvertently illustrates that the girl star is pervasive in and germane to the star system, a figure in need of careful attention. In the next section, I offer a case study of Tatum O'Neal, her first film (*Paper Moon*, 1973), and press response to the film. I argue that whiteness and ambivalent anxiety (primarily about the relationships among childhood, sexuality, and/or gender) precondition her visibility in both the film and contemporaneous press coverage. In other words, O'Neal is spectacular both because of her whiteness and because of her ability to elicit ambivalence and anxiety about her status as girl, particularly in relation to gender ambiguity and sexuality. Finally, in the conclusion, I return to a discussion of star theory, drawing on my analysis of O'Neal to argue that given that the girl star is pervasive in and germane to the star system and that she activates attention to and anxiety about the gender, sexuality, and race status of the social subject, she epitomizes that system. In short, the girl star embodies many of the contradictions and ambiguities of the star figure generally, particularly whiteness, the boundaries of the individual in relation to society, and the scandal—a sexual scandal—at the heart of the star as cultural object. Through analysis of both previous star studies scholarship and Tatum O'Neal as a case study, then, this chapter argues that the girl star elucidates the star system itself—that she is an ideal example of its operation.

Star Studies and a History of the Girl Star

Although I am sorely tempted, I am not quite willing to argue that the emergence of girl stars initiated the star system in the United States or that the U.S. star system requires girl stars in order to function. Nevertheless, I do argue that girl stars have occupied a profoundly important position within the U.S. star system and that studying them is instrumental to understanding that system. It is therefore curious that star studies—even feminist star studies—have not more closely examined the girl star and her role within the overall star system.[15] That said, there are three ways in which star studies have at least indirectly addressed girl stars, and it is useful to draw on this material to illustrate the emergence and then the ubiquity of the girl star throughout the twentieth century.

First, some previous scholarship illustrates the role the concept of the girl played in the formation and early structure of Hollywood. For example, Richard deCordova makes clear that the concept of girl in the 1910s has become central to the story film studies tells itself about the emergence of the star system.[16] While this is a narrative he challenged and complicated in the early 1990s, it is still common[17] to read the story of the battle for market dominance between Biograph and the independents, particularly Independent Moving Pictures (IMP). As the story goes, IMP won the battle when it invented star marketing by staging a publicity stunt in which it claimed there were false reports of a famous "Biograph Girl's" death. The death was a hoax, and IMP would later not only reveal that she was very much alive, but also publish her name for the first time: Florence Lawrence, now the new "IMP Girl." While deCordova shows that this particular publicity stunt was not, in fact, the "beginning" of the star system, nor the first time a film actor's name was revealed, he also establishes the fact that the publicity stunt did happen and thereby illustrates (but does not remark on) the fact that the concept of "girl" was a key marketing tool in the early star system.[18] Through deCordova, then, I would suggest that "girl," even at this very early point, could be understood to be synonymous with "star" (as in "Biograph star," "IMP star") and therefore to be central to the evolving star system and the eventual solidification of the entire Hollywood structure.

Like deCordova, Heidi Kenaga does not comment on the use of the term "girl" in her discussion of the "movie-struck fan" and the "extra girl" in the 1920s, but she does illustrate that these figures articulated social anxiety about single women/girls in the context of labor, public space, and the growing Hollywood film industry.[19] Kenaga shows that in 1925 a narrative about the management of the girl helped connect the Central Casting Bureau (CCB) to the Motion Picture Producers and Distributors of America's role in the representation of Hollywood as self-regulating. As early as 1914, religious and civic organizations, as well as newspapers and fan magazines, worried about "hoards" of girls coming to Hollywood in hopes of becoming movie stars. Hollywood's response was to regulate these girls/women, establishing the CCB to screen, manage, and provide extras (primarily conceived of as women and children)[20] to all the major studios at set wages and working-hour limits. Additionally, the CCB worked in concert with the YWCA to establish the Hollywood Studio Club, providing housing for the movie star hopefuls, as well as education designed to help them find employment. In short, through the CCB and the Hollywood Studio Club, the figure of the girl helped to produce an industry structure that both controlled the labor of the "extra"—regardless of gender or age—and publicly defined the industry as self-regulating and protective of the social good, particularly of young women and girls as laborers: both movie star hopefuls and working extras.

In both the cases examined by deCordova and Kenaga, the use of the word "girl" did not necessarily refer to children or even teens. Often, those labeled as girls were no longer teens or even in their early twenties, but were defined as girls because of their relative youth, their status as single, and/or the child or childlike roles they played.[21] Nevertheless, regardless of the actual age of the early stars, movie-struck fans, and extras, both deCordova's and Kenaga's work illustrate that the concept of girlhood played a conspicuous role in the formation of the early U.S. film industry. That the age boundaries around "girl" in the 1910s and 1920s were different than they are today simply illustrates the historical specificity of this process. Further, very young girls did contribute to the formation and maintenance of the Hollywood star system. For example, in the 1920s, Baby Peggy (Diana Serra Cary) was a major star; born in 1918, she made more than one hundred films before the age of seven (including many high-profile "Universal Jewels")[22] and was available for purchase as a doll. More famously, scholarship on Shirley Temple's role in the 1930s as "the biggest-drawing star in the world"[23] suggests that as an individual girl star she helped shape the development of the film industry. In this case, a girl under the age of ten reportedly "single-handedly revived Fox and influenced its merger with 20th Century."[24] Like Baby Peggy, Temple was marketed as a doll, and in 1935 she received an honorary Oscar for her "outstanding contribution to the film industry." In short, Temple helped the film industry as it fought to survive—and managed to thrive—during the Great Depression.[25] Both Baby Peggy and Shirley Temple make clear that girl child stars were key economic pillars of the industry (even if the stories about them are likely overstated and in part retell Hollywood publicity material). Overall, then, all these examples from the first third of the twentieth century—from Florence Lawrence as the new IMP girl, to movie star hopefuls/extras, to mega child stars Baby Peggy and Shirley Temple—illustrate that the girl star played a central role in establishing, perpetuating, and protecting the structure of both the star system and Hollywood as a whole.

Not only does previous star studies work illustrate the girl's role in establishing and maintaining industry structure, but it also alludes to her role in defining the meaning of "star" itself, even if these allusions are left frustratingly (for me) underdeveloped. For example, in Diane Negra's excellent analysis of white ethnicity in Hollywood cinema, she complicates our understanding of cinematic whiteness by addressing a tension between the white ethnic childlike star (coded as virginal, demystified, assimilable) and the white ethnic womanlike star (coded as sexual, mystified, troublesome). She writes, "Throughout this book, I employ the dichotomy of girl/woman as a functional conceit, in part to draw attention to a broader pattern of differentiation in Hollywood between the safe sexuality of the girl and the often troublesome sexuality of the woman, but also to indicate how female ethnicity has been particularly subject to representation on these polarized terms." More specifically, she suggests that a girlish white ethnic star can more easily be "celebrated as an exemplary American; even if her ethnicity is prominently displayed, the very fact of her girlishness promises that it may yet be traded away."[26] While other work on girl stars (including my analysis of Tatum O'Neal below) would challenge Negra's claim that the girl's sexuality is necessarily safe,[27] her point that the girl/woman dichotomy is central to the representation of the ethnic woman is provocative, and thus she gestures toward the importance of a tension between childishness and adultishness in the female star system, emphasizing that tension's relationship to both sexuality and ethnicity.

Like Negra's work, Richard Dyer's influential analysis of Judy Garland and gay men's relationship to her also offers insights about the status of the girl star, although Dyer develops this even less than does Negra. For example, he argues that Garland's pre-1950s "ordinariness," which—post-1950—turned out to be not so ordinary, was analogous to gay men's experience: "To turn out not-ordinary after being saturated with the values of ordinariness structures Garland's career and the standard gay biography alike."[28] While Dyer does not refer specifically to girlhood here, the pre-1950s Garland included all her childhood roles, as well as the roles that addressed her transition to adulthood. Thus it is Judy Garland as former girl star that provides much of the ordinariness on which Dyer builds his argument, although he does not say so. Later in the chapter, he mentions her "in-betweenness" and suggests that the experience of being a teenage girl is akin to being a "gender misfit . . . 'too old for toys / too young for boys.'"[29] At this point in his argument Garland's identity as a teenage girl, in particular, and Dyer's concept of the girl as a gender misfit by definition explain the special affinity between Garland and gay men. As I suggest below in my analysis of Tatum O'Neal, in fact, gender ambiguity is definitive of the girl star, something Dyer tantalizingly alludes to but does not explore.

Not only has previous scholarship at least implicitly (1) illustrated the role of the girl star in the formation of the film industry and (2) gestured toward the role of "girlhood" or "girlishness" in the very definition of the star (particularly in relation to ethnicity, race, sexuality, and gender ambiguity), it also has (3) explored specific girl stars as individual case studies that show a connection between that star and some aspect of her historical context. This collective work is indebted to Dyer's[30] argument that, as Christine Gledhill explains it, stars embody contradictions regarding social values "under threat or in flux at a particular moment in time."[31] A review of some of this work offers a brief history of some of the issues girl stars have activated throughout the twentieth century.

Scholarship on Mary Pickford in the 1910s and 1920s, for example, links her to progressive era processes of social and cultural reform. John C. Tibbetts argues that Pickford repeatedly portrayed a "growing girl" who made a "transition from the relative brevity and innocence of girlhood to the complications of adolescence." The narratives worked "to maintain the innocence of the child, while making the reader[/viewer] aware of the surrounding evil" from which the child/girl needed protection during her transition.[32] Alternatively, Gaylyn Studlar reads Pickford as in a perpetual childhood/adolescence (rather than in transition, as Tibbetts suggests), ultimately becoming a "child impersonator" later in her career. Given the context of the "overtly sexualized flapper" and the "new woman," who were part of a "perceived crisis in feminine sexual behavior" in the early twentieth century, Studlar argues, "Pickford appealed to and through a kind of cultural pedophilia that looked to the innocent child–woman to personify nostalgic ideals of femininity."[33] Thus Pickford was an erotic object in this historical context, but this eroticism was made safe through both her characters' childlike innocence and the audience's knowledge that she was *really* an adult portraying a child (as opposed to an actual child functioning as an erotic object). Thus, paradoxically, as Studlar has it, Pickford films drew on discourses of sexuality and the new woman while simultaneously evoking nostalgia that distanced Pickford from the perceived crisis of contemporary femininity.[34]

Tibbetts and Studlar read Pickford differently—either as in transition and therefore in need of protection, or as in stasis and therefore available for erotic nostalgia—but together they illustrate two principal tensions that, as my analysis of Tatum O'Neal shows, persist in relationship to girl stars: (1) protection of, yet also desire for, the girl, and (2) the girl as simultaneously in transition and static/nostalgic. Yet they also clearly place Pickford in the context of early twentieth-century discourses about reform, femininity, and women's evolving public sexuality, hence illustrating historical specificity. Thus this scholarship helps illustrate both the ongoing importance of the girl in media culture and the specificity of a particular girl's historical moment.

Scholars focusing on girl stars in the 1930s and 1940s—such as Shirley Temple, Deanna Durbin, and Judy Garland—draw on a similar methodology to address the historical specificity of discourses of nation and nationalism. For example, Georganne Scheiner argues that in many 1930s films it was girls who were capable of "'fixing' the problems of their elders," problems that were often figured as problems of the nation.[35] And, focusing on the 1940s, Ilana Nash argues that sexual tension in girl star films—such as coming-of-age comedies that include a troubling potential attraction between a teenage girl and an older man—ultimately was nonthreatening because it was resolved through patriotism coupled with what always turned out to be the girl's actual sexual innocence.[36] Like Studlar, Nash sees the films as both evoking and disavowing child sexuality, and Nash then links that ambivalent sexuality to the postwar U.S. context.

Unsurprisingly, with the explosion of discourse about the teenager and the related category of juvenile delinquent after World War II and up through the 1960s, girls appeared as objects of vulnerability resulting from the tumultuous changes of the postwar era. Timothy Shary considers exploitation and delinquency films in particular in his work.[37] The big-budget film *Splendor in the Grass* (1961) is a good example here, in which destruction and despair result from delinquency and (girls') teenage sexuality. Another scholar of the postwar period, Alison Whitney, shows how the concept of the (girl) teenager both addressed and assuaged postwar cultural and social anxiety. Even a "clean teenpic"[38] such as *Gidget* (1959), Whitney argues, "carries with it substantial cultural anxiety about the new phenomenon of teen identity"[39] as distinct from and even opposed to the child figure as an integral part of the family unit. The film, nevertheless, resolves that anxiety through Gidget's relationship with and ultimate capitulation to her father's perspective on family (good) and teenage girls' sexuality (bad), and thus *Gidget* "reassur[es] us that bourgeois patriarchy is still the code of the land and that its corresponding social boundaries remain intact."[40] This shift from the girl's role in patriotism to her place in the conservative patriarchal family[41] continued well into the 1960s, I would argue, for example with the 1965–1966 TV series *Gidget* (based on the film) and the 1965 film *Billie*, in which an athletically gifted and gender-confused girl, Billie, finds a way past her masculinity to embrace her father's version of the girl's role in the family as a future wife and mother.

The 1970s, the era I focus on in this chapter, featured two mega girl film stars—Tatum O'Neal and Jodie Foster—with Brooke Shields emerging as a child star toward the end of the decade. Several scholars have written about this decade, including Kristen Hatch, who argues that these stars often portrayed an accelerated adulthood to which there were two cinematic responses. The first was nostalgic: she identifies "tomboy films" (such as O'Neal's *Paper Moon*) as about holding onto childhood just a little bit longer in the face of an accelerated movement toward adulthood. Simultaneously, however, Hatch finds a second response: intense anxiety about girls' adultlike personae. She shows that popular press coverage often worried about girl stars' wise-beyond-their-years personae, specifically in relation to sexuality.[42] For example, Hatch argues that responses to Shields's role as a child prostitute in *Pretty Baby* (1978) illustrated cultural anxiety about a girlhood vulnerable to corruption by a male gaze.[43] Shields was innocent, but precariously so. There was a tension in the 1970s, then, between girls who remained girls (just a little longer) and girls who never really were girls in the first place, sometimes embodied paradoxically in one girl star's persona: take, for example, Jodie Foster as a young prostitute in *Taxi Driver* and then as a confused tomboy in *Freaky Friday*, two films released only ten months apart in 1976.[44]

Based on my girls' studies–focused analysis of this previous star studies scholarship, it is clear that the girl star is an important and consistent cog in the wheel not only of the star system and the structure of the Hollywood industry in general, but also of the discursive and ideological relationship between Hollywood films and the cultural and social context of their moment of production and distribution. I argue, then, that given the frequent relationship between girl stars and cultural discourses of feminism, gender, and sexuality, feminist film studies needs to take girl stars seriously, not only as markers of particular historical moments, as the bulk of the research has done, but also as a Hollywood system and structure, as some of this research does at least implicitly. My argument here for theoretical attention to the girl star is analogous to Negra's argument for attention to the white ethnic star. She writes, "I envision this project as part of an ongoing effort by feminist film theorists and historians to understand women's representational history, and thus it is deliberately centered around actresses whom traditional film histories have tended to overlook or dismiss."[45] Here, then, I deliberately center the girl star, a figure traditionally overlooked in star studies; and I deliberately focus on Tatum O'Neal, a figure traditionally overlooked in studies of 1970s girl stars.

In the next section, I further develop an understanding of the girl star by addressing two conditions of visibility that become clear through a close analysis of O'Neal: whiteness and ambivalent anxiety. By considering O'Neal in part in relation to other girl stars, I argue that these conditions of visibility are not unique to O'Neal but rather are part of the very structure of the Hollywood star system, a structure that becomes particularly clear when examined through the lens of the girl star.

Conditions of Visibility

While previous scholarship on girl stars looks at cultural anxiety, little of it (other than Negra's) addresses race and the production of whiteness. In what follows, then, I turn first to a history of the requirement of whiteness for the girl star and then illustrate how the example of O'Neal in *Paper Moon* (a film that deals explicitly with a relationship between a black girl and a white girl) crystalizes this requirement. Here, I build on and add to the history of the girl stars I present above, both

by reviewing the spotty appearance of girl stars of color leading up to
the 1970s and by looking more closely at the ways in which *Paper Moon*
and some of the public discussion surrounding it implicitly articulate
the girl star as white. Second, as previous research on girl stars illustrates, ambivalence and anxiety also precondition the visibility of the
girl star. Not surprisingly, then, anxiety and ambivalence dominate in
the public discussion of O'Neal and *Paper Moon*, emerging in relation
to a variety of different gendered and sexualized issues. My analysis of
O'Neal provides a detailed look at this requirement. By calling whiteness and ambivalence/anxiety conditions of visibility, I mean to suggest
that the girl star—as a category—cannot exist without them. This is not
to say there might not be individual exceptions to the rule. Rather, it is
to say these aspects of the girl star are definitive of her girlhood.

Whiteness

Most simply, empirically the overwhelming majority of Hollywood girl
stars are white, particularly up through the 1970s. As I discuss throughout the rest of the book, while high-profile African American—and,
to a certain extent, Latina and Asian American—girls have appeared
with some regularity (but not dominance) in media culture since the
late twentieth century, in film in particular girls of color have rarely
had central roles, let alone become well-known stars. My review of the
racial and ethnic identities of girl actors up through the 1970s[46] revealed
only five girls of color who could be considered girl stars, only two of
whom worked in film regularly as children. In the early 1920s at the
age of five, African American Lucille Brown performed in *Our Gang*
(*The Little Rascals*) for one year; she then went on to make several more
films. However, Brown never achieved crossover fame.[47] Asian American Anna May Wong (born 1905) began working as an extra at age
fourteen and received her first billed role at the age of sixteen in the
1921 film *Bits of Life*. This film led to several fan magazine articles that
defined her as a "new star." Importantly, however, despite her youth, she
was never defined as a *child* star, nor did she play child characters. In
fact, in these early roles she often played an Asian character's wife or
mistress, and she was even known for having had an affair at age sixteen with one of her directors.[48] In addition to Brown and Wong, who

performed regularly while they were still children, Dorothy Dandridge (African American, born 1923) and Rita Moreno (Puerto Rican, born 1931) each made one film before the age of eighteen. And Cuban singer Estelita Rodriguez (born 1928 and known as "the Cuban Shirley Temple")[49] moved to the United States and made two singing Westerns for Republic Pictures before the age of eighteen; she then went on to a successful career as an adult, as did Dandridge and Moreno. Other than these five, however, I was unable to find a pre-1980s nonwhite star who appeared in leading film roles while still a girl.

Anna May Wong's non-child roles (performed when she was sixteen and seventeen) stand in sharp contrast to Mary Pickford's perpetual-child roles (performed well into her adulthood). As many scholars have argued, women of color are defined culturally as always already and perpetually sexual[50] and as adultlike even as very young children.[51] Thus, teenage Wong's sexualized adult roles should come as no surprise. Relatedly, even as the films and fan magazine discourse naturalized Wong's mature sexuality, there was public anxiety about white girls' ambiguous sexuality, as Tibbetts and Studlar explain in relation to Mary Pickford. In other words, juxtaposing Wong's stardom to Pickford's highlights that the cultural anxiety surrounding Pickford is not about girls' sexuality, but rather about white girls' sexuality.[52]

Shirley Temple, of course, is a key example here in the history of sexualized white girl stars, and, again, thinking about her sexuality in relation to a star of color—in this case the famous African American dancer and actor Bill "Bojangles" Robinson—is instructive. In her study of the screen relationship of Temple and Robinson, Karen Orr Vered addresses the way Temple's films and iconic status produce and maintain whiteness.[53] Specifically, she looks at the nearly complete absence of material on Robinson in the white press coverage of Temple. A *Modern Screen* spread from 1938–1939, for example, features "The Men in Shirley Temple's Life!" but does not include a picture of Robinson, despite the fact that Temple appeared in four films with him. The only picture of Temple and Robinson together that Vered found in the mainstream press was in an article about Temple's "physical condition." The article pairs pictures of Temple and Robinson dancing with a picture of Temple playing tennis and another of Temple running with a dog. Vered argues persuasively that this layout "relegates the professional dancing of Temple and Robinson to the same status as Shirley's other physical activities."[54] If blackness is correlated with the physical, "girlness" escapes a similar fate because this is just one of many articles to appear about Temple. Understood most often as both "daughter" of and "partner" to white men in other articles, Temple defines a white innocence that is childlike, but nevertheless sexual and therefore adultlike. Vered argues, because of Temple's implicit sexuality[55] and because of the cultural anxiety about miscegenation at the time, Robinson could not have been featured as "one of the men" in Temple's life without both making her sexuality explicit and destabilizing the centrality of whiteness in her persona.[56]

Forty years later, Tatum O'Neal's whiteness does similar work to Temple's. While almost every article about O'Neal emphasizes that she is *not* like Temple, those same articles often also say something about her blonde hair. In his study of Marilyn Monroe, Dyer argues that blondeness "is the ultimate sign of whiteness"[57] because it is "racially unambiguous."[58] Thus references to both Temple's and O'Neal's blondeness implicitly highlight the girls' definitive whiteness.[59] And while O'Neal did work with actors of color (e.g., P. J. Johnson in *Paper Moon*, and Jaime Escobedo and George Gonzales as the "Aguilar boys" and Erin Blunt as Ahmad Abdul Rahim in *The Bad News Bears* [1976]), I was not able to find her pictured with them in the popular press. Thus, as it did for Temple, the press ostensibly protects O'Neal's public whiteness by absenting pictures of her with racially and ethnically diverse figures.

To work against the dominance of Temple's whiteness, Vered turns to the black press, where she finds discussions of the marketing of Robinson in relation to Temple; Vered thereby develops a complex understanding of both Robinson's and Temple's interdependent racializations. Like Vered, I want to use my critical method both to elucidate the operation of the girl star's whiteness and to call attention to the cultural production of blackness. To do this, I analyze two examples: first, director Peter Bogdanovich's commentaries about O'Neal and the only other girl actor in the film, African American P. J. Johnson; and second, one scene in particular from *Paper Moon* that depicts intimacy between Addie and Imogene (the characters played by Tatum O'Neal and P. J. Johnson, respectively). In other words, by reading O'Neal's white girlness in relation to Johnson's black girlness, I seek to center racialization in my definition of the girl star as articulated by O'Neal and through *Paper Moon*.

Multiple articles about the film quote Bogdanovich recalling the following, somewhat long-winded story about Tatum O'Neal and her implicit relationship to sexuality:

> I went to see [Tatum O'Neal and her father, Ryan] on the beach where they live and apparently Ryan hadn't told her anything. Tatum was just herself, a nice little girl, a little bit precocious. Ryan was standing behind the bar in his bathing suit. I'm dressed, like normal, but everyone else is dressed like for the beach. Ryan tells me that I should get into shape, do some exercises. And Tatum pipes up, sort of in disgust, "Oh, Daddy, he's not the type!" I told her to go play in traffic and told Ryan that she got the part. I never saw another girl; that was it, Ryan and Tatum. Perfect.[60]

Tatum's[61] reported comment, "Oh, Daddy, he's not the type!" can be understood to be about adult anxiety about body image and, tangentially, sexuality. It is an earnest, confident, powerful, and dangerous comment (leading to Bogdanovich's suggestion that she go play in traffic). But it is not particularly "knowing" or "conscious" about sexuality: it is precocious. Tatum is sexual and forward; she is ahead of herself. In other words, Bogdanovich eroticizes Tatum by representing her as a child who comments on male sexuality, but he does not represent her as really understanding what she is saying, even as her words bespeak both self-awareness and self-possession.

Bogdanovich's representation of Tatum as precocious child deviates sharply from his comments about the process of hiring teenager Johnson: "P. J. Johnson played Trixie's maid. And we saw about seven girls. They were OK. Nobody was great. They all did readings. P. J. came in. And as she's walking, she's sixteen-years-old, and she looks at me, she says, 'Oowhee, you good-looking.' I said, 'You just got the part.' [big laugh] That was it. I thought, 'If that girl has the guts to say that, she'd be all right.'"[62]

For Bogdanovich, both Tatum and Johnson are "naturals," but in different ways: Tatum because she unconsciously knows something of sexuality and uses it to challenge someone else's adult white masculinity; Johnson because she consciously uses her own sexuality to praise adult white masculinity. Of course, at the time the film was made Tatum was a child and Johnson was a teenager; nevertheless, a racial binary structures Bogdanovich's comments, raising questions and implicit anxiety about Tatum's relationship to adult sexuality while naturalizing Johnson's. And, I would argue, this ambivalence about a white girl's implied premature reference to sexuality is part of what authorizes Tatum O'Neal—but not P. J. Johnson—as the star of this film and as a girl star of the 1970s. That is to say, O'Neal's very stardom is dependent on her being marked as a troubling—but nevertheless entertainingly sexual—white girl.

O'Neal's whiteness is key to the film's narrative as well. A film made in the 1970s about the 1930s, *Paper Moon* directly addresses racial politics through Johnson's character, Imogene. Imogene is a maid for Trixie, a "dancer" and temporary companion for Moses Pray ("Moze"), Addie's reluctant father(-figure) with whom she travels and carries out cons throughout the film. In one particular scene, shot in one take that frames Imogene and Addie together during an intimate moment when Moze and Trixie leave them alone for the first time, Imogene articulates an explicit critique of racism: both Trixie's individual racism and

Figure 1.1. Addie and Imogene discuss racial politics in *Paper Moon.*

the racist structure of the environment in which Imogene lives. Imogene tells Addie she became Trixie's maid because Trixie promised to
pay her four dollars a week, but that she never has paid more than "a
nickel or a dime," every so often. When Addie asks, "Why don't you
quit?" Imogene says she can't because she "ain't got no money to get
home to mama." This scene, then, acknowledges the legacy of slavery,
Jim Crow, and domestic work for African American women and girls,
and it depicts Addie as naive, yet teachable and sympathetic.

Regardless of the film's liberal critique of (former) racism, in the context of the 1970s star system and this film in particular, which centers
Ryan O'Neal (Tatum's real-life father) as its star and "introduces" Tatum
O'Neal as a new star in the opening credits, Addie/O'Neal's whiteness
ensures her survival and centrality in the film, while Imogene/Johnson's
blackness, even though it functions to critique racism and to problem-
atize whiteness, ultimately serves a supporting role to Addie/O'Neal's
white centrality and ensures that Imogene/Johnson will disappear.
This structure is particularly clear in Imogene's final scene. In the first
extremely long sequence of a con in the film, orchestrated by Addie and
carried out by Addie and Imogene, the two girls conspire to break up
Trixie and Moze. For Addie, this means getting her father/friend back,
and for Imogene it means an escape from Trixie. (Addie has promised
to give Imogene thirty dollars to get home to her mother if she helps
with the con; unlike Trixie, Addie keeps her economic promise.) The
sequence ends with a wide-angle tracking shot, quickly pulling away
from Imogene as she stands still in the middle of the elongated hall-
way and waves a small, slow wave to Addie, who is rushing forward
in concert with the camera, looking over her shoulder, smiling and
waving energetically to Imogene. Despite the fact that Addie and Imogene bond more directly and more quickly than even Addie and Moze,
this shot emphasizes an insurmountable literal and figurative distance
between Addie and Imogene. Because Addie is close to the camera, she
appears large in the frame and remains so as she moves with the camera, while Imogene appears to become smaller and smaller in the frame
as she stands still and the camera pulls away: the girls are now separated
and, as their size difference in the frame symbolically implies, will likely
never see each other again. For me, Imogene's little wave at the end is
sad, while Addie's is jubilant. While Imogene now has enough money to

Figure 1.2. Addie and Imogene say good-bye in *Paper Moon.*

get home to her mother, she has lost a friend and, as she states earlier, has no real economic prospects other than going to work for another white woman. Addie, however, regains her friend/father.

Extratextually, P. J. Johnson is also waving good-bye to cinema, while Tatum O'Neal is walking forward into (admittedly, brief) mega stardom. For Johnson, this was her first film; the only other credit I could find for her listed on IMDb.com was as a Dairy Queen waitress in the 1990 film *Texasville.*[63] For O'Neal, this film led to an Oscar as Best Actress in a Supporting Role. At age ten, she was (and still is) the youngest actor to win a competitive Academy Award. Thus, while Johnson's character, Imogene, articulates a specific critique of racism and its relationship to sexism and exploitation, within the context of a historical film her critique is weak and nostalgic, suggesting, as do so many other historical texts that address race and racism, "Yes, it was bad back then, but that's just the way it was. Things are better now."[64] This displacement of racism onto the past effectively bolsters whiteness in the present, as O'Neal remains the center of the film and goes on to be a key player in 1970s girl stardom.[65]

My point in relation to Lucille Brown, Anna May Wong, Dorothy Dandridge, Rita Moreno, Estelita Rodriguez, Mary Pickford, Shirley Temple, Tatum O'Neal, and P. J. Johnson is not so much that the only girls who become film stars are white (although this is most often the case) but that "girl star," as a category, defines and reinforce whiteness. By comparing Addie/O'Neal to Imogene/Johnson and Anna May Wong to Mary Pickford, and by drawing on Vered's comparison of Temple to Robinson, I mean to illustrate the production of whiteness through the structure of "girl star," a process that draws on blackness to shore up whiteness. While Robinson and Johnson make explicit and therefore destabilize Temple's and O'Neal's whiteness momentarily within the diegesis and (potentially) long term for the spectator, the films and the mainstream popular press surrounding Temple, O'Neal, and *Paper Moon* solidify an unspoken whiteness. By drawing a connection between Temple and O'Neal, who function so similarly in two very different time periods, I want to suggest that girl star as a cinematic category produces, maintains, and requires whiteness. As many other scholars have shown, the production of whiteness is certainly not unique to the girl star, but arguably it is a condition of her visibility.

Ambivalence and Anxiety

Why might anxiety and ambivalence also be a condition of visibility for the girl star, a key piece of her structure? I would argue it is because the terms "child" and "star" do not fit seamlessly together. Child stars are loved (in large part) because they are children, but if the adoration is for childhood, the love (and therefore often the stardom) will disappear when the children inevitably become adults. Thus, attention paid to a child star always includes an ambivalent nostalgia for the fleeting present combined with a threat of future abandonment by one's object of adoration (and an embedded despair about that future loss). Additionally, both media discussions of child stars and public and legal policy about them (e.g., labor laws, number of hours allowed on the set, educational requirements) express anxiety about the very existence of child stars. In other words, if we love them so much, how can we torture them by making them work long hours, encouraging them to perform scenes with adult themes, and stealing their childhoods even as they come to embody through their performances an idealized childhood? How can we allow their parents to exploit them for economic gain and thereby acquire vicarious and sometimes actualized personal fame? Further,

given that "child" signifies sexual innocence but (female)[66] "star" signifies erotic to-be-looked-at-ness, the girl star embodies the unresolvable
contradiction of childhood sexuality, thereby producing anxiety about
the prospective erotic threat posed by the male gaze at the girl child.[67]

Here, I explore this anxious ambivalence in the press coverage of
O'Neal surrounding the release of *Paper Moon*, especially in the contexts of feminism, gender, and the 1970s. My goal is to point both to
the specificity of O'Neal and the 1970s and to ambivalence and anxiety in the figure of the girl star, regardless of her historical moment.
In reviewing 1970s newspaper and magazine articles about O'Neal and
Paper Moon, I found five key ways in which anxiety and ambivalence
emerge: ironic binaries (child/adult and feminine/masculine); tortured
childhood; the difficulty of combining "child" with "star"; sexuality; and
hostility toward the girl star. As I illustrate below, each of these categories points to a difficulty at the heart of the girl star: simultaneous adoration and abhorrence, concurrent delight and despair.

IRONIC BINARIES: CHILD/ADULT
AND FEMININE/MASCULINE

Several articles offer one-liners that capture the irony in O'Neal's child/
adult persona. For example, *Time* reports she has "a cunning apple pie
face":[68] she is both adult (con-artist cunning) and child (Middle America
apple pie). Similarly, Lorraine Davis reports in *Vogue* that O'Neal has a
"voice that ranges from nightclub husky [adult] to grade-school shrill
[child]."[69] More generally, authors describe her as "pint-sized" and "precocious"—in other words, small but adultlike. Making the child/adult
irony crystal clear, many of the articles quote Bogdanovich saying "she
is ten going on thirty."[70] Articles often end with a naive claim from her,
suggesting she sees herself as much more grown-up than she really is.
Again, she is child/adult. For example, a *Time* article ends with this quotation: "I'm spoiled. I wasn't spoiled when I was younger. But I think that
the present for me is to be a little spoiled."[71] Here she appears naive of the
vicissitudes of time as a nine-year-old who thinks of herself as "older"
than she used to be; simultaneously, she draws attention to the profound
changes she actually has just experienced in her life, changes that might
help (or force) her to "grow up." Thus she is both child and not-child, and
each characterization anxiously masks or disavows the other.

Explicitly defining O'Neal as woman, *Vogue* chose her for its June 1973 column on "The American Woman in the Movies." Claiming that O'Neal plays "the American woman at her strong-headed, firm-hearted best: intelligent, independent, ready for anything," Davis also assures *Vogue* readers that O'Neal has "a private store of feminine self-doubt, of love for pretty clothes, of devotion to the man she loves." Thus she is both independent (an adultlike feminist) and typically feminine (with adultlike concerns). Later in the short article, Davis writes that O'Neal "must have been weaned on diet soda, because there is no sugar anywhere in her system," and thereby implicitly suggests she is a *Vogue*-style independent woman who eschews traditionally feminine ways (sugar) while perhaps embracing modern femininity (dieting). The article ends by implying that O'Neal's skill and appeal mean that she will make many more films, "unless, of course, she decided to be President, instead."

Davis's implicitly feminist comment about a future woman president points to another important binary in O'Neal's persona: femininity/masculinity. Bit characters in *Paper Moon* mistake her character for a boy, and, in fact, the film invites the audience to make the same mistake as well: the first image of Addie is a low-angle shot of her face with a pageboy haircut, looking down at the camera, with an open landscape and wide sky in the background. This shot, including a distinctly Western genre setting, suggests a masculinity that Hatch reads as tomboyism.[72] Addie explicitly objects to similar mistakes within the diegesis, and Moze responds by buying her a dress and hair ribbons. Nevertheless, she dresses in her masculine overalls through most of the film. And, of course, O'Neal famously wore a tuxedo to the Academy Awards. In the press, O'Neal expresses her displeasure with being mistaken for a boy, but the articles nevertheless play up the gender tension. For example, *Time* reports, "Her perky performance in *Paper Moon* is being compared with the classic childhood performances of Jackie Coogan and Jackie Cooper. Still, such mega praise does not entirely please nine-year-old Tatum O'Neal. 'It's not the funnest thing in the world being called a boy,' she laments in her husky voice."[73] Not content to allow her complaint to stand, the article mentions her husky voice, reminding readers of her masculinity. Nevertheless, this same article includes the detail that O'Neal likes "big elevator shoes and great clothes," thereby suggesting

Figure 1.3. Cross-dressing Tatum O'Neal: the youngest person ever to win a competitive Academy Award.

that her voice's huskiness is more like fashion icon Marlene Dietrich's masculinity than like, say, John Wayne's.

Overall, then, O'Neal can be both child and adult, both masculine and feminine. While admittedly, many of the articles do not necessarily represent these binaries in O'Neal's persona ambivalently, but instead embrace both sides of the binary as fascinating, much of the press coverage *is* particularly ambivalent. As I explore below, this ambivalence is often tied to questions about O'Neal's childhood and/or femininity, questions that are set up and authorized by the adult/child and feminine/masculine binaries.

A (FORMER) TORTURED CHILDHOOD

Many articles articulate anxiety about Tatum's difficult childhood, but then displace the concern by suggesting that her difficulties are all in the past. In one article, Ryan reports that Tatum used to "take a scissors to herself," cutting out clumps of her hair.[74] *Time* says that "Tatum's childhood has been more gothic than glamorous"[75] and that her mother used drugs, but it then reports that her parents are now divorced. Similarly, Ryan "used" to be a playboy, "but those ruffian days are all over."[76] The articles have it both ways, then, reporting on the titillating details of Tatum's tortured childhood and Ryan's playboy lifestyle while simultaneously insisting that this odd father/daughter pair has achieved some kind of nuclear family–like normality.

Making the film *Paper Moon*, in particular, has presumably helped them settle into family life. For example, Tatum reports, "What was good about the film was that I got to know my father better." The same article quotes Ryan saying "I felt if we did this movie together . . . my God, we'd be connected for life. It would undo the years we were not together."[77] Another article emphasizes the tortured childhood, but nevertheless ends with a happy present. In "The Real Love Story," Ryan reports that "Tatum had fallen off a roof and broken her foot and nobody had done anything about it." In the end, Ryan says, Tatum and her mother had a "fist fight" and Tatum left. The article ends, however, with Ryan claiming that Tatum and her mother have reconciled and, "since then, all has been well between them."[78]

Overall, the articles work to suggest that things are better now, although the many details about Tatum's troubled childhood (which, of course, she is still in, given that she is only nine years old) that emerge either within each article or across multiple articles keep the anxiety very much alive. Thus there is ambivalence about tortured childhood: both a concern about it, and a pleasure in reporting it; both an insistence that it is in the past (hence authorizing the titillating pleasure), and an almost obsessive impulse to report it repetitively and in detail, thereby keeping it in the discursive present. Given that this ambivalence is specifically about Tatum's relationship to childhood, it is a key part of the production of her girlhood as contradictorily torturous and fabulous.

THE STRESS OF FILMMAKING:
CAN A STAR REALLY BE A CHILD?

Press and magazine writers often express anxiety not only about Tatum's former childhood, but also about the effects of her participation in filmmaking as a child. They ask if she's hooked on cigarettes, which she had to learn to smoke for her role in *Paper Moon*, and if she goes to school or has tutoring (the answer is "occasionally").[79] Sam Blum says that Tatum shares certain problems with the character Addie, and that those problems "leave one uneasy." Life has been "hard going" and "whatever 'normal' childhood is, neither will ever know it."[80] Blum spends a good deal of time on anxiety, in fact. He reports that during their interview Tatum was in "agony" because of stomach pain, and he depicts Ryan as uncaring. When Blum offers to postpone the interview, Ryan says, "No, no . . . she can do it. She always comes through. Tatum works regardless of her physical condition. But she's a complainer, you know, and I'm kind of used to it. She often gets stomach-aches, but they generally go away. This one's swelling and puffing, but we . . . will go down to the drugstore and get something."[81]

The anxiety is doubled here in that, presumably, both working in the film industry and living with this particular father—who downplays pain, ignores physical symptoms, and blames his daughter for complaining—could give a child a stomach-ache (or ulcer, as other articles report). That Blum included the detail of the "swelling and puffing" in Ryan's voice creates a shocking image, again, both because it seems like a serious medical condition and because Ryan ignores it. Blum ends the article by saying "For whatever glory it earns me, I was one of the last human beings to meet Tatum O'Neal as a little girl. She wasn't a completely happy little girl. But she hadn't yet known, as her father put it, 'the recognition . . . the notoriety.' People still mistook her for a little boy. . . . Now she is a movie star. . . . I hope she's a happy movie star, but I don't know that movie stars are happier than little girls."[82]

Such statements indicate that filmmaking and subsequent press interviews themselves pose a danger to the innocence and fluid gender identity of the "little girl," and that parents can be part of the danger, too, even as filmmaking, press interviews, and stage parents are all nevertheless required for the very existence of the "[girl] movie star." Importantly, being mistaken for a boy is somehow part and parcel of being a little girl, which in turn is antithetical to being a movie star. For Blum, child and movie star are separate categories. While Tatum has been both, she cannot be both at one time. Thus the category "girl star" is an oxymoron, and the fact that Tatum O'Neal is in fact both a girl and a star is a contradiction impossible to resolve. That contradiction, then, means that ambivalence is always at the heart of the girl star.

HOW SEXUAL *IS* TATUM O'NEAL?

Thus far, I have discussed the anxious ambivalence surrounding O'Neal in terms of ironic binaries, a tortured childhood, and the oxymoron of the child star. In each case, the fact that she is a girl (not a boy) is not central to the cultural anxiety, even when it is a topic for discussion. In other words, even for the ironic masculine/feminine binary, the child star in question, hypothetically, could be a boy and the anxiety could still operate. In terms of sexuality, however, the fact that O'Neal is a *female* star, a *girl* star, is crucial. It is, after all, anxiety about a heterosexual male gaze at the too-sexual girl that drives much public discussion of girl stars, and O'Neal is no exception.

Importantly, however, the film *Paper Moon* itself does not emphasize a feminine sexual to-be-looked-at-ness for O'Neal or for Addie. While Addie and Moze are close, and while, for example, they do engage in frequent testy exchanges that might be associated with the erotic sexual banter commonly found in screwball comedies, Moze is interested in other women and spends much of his time trying to get rid of Addie. Further, Moze's adult companion, Trixie, *is* hyper-sexualized (through costume, performance, references to prostitution, and the depiction of an erotic relationship between her and Moze), serving as the feminine sensual center of the film and thereby deflecting sexuality away from Addie. The press nevertheless proceeds to sexualize O'Neal, constructing her as sexually available and thereby authorizing her stardom.

The starkest and most unapologetic example of her sexualization appears in a *Vogue* article with the double-entendre title "Tatum Takes Off." Primarily a photo spread, O'Neal appears dressed as Raquel Welch, with balloons as false breasts, and as David Bowie, with an exposed stomach and a sloping waistline. Not only do these impersonations draw attention to her as a sexual being, but they also destabilize her racial and gendered identity as she impersonates first a Latina and then an adult male, making the sexuality all the more provocative. Other examples of her sexualization in the press include the descriptions of her voice as husky that I discuss above, as well as a more explicit claim by Valerie Wade that she has "the sexiest voice since Monroe."[83] Relatedly, Blum writes that she is a "little blonde who makes women want to adopt her and men want to marry her."[84]

Anxiety about the O'Neals' father/daughter relationship is at issue in many of the articles and often bleeds over into both implicit and explicit anxiety about sexuality. For example, Blum writes, "A father whose daughter reminds him of Marilyn Monroe—a beautiful and talented, yet insecure and suicidal woman—suggested a relationship I wanted to know more about."[85] Blum also says that "Tatum has more and more taken over her father's life—moving into his home, his profession, his consciousness," and he quotes Ryan as saying "I haven't had a very good reputation when it comes to women. But I've had much less action than is reported; and when Tatum came into my home I had even less, because I no longer needed someone to fill the loneliness, the void. I had Tatum."[86] Not leaving that statement alone, Blum follows it by asking Ryan what Tatum thinks about living the Oedipal fantasy. Ryan has to ask what that means, and then he denies there is anything Oedipal about his relationship with Tatum. Blum does not comment further, but given his previous depiction of the father/daughter relationship, he gives the distinct impression that Ryan is in denial about at least a metaphorical sexual relationship between father and daughter. In fact, Blum's article is titled "The Real Love Story: Ryan and Tatum O'Neal," obviously referring to Ryan's 1970 film *Love Story*, and thereby eroticizing his relationship with his daughter.

While some examples in the press seem to celebrate Tatum's sexualization (such as the *Vogue* photo spread), many more are anxious that her father and/or her work in filmmaking have made her sexual. In the process of raising the issue, of course, the articles themselves contribute to the discursive production of Tatum as a sexualized girl child star. As Hatch reports, there was significant discussion in the 1970s press about the supposed dangers of the representation of girl stars as sexual.[87] I want to reflect on one 1977 *Ms.* magazine article by Molly Haskell, in particular, because it raises questions about the representation of sexual children in a more explicitly feminist way than does any of the other coverage. The title, "Tatum O'Neal and Jodie Foster: Their Combined Age Is 27—What Is Hollywood Trying to Tell Us?" initiates a common critique of the very existence of girl actors in Hollywood. Haskell does not waste any time telling us what she thinks Hollywood is trying to tell us. She says that the girls are "kiddies, moppets, and nymphets." They are "teenybopper sex symbols," and O'Neal and Foster in particular are a "baddy-baddy" and "teenage temptress," respectively.[88] These girl stars use "suggestive looks and gutter language [and] seem to have been there and done it all." Articulating what appears in much of the press coverage of O'Neal, Haskell argues that these girl stars offer a "double titillation, the extremes of innocence and depravity."[89]

Not only Haskell's contemporary journalistic feminism, but also more recent feminist scholarship sexualizes O'Neal. For example, in an essay focused primarily on Brooke Shields, Hatch also lists O'Neal, along with Melanie Griffith, Nastassja Kinski, Linda Blair, and Jodie Foster, as having "all achieved stardom through a sexual precocity that led them to be labeled at one point or another as a new incarnation of Lolita."[90] But, as I illustrate here, unlike the other actors Hatch lists, O'Neal's sexuality is raised only in the press during the early 1970s, not in the film *Paper Moon*.[91] The fact that both scholarship and the popular press nevertheless eroticize O'Neal suggests that—by definition—the girl star is both sexual and in danger because of that sexuality. Anxiety and ambivalence about that sexuality is a condition of her visibility and will be ascribed to her, regardless.

CRITICS LOVE/HATE THE GIRL STAR

In her *Ms.* article, Haskell not only points out the sexualization of the child star, but also argues that, in the context of 1970s feminism, this emphasis on the sexual girl child is a way for Hollywood to avoid making films with "full-fledged honest-to-goodness thinking and talking grown-up women. . . . For the man whose ego is sustained not by inherent worth, but by a sense of superiority over the weaker sex, there is a need for constant worshipful glances from the 'little woman.'

Since there are few grown women left who will perform the shrinking act for this purpose, he will have to resort to little women in the literal sense."[92] On the one hand, it is easy to agree with Haskell. On the surface, certainly women are underrepresented and underpaid (in comparison to men) in Hollywood, both in front of and behind the camera.[93] On the other hand, Haskell is not only dismissive but also derogating of girls. Haskell seems particularly contemptuous of girls as "unskilled" in her pursuit of a feminist critique of the absence of women in Hollywood. Girl actors do not think, none (except, Haskell claims, Jodie Foster) has "real" star quality, and they are willing to perform "shrinking acts." Similarly, while many articles about O'Neal and *Paper Moon* praise her acting ability and do not question her Academy Award, they nevertheless wonder whether she will ever be able to follow up this performance, and they suggest that she was able to play the part only because she could be "authentic" or "herself." Hence, she may not be a "real" actor; she may not have even been performing. In short, she may not have any real skill at all. For example, while Davis does praise O'Neal's acting ability in *Vogue*, she does so primarily by claiming that she is an adult or at least adultlike. Further, negative associations with children run throughout the three-paragraph article, from claims that O'Neal is a "match" for Shirley Temple because she is "tough," to insulting sweet and cute portrayals of children, to calling a grade-school voice "shrill."[94]

This theme in the press, then, works to diminish the girl star, to represent her as "less than" women, actors, and regular girls. The authors love to watch *Paper Moon*, but they distrust Tatum herself for having the capacity to make the film. And they distrust her father for putting her in the situation, as well as the audience for making her a star by adoring her and thereby stealing her childhood. While Haskell suggests—with anger—that the attention paid to girl stars in the 1970s was at the expense of adult women, this claim ignores the long history of the girl star that I argue feminist film critics and scholars need to address.[95] My point here is that by ignoring the history of girl stars and defining them as lesser than "true" adult stars, despite offering an important feminist critique of Hollywood, Haskell draws on and contributes to a cultural hostility toward girls that runs throughout much of the coverage of O'Neal and *Paper Moon*.

Part of the girl star phenomenon, then, is not only adoration of but also hostility toward girls, if not in the films themselves then certainly in the marketing and press surrounding them. Again, ambivalence dominates and drives the discourse about the girl star; along with anxiety about sexuality and the deleterious effects of stardom on the childhood of a girl, it is a condition of her visibility.

Conclusion: The Girl as the Epitome of the Star System

Much of the anxiety and ambivalence about O'Neal is tied, in particular, to her status as girl. The tension between child and adult—sometimes linked to a tension between masculinity (childish tomboy) and femininity (knowing erotic object)—the anxiety about lost childhood and early sexualization, the hostility toward and disdain for the girl, and the impossibility of imagining that a childhood innocence can be maintained once a girl becomes a star, all illustrate the specificity of the girl star, both child and female. Similarly, the history of the girl star I tell through previous scholarship on the film industry, the star system, and the relationship between girl stars and their historical context emphasizes the specificity of the girl star. In other words, thus far this chapter has identified the particularities of the girl star. I turn now, however, to a discussion of how those particularities can be seen to epitomize the star system, in general. This move returns to my interest early in the chapter in illustrating the centrality of the girl to the U.S. star industry. By arguing that the girl star can be understood as the epitome of the star system, I mean that she is the perfect example, the distillation, even the intensification of several aspects of the U.S. Hollywood star system. I see this as being the case in at least three ways.

First, not only is the girl star usually white, but her whiteness is deepened. Of course, statistically, for both children and adults, there are obviously many fewer stars of color, particularly up until the 1970s when Tatum O'Neal emerged. Yet, if we think of the many, many important exceptions to that rule, the names that come to mind are adults: for example, Philip Ahn, Sessue Hayakawa, Rita Hayworth, Nancy Kwan, Carmen Miranda, Hattie McDaniel, Ricardo Montalbán, Sidney Poitier, Paul Robeson, Bill Robinson, and Raquel Welch. Despite the dominance of whiteness, there is an important and complex history of adult stars of color throughout the twentieth century.[96] This is not the case for girl stars. In fact, every single one of the high-profile girl stars up until the 1970s is white. Further, not only is the girl star white, but she also is often blonde, intensifying her whiteness. And she exists at the center, with actors of color—such as Johnson/Imogene in *Paper Moon* and Bill Robinson in the four films he made with Shirley Temple—functioning as narrative support, as sidekick, as a discursive backdrop. The girl star, then, is a promise of the continued dominance of whiteness. She is a symptom and effect of racism, one that reveals the continued operation of this force. And she reveals the depth of whiteness's roots in the star system.

A second way in which I would argue the girl star epitomizes the star system is in her relationship to the representation of the individual. Gledhill argues that stars work through questions of the "person." Stars contain contradictions between exteriority and interiority, excess and reality, and the extraordinary and the ordinary, and these tensions are productive for processing various social and ethical issues.[97] Relatedly, Judith Mayne argues that the "appeal of stardom is that of constant reinvention, the dissolution of contraries, the embrace of wildly opposing terms."[98] Because girl stars, in particular and by definition, manage a tension on the line between child and adult, they incessantly work through the concept of full subjectivity. Dyer writes, "Stars articulate what it is to be a human being in contemporary society; that is, they express the particular notion we hold of the person, of the 'individual.' They do so complexly, variously—they are not straightforward affirmations of individualism. On the contrary, they articulate both the promise and the difficulty that the notion of individuality presents for all of us who live by it."[99] This describes the girl star just as it does any star, but the girl star takes this tension further, because she is not fully human: she is not an adult, but neither does she get a "normal childhood." Further, she is capable of breaking down the barriers drawn around appropriate humanness—for example, when she is figured as child/adult and when she is a sexualized child. The girl star is about the problem of what it means to be an individual: where childhood ends and adulthood begins, what the fullness of the individual or subjectivity is.

All this is about boundary crossing: the girl star is an emblematic figure that illustrates the dangers of crossing boundaries and the complexity of being a full subject in the world, and she is also an individual example of the pleasures of boundary crossing, of either inhabiting a not-fully-individualized-childlike subjectivity or inhabiting a fully-individualized-adultlike subjectivity ahead of time, precociously. That she poses risks and threatens to destabilize social conventions and norms makes her a highly intriguing site of negotiation over the meaning of the social subject. If the whiteness of girl stars functions to intensify the overall whiteness of the star system, one that disavows the complexity and importance of race and ethnicity, here the girl emphasizes a central tension of the star system, heightening the anxiety at the heart of the conflicts between the individual and the social and between the exceptional and the everyday that Gledhill, Mayne, and Dyer identify in the star system.

The issue of anxiety leads me to the third way in which girl stars can be understood as the epitome of the star system: as a scandal. In his history of the star system, deCordova lays out four stages to the development of the star system, beginning with the actor, then the picture personality, then the star, and finally the "star scandal." He argues that in the 1920s the coverage of the star shifted from adoration of the person both on- and off-screen (the third stage of the star, proper) to the fourth stage, including scandal and anxiety about star behavior. He suggests that, in part, this shift took place because of increased media coverage, as daily newspapers (tied less directly to Hollywood industries) began to cover star behavior. While some of this coverage was about high-profile scandals, most infamously Roscoe "Fatty" Arbuckle's trial for the manslaughter of Virginia Rappe,[100] deCordova also points out that high-profile divorces (e.g., Mary Pickford and Owen Moore) and remarriages (e.g., Mary Pickford and Douglas Fairbanks, one month after Pickford's divorce was final) were part of the coverage of scandal. In his book's conclusion, deCordova argues provocatively that the ongoing eruption of various star scandals illustrates that little changed in the fourth stage of the star system between the 1920s when it emerged and his contemporary moment of the 1980s.[101] Regardless of whether one is persuaded by this expansive historical argument, it seems clear that the concept of the "star scandal" was very much a part of the production of Tatum O'Neal as a star in the 1970s, particularly in the anxiety about her relationship with her father and the "danger" of filmmaking for Tatum as child. The scandal here, however, is primarily the scandal of the girl star, the scandal that a girl child could become a public star. In other words, the girl star crystallizes what deCordova defines as the culminating stage in the star system: the star scandal—not because she may get caught up in a scandal, per se, but because *she herself is the scandal.*

   And this is a sexualized scandal. DeCordova argues that the emergence of the full-fledged star depended on a discourse of secrecy—primarily sexualized—and that the job of discourse about the star was to insist on a secret and then work tirelessly to reveal the "truth" behind the persona. The secret of sexuality, then, is required of the star. For the child star, of course, there must be at least a surface distrust of sexuality. Thus, again, simply the fact that she is a star—and therefore by definition has a sexualized private self that must be pursued—is itself the scandal. The scandal for the girl star is intensified because she is a child, sexualized too early. The girl star, then, is the quintessential star—a hyper-white, highly sexualized, and highly scandalous individual in conflict. The girl star may not determine the star system, but arguably she is the distillation of it.

2

"It's Like Floating" or Battling the World

Mass Magazine Cover Girls

One way to study the increase in attention to girls since the early 1990s is to track the number of girls to appear on the covers of mass-market magazines. In a previous study of *Time* and *Newsweek* since they began publishing in 1923,[1] I discovered that girls have always appeared on the covers of these mainstream news magazines. Almost every year since 1923, at least one issue of each magazine has featured a girl. Thus, as in other areas of media culture (including film, as I discuss in the previous chapter), mass magazines throughout the twentieth century drew on and contributed to a public fascination with girls.[2] Nevertheless, it is also the case that the number of covers depicting girls has ballooned since the late 1980s, in concert with the increase in representations of girls in media culture generally, as I discuss in this book's introduction. Collectively, these depictions spectacularize turn-of-the-twentieth-first-century girls as worth looking at and thinking about—indeed, as fascinating.

For this chapter, I examined every *Time*, *Newsweek*, and *People* cover from January 1990 to July 2012. I identified 242 covers featuring girls and use them here to map the field of spectacular girlhood in contemporary media culture. Thus this chapter provides a broad context in which to understand subsequent chapters focused on more specific case studies. Why these three magazines for my outline of girls in turn-of-the-twenty-first-century media culture? I could have included *Us Weekly* and other tabloids, or fashion magazines such as *Glamour*, *Vogue*, and *Teen Vogue*, all of which are also available at the checkout stands of my local grocery stores. However, by focusing on *Time* and *Newsweek*—news magazines ostensibly aimed at a generic reader— I mark the moments when girls reach saturation, when they appear everywhere, not "just" on magazines aimed specifically at girls and/or defined by their investment in celebrity, scandal, and/or supposedly feminine concerns such as fashion. Nevertheless, I also include *People*—the best-archived contemporary celebrity magazine—in order to foreground this book's interest in celebrity culture.

More generally, I choose magazine cover girls because they insistently insert themselves into our field of vision: if we go to the grocery store or pass a newsstand we see them regardless of whether we want to, looking out at us as we pass by. Certainly, girls are also insistently present in other areas of media culture: If we turn on the television and flip channels—passing by or pausing at the Disney Channel, Nickelodeon, or MTV—or listen to CNN or Fox News or follow celebrities on Twitter, we will see, hear, and read about girls whether we want to or not. If we go to the movies, we will see posters and previews for upcoming or recent releases of films featuring girls. If we go to Barnes and Noble or Amazon.com, displays for teen novels and self-help books or suggestions for purchases will place girls in front of our eyes. Simply by moving through our daily lives, we will see AMBER Alerts on billboards and flyers posted at our children's schools, and as tickertape running along the bottom of our television screens.[3] Magazine covers are a part of this large field of unavoidable representation, contributing to a cluttered landscape of spectacularized girls that seemingly seek us out, call for our attention, encourage us to make a purchase, or interrupt our everyday lives to insist that we think about them.

It would be impossible to write about the entire field of girlhood; it is just too large, too everywhere, to capture in its entirety. I therefore have to make choices in order to say anything. I choose magazine covers because they are central to celebrity culture: they provide snapshots documenting and, in fact, producing girls as celebrities, sometimes preestablished celebrities (those who appear most frequently are Chelsea Clinton, Mary-Kate Olsen, Lindsay Lohan, Miley Cyrus, and Vanessa

Hudgens) and sometimes "fifteen-minutes-of-fame" "accidental"[4] celeb-rities who are thrust into notoriety because of something that happens to them (JonBenét Ramsey appears most frequently in this category). In either case, when these girls appear on magazine covers they are spectacular figures we must care about, at least for the time they occupy our conscious attention, even if we are just passing by.

In the previous chapter, I explore theories of the star, concentrating on film studies and the film industry. There, I argue that the girl star epitomizes the whiteness, the status of the individual in society, and the pursuit of the (sexualized) scandal/secret at the heart of the star, par-ticularly in the context of twentieth-century U.S. film history. In this chapter, I build on this work but also shift to a broader, more contem-porary concept of the "celebrity." As Sean Redmond and Su Holmes argue, "There is now a vast range of media sites through which mod-ern celebrity can emerge. Mass, digital and narrowcast media outlets, often in a synergetic relationship, enable the famous to be pictured, photographed, broadcast, podcast, and filmed in real time, offering a 24/7 relay across the globe."[5] Further, they address how, in the context of multiple contemporary media platforms that enable incessant access, the contemporary celebrity is often gendered female and concomitantly "devalued."[6] As Milly Williamson puts it, "Widespread scorn and deri-sion directed at celebrities is aimed predominantly at a particular kind of *female* celebrity," one who violates rules of appropriate femininity and motherhood.[7] This celebrity studies scholarship therefore suggests that the ubiquity of images of girls does not necessarily mean girls have power, but rather that the contemporary media's fascination with girls is linked to a feminization of the concept of celebrity, and that the tension between can-do and at-risk in depictions of girls relates to a "dichotomy between idolization and denigration of stars" that Leo Braudy points out "has long been with us."[8]

For Christine Geraghty, this is the "star-as-celebrity," with an intense "emphasis on the private life" regardless of what professional work the individual may (or may not) be producing.[9] In the context of this chapter on magazine cover girls—which includes celebrity girls who appear on television and in politics and who play sports, but also girls who become celebrities not because of something notable they do but rather because of something unexpected that happens to them (e.g., kidnapping and/or death)—the concept of celebrity encapsulates the importance, and often scandal, of the girl's private life. As celebrities, even if they are only celebrities for fifteen minutes, these cover girls seem to be entirely available to us; both their bodies and their selves are public—they belong to us.

Further, because they are girls, that availability is not only for our consuming pleasure. It also often insists on a protectionist response from us—one, I argue, that values innocent prepubescent white girlhood, in particular. As I show below, the covers define most girls either as what Anita Harris calls can-do, able to maintain a perfectly balanced and successful life, or as at-risk, unable to manage the pressures and dangers of girlhood and femininity.[10] In this landscape, it is most often very young white (usually blonde) girls who most need protection and most deserve adoration. Celebrity girlhood at the turn of the twenty-first century, then, is at least in part about loving and protecting imagined young white feminine innocence, just as it was in the 1970s in relation to Tatum O'Neal (as I argue in chapter 1).

In the analysis that follows, I first describe the dominant themes on the covers, specifically whiteness and the can-do/at-risk binary. In this section, I draw representative examples from every cover girl to appear on *Time*, *Newsweek*, and *People* since 1990. My goal here is to map, as objectively as possible, the magazine covers' dominant or normative versions of girlhood. In the second, longer section of the chapter, however, I turn to the book's primary interest in identifying alternative girls, insisting on finding them even here amid mass-market magazine covers.

In his analysis of *That's So Raven* (2003–2007)—whose central character is a teenage African American girl with psychic powers—Hollis Griffin argues that "when black characters are offered as main points of audience identification, the ways they navigate common narrative problems . . . [offer] a distinctly black epistemology."[11] Working from this perspective and drawing on Patricia Hill Collins, Griffin finds racial knowledge "rooted in the experiences of black women" in Raven's magical sixth sense and intuition. Acknowledging that her intuition is often played for comedy, he nevertheless insists on "the possibility [of] . . . a transformative politics of racial difference" in *That's So Raven*.[12] Similarly, here I pursue the possibility of a transformative politics on these magazine covers, even while acknowledging that to do so is to work against the statistically dominant girls on the covers. I ask: How might one complicate the pervasive depictions of whiteness and the can-do/ at-risk binary? What alternatives are there, even if they appear rarely? And how much of an against-the-grain reading is possible when we look longest at those few covers that open up questions about sexuality, race, and girls' agency outside a can-do/at-risk binary? In other words, in this chapter, I first (empirically) count, acknowledge, and document all the cover girls to appear on *Time, Newsweek,* and *People* from January 1990 to July 2012, but I then turn to the examples that I define as alternative and see as articulating the most diversity and complexity. In the process, I argue that the statistically dominant girl on these magazines is white and caught between anxiety and adoration, but that several alternative girls also emerge, girls who complicate the can-do girls' racial identity, challenge nationalism, and at least in part escape the oscillation between at-risk and can-do. While I have to work relatively hard to find these alternative girls, a key goal of this chapter is to argue for and illustrate the importance of approaching *all* instances of girlhood in contemporary U.S. media culture in a way that makes it possible to see these girls, to see those girlhoods that do not so much resist the anxious adoration and whiteness of the can-do/at-risk dichotomy, but that make them—if only temporarily—beside the point.

Cover Girls

The girls who appear on the covers of *Time, Newsweek,* and *People* from January 1990 to July 2012 can be organized into three categories, the first two of which include celebrity girls: (1) athletes, teen celebrities, or children of political figures (girls who are famous because of who they are or what they do); (2) girls who are dead, kidnapped and dead, or kidnapped and rescued (famous because of what happened to them); and (3) girls who function as symbols of some social ill or good (unlike the other two categories, these girls are nameless, on the cover not because of who they are but because of what they represent). All three types of girls are offered as objects of concern, adoration, or both. The bulk of my analysis in the subsequent section of this chapter focuses on the first two categories in order to foreground the spectacular girl celebrity—whether she is a full-fledged celebrity actively engaged in celebrity culture, or she is a fifteen-minutes-of-fame celebrity, inadvertently drawn into celebrity culture for a brief time. In this first overview section, however, I also include some discussion of the "symbol girls" in order to describe more fully the context in which the celebrity girls—especially the alternative celebrity girls—appear.

To begin, it is important to recognize that the tension between the can-do/at-risk girl is palpable across all these magazine covers: 80 percent of the 242 covers engage this tension. Perhaps the best example of this comes from 1992, when sixteen-year-old Olympic gymnast Kim Zmeskal appeared on two covers. First, on the eve of the Olympics, a *Time* cover headline read "Gym Dandy!"[13] Two weeks later, after having not fulfilled her promise at the Olympics, Zmeskal appeared on the cover of *Newsweek*, but with the headline "It Hurts: Do We Push Teen Athletes Too Hard?"[14] Zmeskal's almost simultaneous appearance on two different national news magazine covers, representing two diametrically opposed arguments about girl athletes, is a particularly stark example of the dialectic the magazines embrace between adoration for and anxiety about girls.

And there are many more examples. For instance, compare *Newsweek*'s 2002 "In Defense of Teen Girls" cover ("They're not all 'Mean Girls' and 'Ophelias'" and "How to raise a well-balanced 'Gamma Girl'"),[15] on which a smiling, red-haired teen girl wearing jeans and a modest long-sleeved T-shirt and whose head blocks part of the magazine masthead leans forward and looks directly into the camera; to *Time*'s 2000 "Early Puberty: Why Girls Are Growing Up Faster" cover ("Is it hormones? Is it fat? Is it something in the water? How parents and kids are coping"),[16] on which a slight, dark-haired, light-skinned girl wearing a plain white bra with the price tag still attached stands with her back to the camera and her head partially obscured by the magazine masthead, lit harshly from the side so that half her body is in dark shadow and half her body is so well lit the feathery hairs on her shoulder are visible. Gamma girl is big, powerful, and happy. Her body spills forward, almost escaping the borders of the magazine as she engages directly with us. Early-puberty girl is small, vulnerable, and withdrawn, faced with the trauma of buying a bra at an early age and trapped by the borders of the magazine. The masthead and her position with her back to us obscure her identity, yet harsh lighting and scant clothing reveal her body in excruciatingly fine detail.[17]

In addition to concern about pushing teen athletes too hard and early puberty, cover girls mark anxiety about general social issues such as school segregation,[18] lead poisoning,[19] and September 11.[20] They also encourage worry about issues directly related to girls, such as child beauty pageants,[21] eating disorders,[22] and global prostitution.[23] Yet numerous cover girls also illustrate social successes such as homeschooling,[24] the joys of fatherhood,[25] and the best high schools in the United States;[26] and they illustrate just how well girls are doing not only as well-balanced gamma girls but also as everyday heroes[27] and Harry Potter fans.[28] In short, collectively these many covers contribute to a cultural investment in the can-do/at-risk dichotomy of girlhood, one that ensures a persistent oscillation between celebration of and anxiety about girls.

Importantly, regardless of their characterization, the vast majority of the girls appear to be white—78 percent—and the most vulnerable at-risk girls in need of the reader/viewer's protection are very young and white, usually blonde with blue, green, or hazel eyes, looking into the camera as if asking for help, often from beyond the grave. The best-known example here is likely JonBenét Ramsey, who appeared on more covers (seven) than all other individual girls during the twenty-two and a half years of *Time*, *Newsweek*, and *People* covers I analyzed. Their blondeness makes them unequivocally white,[29] and concomitantly, their innocence makes the girls who matter—the girls who qualify as "lost girls," the girls who stand in for "every parents' worst nightmare"—white.[30] This is an unspoken, yet excessive, white and innocent girlhood. Thus girls of color are doubly marginalized: they appear infrequently, and when they do appear, they are often spectacles of anxiety, not adoration or protection.[31]

Generic teen girls, who face issues such as eating disorders and sexual exploitation and the dangers of the Internet, most often also appear to be white, but they more often have dark hair and sometimes appear to be generically ethnic: Jewish? Latina? Mixed?[32] They usually face away from the camera, often looking down, and seem to bear some (but not all) responsibility for their troubles. For example, a *People* cover about eating disorders features a girl who appears white–ethnic: the small print reveals that her name is Wendy Levey from New York City, which one might imagine could mean "Jewish." She looks down—perhaps at a mirror off camera or maybe at a television set or magazine cover such as the one on which she appears—as she holds her hands to her back and her stomach, as if measuring the size of her waist. Next to her, but much smaller, images of hyper-thin media stars Courteney Cox, Pamela Lee, and Heather Locklear support the headline's Ophelia Thesis claim that "media images of celebrities teach kids to hate their bodies." One reading here, then, is that this generic girl is overly obsessive about her perfectly fine body and that she engages in behaviors she should change, but that those behaviors are the result of media consumption. Presumably, if she took responsibility for her media consumption and cut back (on media consumption rather than food), it would be easier for her to stop hating her own body.

This brief analysis illustrates the dominant representation of girls on these magazine covers: they are primarily white and caught in a tension between adoration of their girlish success and/or innocence, and anxiety about what they represent or how they behave.[33] Further, the most vulnerable (at-risk) girls—those who need protection—are white, blonde, and very young. Empirically, then, mass magazine cover girls depend on and contribute to the dominance of whiteness and the abjection of people of color. Further, this racialized structure links to a can-do/at-risk dialectic in such a way that the girls we are encouraged to love—regardless of whether we adore them or worry about them—are white.

And yet, what if we turn away from the can-do/at-risk dichotomy and pursue additional readings of the few girls of color who do appear on these covers? What if we move away from empiricism and toward a critical investment in finding and exploring alternative girls, even in the heart of the mainstream mass media to which *Time, Newsweek,* and *People* covers contribute? In the next section I ask: What are the exceptions to the dominance of whiteness and the Möbius strip of can-do/ at-risk and adoration/anxiety? And why is it important to center those exceptions in feminist media analysis?

Alternative Cover Girls

Two kinds of alternative girls appear on these magazine covers: those who are not white and/or those who can be read beyond the bounds of anxious adoration, who may activate the can-do/at-risk dichotomy but can also be understood to do something more than simply reproduce that dichotomy. In other words, here I am interested in girls who are spectacular in part because of their difference. Additionally, my focus here is on the first two categories of girls that I mention in the previous section: girls who either were well-known before appearing on the cover (daughters of politicians, teen celebrities, and sport stars) or who drew sufficient attention at the time they appeared on the cover that a casual viewer might already know a few details of their stories when seeing the cover (kidnapped and/or dead girls). By emphasizing girls who are (at least temporarily) spectacular in their fame, my goal is to address a more complex girlhood than those represented by the fleeting symbolic girl (the third category in the previous section), to consider girlhoods that can be imagined to escape the bounds of the magazine covers. Further, in pursuit of more complexity, multiplicity, and resistant/feminist readings when examining girls I define as alternative, in this section I analyze the cover story along with the cover image. By looking closely at alternative cover girls on and in the very same magazines that produce the dominant cover girl, I seek to use the magazines against themselves.

I organize my discussion by separating the celebrity girls into four more specific types: (1) daughters of high-profile politicians, (2) teen celebrities, (3) sports stars, and (4) girls who become (temporarily) famous through vulnerability: death and/or kidnapping. In each section, I first discuss the majority girls and then move on to a fuller, more subjective discussion of the ways in which some of the cover girls offer alternative girlhoods. I start with the two categories that seem to offer the least opportunity for challenging the dominant white, can-do/at-risk version of girlhood: the daughters of politicians and the teen celebrities. From there, I turn to the sports stars, who I argue have the potential to open up a critique of nationalism, and then conclude with an analysis of the kidnapped and/or dead girls. These girls, despite (or maybe because of) their trauma, allow me to develop the most resistant reading of some mass-magazine cover girls as nonnormative girls who, despite their spectacularization, can be read as making choices that cannot fully be reduced to can-do/at-risk.

Daughters of Political Figures

Between January 1990 and July 2012, the children of the three U.S. presidents with school-age or teenage children appeared on the cover of these magazines: Chelsea Clinton on *Time*[34] and twice on *People*,[35] Barbara and Jenna Bush on *People*,[36] and Sasha and Malia Obama twice on *People*.[37] Additionally, Bristol Palin—vice-presidential candidate Sarah Palin's teenage, unwed daughter—appeared on the cover of *People* after she had her baby.[38] On the one hand, the appearance of the Obamas— the girls of color in the group—is not particularly alternative. After all, during these twenty years every (non-adult) child of a seated U.S. president appeared on at least one cover. On the other hand, one difference between their representation and that of Chelsea, Barbara, Jenna, and Bristol is significant: Sasha and Malia are not associated with the scandal that is typical of star and celebrity culture, whereas each of the other daughters of politicians is.

The 1998 *Time* Clinton cover features Chelsea with her parents, sandwiched between them as they leave "the White House for Martha's Vineyard": all three of them smiling. The headline declares "It's Nobody's Business but Ours," referring to the ongoing Lewinsky scandal. Chelsea's parents flank and protect her, and the headline further suggests that if the public and the politicians were to leave her father alone, they would—by extension—be leaving her (and her mother) alone. In contrast to Chelsea—who is affected by someone else's inappropriate choices—the Bush daughters appear on the cover of *People* ostensibly because of scandals directly involving them, with the headline "The Bush Girls' Latest Scrape: Oops! They Did It Again," emphasizing both the current and former scandals in which they were involved. This time, they had been caught "trying to sneak a drink."[39] Like them, Bristol Palin appears because of a scandal, holding the evidence of her "mistake": her newborn. All but Chelsea appear in relation to their inappropriate choices; they are worth looking at as cover girls because of their fascinating at-risk behavior. Chelsea nevertheless is also at-risk; her depiction as innocent simply calls for a protectionist response.

Unattached to scandal, the Obama girls appear with their parents in a relaxed home setting on both 2008 *People* covers. The headlines read "The Obamas at Home" (in Chicago)[40] and "The Obamas' New Life" (in the White House).[41] Both covers associate Sasha and Malia with idealized domesticity and depict them as regular girls, despite their fame, through references to chores and piano practice on the first cover and new friends and a new puppy on the second cover. Both images feature

Figure 2.1. Sasha and Malia with their parents on the cover of *People*, November 24, 2008.

the family clustered together, smiling and touching in a casual pose. Sasha and Malia are on the cover, but unlike the other daughters-of-politicians girls—particularly Jenna, Barbara, and Bristol, who represent girls' bad behavior—Sasha and Malia are supplemental, contributing to the definition of a domesticated presidential nuclear family.

Inside "The Obamas at Home" issue additional casual family snapshots appear, along with a picture of the girls playing with a Hula-Hoop at a Fourth of July celebration.[42] In "The Obamas' New Life" issue, interior photos again show them with their parents, hugging, kissing goodbye at school, and greeting a puppy.[43] Like the images, the articles themselves offer only joy and calm regarding Sasha and Malia. An enlarged quotation from Michelle paints a picture of girls who seem to be able to achieve anything: "Our girls love to talk. . . . They feel confident in their own opinions because we value them even if they're silly or wrong or a little off."[44] They are achievers; collectively they take classes in soccer, dance, drama, gymnastics, tap, tennis, and piano. When they learn to read on their own their reward is an extra half hour before lights out—for more reading.

Yet these are not spoiled girls; they do not even face that minor risk. The article reports that the girls "set and clear the dinner table," and that they follow the rules by taking off their shoes in the living room.[45] A sidebar reports the "Obama house rules: no whining, arguing, or annoying teasing; make the bed, set your own alarm clock; keep playroom toy closet clean, lights out at 8:30." It also reports that their allowance is one dollar a week for doing chores.[46] Neither are they lacking for fun—again, no risk of overbearing parents here. While they take their shoes off downstairs, upstairs they have a playroom in which they are allowed to jump on the couch. Nor, the article and Barack assume, will they face a risk of being damaged by the campaign trail or the possibility that their father will succeed in becoming president. And this is not just a case of disavowal. The article provides evidence of careful parenting, geared toward self-consciously helping the girls live with their new status as celebrities. When Malia hears television pundits attacking her mother, Barack reports, "'we talked it through.' . . . 'Fortunately,' he adds with a playful grin, 'she's completely confident about her mommy's wonderfulness.'"[47] In fact, the theme of talking things through frequently appears in the article, including mornings in bed for all four family members (or three if Barack is out of town), and talking, as Michelle reports, "about Daddy being President, about adolescence, about the questions they have."[48] The second article focuses less attention on the girls, but carries over the theme of the girls being the "top priority." The "Obamas' To-Do List" includes "holding life steady for their two daughters," finding a school so the girls can feel "settled," and making "the White House their own" so that the girls "feel comfortable."[49]

As African American girls in the public eye, Sasha and Malia Obama function as both evidence that "all people" can achieve the American Dream—hence as the most model of model minorities—and as postracial girl role models who maintain a healthy, balanced, and modest lifestyle, regardless of their surroundings or how famous and powerful their father is. Like wish fulfillments, they embody a seemingly postracial future in which their father is president and they are his can-do daughters—of course achieving and maintaining that status with the sage and supportive help of their idealized parents.

How alternative are Sasha and Malia when their cover girl status is as perfect, can-do, postracial girls? Yes, they redefine the idealized girl as African American. As Cheryl Wall argues when writing about President Obama's first inauguration day, "What a wonder it was that surely for the first time in history, if only for a day, the most adored children in the world were two little black girls."[50] Yes, they break with the typical image of the girl of color as at-risk. In these two ways, Sasha and Malia's presence on the covers of these magazines shifts the racialization of the can-do/at-risk dichotomy. Yet the can-do girl is still an impossible ideal—a spectacular image produced for avid consumption in the context of postfeminism and neoliberalism—even if it now includes two particularly famous African American girls. Can-do status, in general, is still beyond the reach of an everyday girl who likely does not have the time, economic resources, and/or political connections necessary to achieve a full can-do identity. Certainly, here, as first daughters, Sasha and Malia's can-do status is abstract and unattainable—it is phenomenal. Further, as Kent Ono argues, the very idea of postracism masks continuing racialized social inequities.[51] Later in her article, Wall develops this idea, backing off her initial optimism and pointing out that the public existence of Sasha and Malia, their celebrity status, is not enough: it may lead to proposed Sasha and Malia dolls for non-presidential parents to buy and children to play with, but it does not lead to change for the many African Americans who face environmental, social, and economic inequities.[52] In short, when considering the Sasha and Malia covers in the context of the hegemony of the can-do girl and her relationship to a postracism that disavows social inequality, I do not read the Obamas as alternative girls.

In the end, my analysis of these cover girls embraces a contradiction. Like Wall, I take pleasure in the fact of Sasha and Malia; I enjoy the fantasy of African American girls as idealized role models for all girls, as girls to notice. Like Griffin's argument regarding Raven, I consider just the appearance of these two African American girls to be significant. Yet, also like Wall, in the end I see only the smallest difference between the magazines' depictions of Sasha and Malia and the same magazines' much more common depictions of a generic, white, can-do gamma girl. Sasha and Malia shift gamma girl's racialization, but—at least on the covers and pages of these magazines—that change does little if anything to redefine the impossible fantasy of perfect girlhood. Gamma girl and the Obama girls remain objects for adoration, overdetermined as can-do and thereby shoring up the can-do/at-risk dichotomy.

Teen Celebrities

Because I include the celebrity magazine *People* in my sample, teen celebrities are a particularly large category of girls on these covers. In fact, while *Time* features eighteen-year-old Asian American singer Utada Hikaru along with several other (non-girl) music stars on one cover,[53] and *Newsweek* features Paris Hilton and Britney Spears when they were in their twenties in relation to a "debate over kids and values,"[54] the rest of the nonathlete teen celebrities appear on the covers of forty-one different issues of *People*. In chronological order, they are as follows: Drew Barrymore;[55] Sandra Dee of *Gidget* (1959), pictured as a teen in an inset photo;[56] Dana Plato, the former child actor from *Diff'rent Strokes* (1978–1986);[57] Shannen Doherty of *Beverly Hills, 90210* (1990–1994);[58] Tracey Gold from *Growing Pains* (1982–1992);[59] the cast of *The Brady Bunch* (1969–1974);[60] Annette Funicello, both as a teenage Mouseketeer (in an inset) and as an adult;[61] Soleil Moon Frye of *Punky Brewster* (1984–1988);[62] Mackenzie Phillips of *One Day at a Time*

(1975–1984), pictured as a teen in an inset photo;[63] Brandy (Norwood) of *Moesha* (1996–2001);[64] Neve Campbell, Lacey Chabert, and Jennifer Love Hewitt of *Party of Five* (1994–2000);[65] Kate Winslet in *Titanic* (1997);[66] Olivia Newton-John in *Grease* (1978);[67] "Brat Pack" members Ally Sheedy and Molly Ringwald in images of them as teens in the 1980s;[68] singer LeAnn Rimes;[69] Dana Plato (again);[70] the *Brady Bunch* girls (again);[71] Britney Spears;[72] girls from *Square Pegs* (1982–1983), *Fame* (1982–1987), and *The Facts of Life* (1979–1988) in a "Where Are They Now?" cover;[73] Tatum O'Neal, with an inset picture of her in *Paper Moon* (1973);[74] Mary-Kate and Ashley Olsen;[75] Mary-Kate and Ashley Olsen (again);[76] Mary-Kate Olsen (again);[77] Lindsay Lohan;[78] Lindsay Lohan (again);[79] Lindsay Lohan (again);[80] Miley Cyrus;[81] Dakota Fanning and Hilary Duff as two of the "World's Richest Teens";[82] Vanessa Hudgens, Ashley Tisdale, and Monique Coleman (along with the boys) from *High School Musical 2* (2007);[83] Vanessa Hudgens (again) with her costar Zac Efron;[84] Miley Cyrus (again);[85] Miley Cyrus (again);[86] the cast of *High School Musical 3* (2008) (again);[87] Brenda Song of *Suite Life on Deck* (2008–2011);[88] Selena Gomez and Demi Lovato;[89] the cast of *Saved by the Bell* (1989–1993), pictured as teens in an inset photo;[90] Miranda Cosgrove from Nickelodeon's *iCarly* (2007–2012);[91] Kristen Stewart of *Twilight*;[92] Kristen Stewart (again);[93] Jennifer Lawrence of *The Hunger Games*;[94] and Jennifer Lawrence (again).[95]

The most common type of cover in this group features beautiful pictures of smiling teen celebrities. By and large, these are happy, adorable, well-adjusted girls. The covers explore the fact and pleasure of teen stardom (the Brat Pack cover, Brandy, Mary-Kate and Ashley Olsen, Lindsay Lohan, Brenda Song, Selena Gomez and Demi Lovato, and Miranda Cosgrove), including the more specific topic of "Raising a Teen Star (the Right Way)!" (Miley Cyrus, featured with her dad).[96] Sometimes the actors appear with their costars, often in ways that conjure images of fun on- and off-screen (*Party of Five* cast) and/or hint at real-life romance (Shannen Doherty with *Beverly Hills, 90210* boys, Vanessa Hudgens with Zac Efron, and Kristin Stewart with the *Twilight* boys). While pleasure and happiness are certainly dominant, sometimes the covers link the stars to personal challenges, such as the decision to have breast-reduction surgery (Soleil Moon Frye), becoming suddenly rich or being one of the "World's Richest Kids" (LeAnn Rimes and Miley

Cyrus,[97] respectively), or—more anxiously—being "Too Sexy, Too Soon?" (Britney Spears), eating disorders (Tracey Gold and Mary-Kate Olsen),[98] or family crisis (Lindsay Lohan).[99] Several covers specifically articulate anxiety about the danger of celebrity for girls (Drew Barrymore and Tatum O'Neal), some by pairing images of the actor happy and smiling in earlier years with more recent, smaller pictures of her in distress (e.g., Dana Plato's arrest for armed robbery[100] and ultimately death,[101] and Lindsay Lohan's DUI[102]). In addition to the can-do/at-risk tension on these covers, reading across multiple covers, *People* produces the same tension for Mary-Kate Olsen: in May 2004 she appears on one of the "Inside Our [wonderful teen stardom] World" covers, only to appear two months later on a cover about her "Eating Disorder Crisis."

As a whole, despite the covers that address anxiety about celebrity girls, the teens appear happy and relaxed, and they come across as romantic (but not erotic) figures. Even the cover featuring Britney Spears uses a subtitle to the "Too Sexy, Too Soon?" headline to soften the anxiety about teen girls' sexuality: "Little girls love her, but her image makes some moms nervous. The controversial teen singer sets the record straight about breast implants (no way!), much older guys (yuck!), and e-mailing Prince William ('He's so sweet!')." She appears lovely, but her gaze arguably is not alluring and her sleeveless top, though tight-fitting, is not skimpy, as it covers most of her upper body. In short, a few of these girls are at-risk, rendered vulnerable because of their celebrity, but the majority are happy and successful can-do girls.

Of the nearly fifty teen celebrities appearing on these covers, only seven are stars of color:[103] African American Brandy, Japanese American Utada Hikaru, Hmong Thai Asian American Brenda Song, African American Kim Fields (*The Facts of Life*), African American Monique Coleman, mixed race Filipina American Vanessa Hudgens, and mixed race Mexican American Selena Gomez.[104] And of these seven, only two—Vanessa Hudgens and Selena Gomez—are the primary subject of their covers and cover stories. Further, while Selena Gomez's name, in conjunction with the mixed race identity of her most famous character—Alex of *Wizards of Waverly Place* (2007–2012)—makes clear she is Latina, like "most Latina/o stars . . . over the last century"[105] she is light-skinned and also often performs and plays characters who read as white or as racially ambiguous, thereby potentially masking her Latina identity. Thus the covers' depiction of the two most prominent of these stars of color—Hudgens and Gomez—contributes to what Angharad Valdivia calls the "fourth stage" of racial representation, one of ambiguity and hybridity. She writes, "With an ambiguously brown image an advertiser [or magazine cover] can potentially appeal to a broad range of ethnicities ranging from white to Latina, Native American, Asian American, Indian, Middle Eastern, and even black if the signifiers are ambiguous enough."[106] In other words, these girls' racialization is a marketing tool, but not a topic of discussion.

As these *Time*, *Newsweek*, and *People* covers would have it, there simply are no significant African American or other explicitly racialized teen celebrities in U.S. media culture girlhood (the five covers including small pictures of relatively unknown and/or ensemble cast girls of color notwithstanding). As I illustrate in the book's introduction, these girl celebrities of color certainly exist; yet, during these twenty-two and a half years, high-profile teen celebrities of color such as Raven-Symoné, America Ferrera, Keke Palmer, and Rihanna, for example, did not appear on the covers. From a perspective invested in examining alternative girlhoods, then, my first argument must be a critique of the systematic elimination of girl celebrities of color from the landscape of the magazine covers at the grocery checkout or newsstand, even though they appear time and again in other mediated spaces. In other words, girls of color are not just absent from these covers, but—given their visibility elsewhere—they are neglected, displaced, and denied. That said, I want to take the opportunity offered by Hudgens's and Gomez's appearance on these covers to look inside the magazines at the articles about these two celebrities of color to understand how they, in particular, are positioned in relation to girlhood, to ask whether the articles make their racialization explicit or implicit, and to explore the possibility of imagining alternatives to whiteness through these two girl celebrities.

The issue on Selena Gomez centers her lifelong friendship with Demi Lovato. We learn that they met while auditioning for *Barney and Friends* (1992–present), appeared together on the show, were homeschooled together, identify strongly as Texans, and stay in touch via Twitter. The issue emphasizes their similarity: calling them "two seven-year-old brunettes" when they met,[107] and featuring them in a

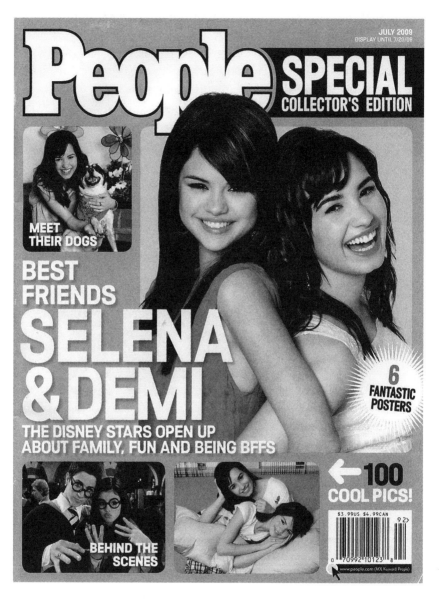

Figure 2.2. Selena Gomez and Demi Lovato as BFFs on the cover of *People*, July 22, 2009.

two-page photo in which they lie on their backs with their hair flowing together and with the title "Two of a Kind!" When they worked together on the 2009 made-for-TV-movie *Princess Protection Program*, "It honestly didn't feel like work. It was fun to make."[108] They are BFFs and "just really connected."[109] Interview questions also pursue Gomez's relatively tame love life: her on-screen kiss with Dylan Sprouse when she was twelve years old, her crush on Shia LaBeouf, and her friendship with Taylor Lautner. The many photos depict Gomez as glamorous but also playful; she is often affectionately touching fellow cast members in the photos, and whenever Gomez and Lovato appear together they are touching (or, in a few cases, hitting each other with pillows in a typical tween girl sleepover pillow-fight scene). Gomez seems to be an ideal/ typical friend, lavishing affection on everyone with whom she works/ plays and staying true to her BFF: she is the kind of girl anyone would want to be around. Nowhere does the issue address how Gomez self-identifies racially, or how she feels about portraying a Latina in *Wizards of Waverly Place*, or what it means to her to be mixed. Instead, the emotional and physical link between Gomez and Lovato—whose entwined hair and lifelong friendship makes them appear almost as one—contributes to an ambiguous racial hybridity for both of them, a hybridity that is part of their appeal, their uniqueness, and, in fact, their spectacularization, but that does not seem to make any real difference in their lives or work.

One of the two Hudgens *High School Musical 2* covers features her with Zac Efron, her on-screen and (at the time) off-screen boyfriend, and offers even less access to an explicitly nonwhite racialization. Both on the cover and in the article and photos inside, Hudgens and Efron are portrayed as fun teens, loving and affectionate but not especially sexualized (only one small photo shows them actually kissing romantically), with nothing scandalous about them at all.[110] Almost all the photos show the couple together in fun poses: at the beach, drinking a frozen coffee drink, on a swing, and simultaneously kissing an Emmy statue won by *High School Musical*. Establishing the romantic but not sexual nature of their relationship and maintaining their success stories—and Hudgens's status as a can-do girl—the article claims, "Like teen celebrities from a gentler era, Efron and Hudgens get spotted out buying Pinkberry frozen yogurt, not stumbling out of nightclubs." And:

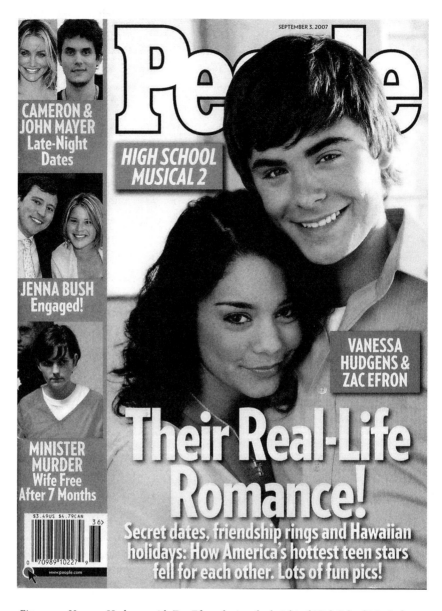

Figure 2.3. Vanessa Hudgens with Zac Efron during the height of *High School Musical* success, September 3, 2007.

"At heart, the biggest teen stars on the planet remain two low-key kids who were raised by middle-class parents and like to do pretty much the same things they did before they were stars." Like Gomez, Hudgens is glamorous (she has "three closets devoted entirely to shoes"), but she is also just a normal kid. The article reports that she wants to go to college (as does Efron) and declares, "Though fame is 'exciting,' says Hudgens, 'it's hard to keep a personal life. I am a teenager. Part of me just wants to be normal.'" The only oblique reference to her specific racialization is a claim that she "dreams of playing Maria in *West Side Story*."[111] Otherwise, she is just an everyday girl dealing in as squeaky-clean a way as possible with mega stardom.

Overall, then, the articles' representation of these two stars of color downplays their distinctly racialized identities. While the articles do ever so slightly acknowledge Gomez's and Hudgens's raciality—Gomez is a "brunette" and Hudgens wants to play "Maria"—they do so only in a way that activates "ambiguous hybridity" and without addressing any specific racialization. Through these stars, then, girlhood is no longer white, but as with Sasha and Malia Obama, that change does not transform the can-do category beyond a—slight—darkening. Griffin argues that "racial difference is an event communicated wherever the signs of blackness are deployed in the name of capital," and he uses that claim to read a black girl epistemology in *That's So Raven*.[112] Similarly, here, I *want* Selena Gomez's and Vanessa Hudgens's mixed identity and racial difference to matter, just as I want racial difference to matter in relation to Sasha and Malia. It matters to me when I look at these covers; and it is there—present—not only for me, but also for anyone interested in questions of racial identity and representation. But, I must admit, racial difference does not matter in the context of the covers and the cover stories. In fact, like the magazines' exclusion of other high-profile celebrities of color, the particular way *People* represents Gomez and Hudgens could be said to deny rather than to acknowledge racial difference. Nevertheless, there it is, smiling out at passersby and subtly (and only ever so slightly) refiguring the image of the can-do teen celebrity girl. In short, like Sasha and Malia, Gomez and Hudgens simultaneously challenge the whiteness of the can-do girl and contribute to a postracial discourse that makes racial difference (only) a commodity.

Sports Stars

As in all the other categories, the sport stars who appear on the covers tend to be white: this is not surprising, given that high-profile sports in which girls typically participate (gymnastics, figure skating, and tennis) are dominated by white athletes. Despite this dominance of whiteness—linked to nationalism in the case of sports—I am nevertheless able to read more developed alternative girlhoods in this category, as I illustrate below.

Between 1990 and July 2012, the following athletes appeared on the covers of *Time*, *Newsweek*, and/or *People* while still teenagers, some of them twice: Olympic gymnasts Kim Zmeskal[113] and Kerri Strug;[114] tennis players Jennifer Capriati[115] and Venus Williams and Serena Williams (together);[116] and Olympic figure skaters Michelle Kwan,[117] Tara Lipinski,[118] and Sarah Hughes.[119] Of these eleven covers, three featured girl athletes of color: *Time*'s Venus and Serena Williams cover and *Newsweek*'s and *People*'s Michelle Kwan covers.

Overall, these sports covers tend to be patriotic and/or celebratory. For example, on a *Time* cover Kerri Strug—who performed a vault on a severely injured ankle at the 1996 Olympics—appears in Béla Károlyi's arms with her ankle taped, wearing her team gold medal and holding a bouquet of flowers aloft.[120] Heightening the celebration of Strug's achievement, her image appears alongside a photo of an injured man, lying on the ground, after the 1996 Atlanta Olympics bombing. The headline reads "Courage and Cowardice." Clearly, Strug represents the former. On an issue of *People*, Strug appears in everyday clothes and wearing her medal, alongside the headline "Encore! Encore! America's Gold Medal Winners Look Back in Wonder—and Begin the Rest of Their Lives."[121] Her sweater is red, her lipstick is bright red, the headline is blue, and the background is white: she is a symbol of the nation. Figure skater Sarah Hughes appears on the cover of *Time*'s Olympic preview edition, pictured in an ice skating jump that seems to have taken her almost above the mountains featured in the background. The subtitle claims "Peak Performance." While she wears a soft orange skating dress, patriotic red, white, and blue dominate the background, the masthead, and the magazine's border. Gymnast Kim Zmeskal and tennis player Jennifer Capriati are also featured on nationalistic and celebratory covers: *Newsweek* declares Capriati "The 8th Grade Wonder" and shows her smiling broadly at the camera while holding and playing with a small dog.[122] And, as I discuss above, *Time* calls Zmeskal "Gym Dandy." Like Hughes, on this cover Zmeskal makes an impossible jump, outside any real space and with no physical place to land. And, again, red, white, and blue dominate the image, including Zmeskal's blue leotard. In short, these athletes are in a perpetual state of overwhelming nationalist achievement; indeed, achievement literally unachievable by anyone (e.g., leaping over a mountain), even the world-class athletes they are.

The two covers that are more concerned than celebratory nevertheless continue to produce affection for the girl athletes while also asking whether "we push teen athletes too hard?" (Zmeskal)[123] and "what went wrong?" (Capriati).[124] Both questions suggest a protectionist stance toward these formerly simply beloved athletes; and *People* follows up with a subtitle about Capriati declaring "At 13, she was a bubbly kid with a booming forehand. At 18, she's burned out, partying hard, and facing a drug charge. Is this payback for a stolen childhood?" Two images appear on the cover, a large image of Capriati at age thirteen, on a tennis court in action and smiling, and a smaller inset image of her mug shot from her arrest for marijuana possession. The two Capriati images on one cover—the large happy image and the small distraught image—make clear that the covers are not giving up on affection for these girl wonders. In fact, the concern for the girls grows out of and depends on that affection. In other words, without the pre-existing affection, there would be no current concern or attention. Overall, these athletes are the nation's darlings, loved and—when necessary—protected.

Turning to an analysis of the athletes of color, neither the Michelle Kwan covers nor the Venus and Serena Williams cover fits completely within these nationalist, celebratory, and/or protectionist modes. For example, Kwan's *People* cover does not use red, white, and blue at all. Kwan's *Newsweek* cover is red, white, and blue, but white dominates both the background and Kwan's skating dress. This color scheme, along with the headline "Soul on Ice," associates her, perhaps, more with figure skating ice than with the nation. Further, unlike Zmeskal and Hughes, Kwan is not in motion in this image. Rather, she poses in a vague figure skating position and smiles for the camera. Her long hair is loose and falls around her shoulders and arm in a way it never would during competition. Both feet touch the ground. In short, while she is lovely, this picture does not portray her as a powerful or accomplished athlete representing the United States. And while the *People* cover does depict her in motion (as though she is skating forward off the cover toward the viewer) despite a smile, her face is pinched (perhaps in concentration or effort). On both covers, then, she is lovely, but neither explicitly Americanized nor completely in control of her athletic abilities.[125]

The article inside *Newsweek* continues the both of and not of the United States tone in its discussion of Kwan. While it claims she is "the odds-on favorite to produce America's iconic moment," it also draws a tenuous connection between her claim that "I control my own Olympic destiny" and what the article calls "the modesty . . . simplicity and genuine friendliness of Nagano itself."[126] While the idea that one controls one's own Olympic destiny does not sound modest to me, the article insists on connecting Kwan to an Orientalist image of a "modest" and traditional Nagano, thereby displacing her from an unequivocal U.S. identity.[127] The *People* article stereotypes Kwan as well, emphasizing that, in comparison to her teammates Tara Lipinski and Nicole Bobek, she is "ultradisciplined" and her parents are "very protective."[128] In short, across these two covers, Kwan is American, but only sort of. She is a sheltered and hard-working Asian (American) beauty, but she is not the stuff of absolute-girlish-wonder and national power (nor a girl in need of—or deserving—protection) as are the white girl athletes to appear on the cover of these magazines.

The covers distance not only Kwan from Americanness, but also the only other girl athletes of color to appear on these magazines during these twenty-two and a half years. "The Sisters vs. the World" declares *Time*, along with pictures of both Venus and Serena Williams in close-up action.[129] One possible reading here is that the Williams sisters are in conflict with everyone, including "Americans." They can be read as isolated, unique players who are aggressive but certainly not adored by the nation. The subtitle suggests an additional interpretation, however: "Taunts! Tantrums! Talent! Why the women, led by Venus and Serena Williams, are pushing the men off center court." Here, the words position Venus and Serena with the other girl and women players, in opposition to the men, who are implied to be "the world" by the primary headline. Yet it is the Williamses who are held responsible for men's displacement. Inside the magazine a third interpretation of "the world" emerges. There, we learn that none of the other players on the tour likes Venus and Serena because they are supposedly "arrogant," "aloof," and "rarely compliment or congratulate an opponent."[130] Thus

Figure 2.4. Venus and Serena Williams battle the world on the cover of *Time*, September 3, 2001.

"the world" could be read to mean "other top women tennis players," including Americans.

In any of these three readings—(1) the Williams sisters are without nation, (2) they lead a displacement of men, or (3) they are isolated from other girl and women tennis players—the headline sets Venus and Serena apart, and it defines them as different and in conflict because of it. As Delia Douglas puts it, "The unmistakable message here is that they do not belong."[131] The article does name race explicitly as one of their differences, claiming that it is part of "their appeal,"[132] and that it brings an expanded fan base to tennis ("blacks are now more than twice as likely to identify themselves as avid tennis fans as whites");[133] but also suggesting that their race leads to animosity because (1) they supposedly socialize only with other African American players in the top one hundred (Chanda Rubin and Alexandra Stevenson), (2) their father often claims there is racism on the tour and in media coverage, and (3) they "get sponsors because they are black" (according to fellow player Martina Hingis).[134] Yet, like for Kwan and the Obama girls, the Williamses' particular racial identity is also a point of affection for the magazine—a difference that can be embraced: Venus and Serena are invested in education and they, "like the equally driven Jackson and Wayans families[,] . . . are Jehovah's Witnesses. . . . Serena, in fact, buys her rap albums at Wal-Mart because the bad words have been excised."[135]

The racialization of Kwan, Venus, and Serena includes both (1) a displacement from patriotic U.S. nationalism and (2) an exoticized affection for quaint and essentialized supposedly Asian and African American characteristics (modesty and valuing education, respectively). I read both depictions doubly. First, I read these athletes' displacement from U.S. patriotism, on the one hand, to produce racial exclusion even as it seems to include racial difference by featuring Kwan and Venus and Serena Williams on the covers. On the other hand, Kwan's, Venus's, and Serena's explicit difference from the white athletes makes it possible to read them as challenging nationalism and displacing whiteness. And, second, in terms of affection for the athletes' racialization, on the one hand the construction of Venus and Serena Williams as African American Horatio Algers in their approach to education implies that African Americans who cannot pull themselves out of poverty—by sheer hard work, good families, high moral standards, and self-sacrifice—are responsible for their own poverty. On the other hand, the fact that as teen girl professional athletes Venus and Serena were able to make the very unusual move to value both education and sport challenges the tennis status quo. Venus and Serena are smart girls, but they are not simply "can-do." They do things differently. In other words, because they are more than just athletes who either succeed (most others) or fail (Zmeskal, Capriati) spectacularly, Venus and Serena escape the can-do/ at-risk dichotomy. Hence Venus and Serena Williams, and Kwan to a certain extent, rewrite what it means to be a cover girl in ways that challenge both unquestioned nationalism and the adoration/protectionist stance of the majority of the magazine covers.

Girls in Peril

Seemingly in direct opposition to the primarily happy and successful daughters of politicians, teen celebrities, and sport stars, girls often also appear on the covers as vulnerable and threatened: either dead as a result of a tragedy, kidnapped and still lost, or kidnapped and rescued. Some of these girls remain nameless and/or function as a symbol of tragedy in relation to other topics, such as teen violence,[136] conflict in the Middle East,[137] and TWA Flight 800.[138] The covers I focus on in this section, however, depict the girls not only as vulnerable but also as celebrities themselves, famous at least for a brief time because of something horrific that has happened to them. These are the at-risk spectacular girls who counterbalance the can-do teen celebrities and sports stars.

All three of the magazines contribute to this category, although *People* provides by far the most examples. For instance, within the space of seven weeks, *People* featured three covers about Jaycee Dugard and Elizabeth Smart, two blonde-white girls who had been kidnapped (separately) but eventually rescued. In August 2009, twenty-nine-year-old Dugard, who had been kidnapped when she was eleven years old, was rescued, along with her two daughters born while she was held captive. *People* ran two cover stories seven weeks apart, both featuring pictures of Dugard as a child.[139] In the interim, it ran a story on Smart, who had been kidnapped in 2002 and rescued in 2003, but was now giving testimony in the competency trial of the man who kidnapped her.[140] *People* also featured Smart just over a year earlier,[141] and twice in 2003 around the time she was rescued.[142] *Newsweek* likewise featured Smart when she was rescued.[143] In addition, *People* ran one more cover on Dugard in 2011, when she published a memoir.[144]

In 2002, *People* ran the only story about girls of color who had been kidnapped and survived: it featured Latina Jacqueline Marris[145] and African American Tamara Brooks, two teens who fought back and escaped their kidnappers.[146]

Stories on kidnapped girls who—unlike Smart, Dugard, Marris, and Brooks—were murdered or were still missing at the time of the cover include the following white (almost all blonde) girls: Polly Klaas, whose kidnapping and murder contributed to the establishment of California's three strikes law;[147] Madeleine McCann, a British girl abducted while her family was vacationing in Portugal in 2007 and who remains unfound;[148] Lisa Irwin, who disappeared when she was only ten months old;[149] and Miranda Gaddis and Ashley Pond, who were both kidnapped in the same Oregon town.[150] In August 2002, both Oregon girls' remains were found and their alleged murderer was arrested, but *People* did not run a follow-up cover story. Similarly, in 1999, when Carole Sund, her teenage (blonde) daughter Julie Sund, and a (blonde) exchange student from Argentina, Silvina Pelosso, disappeared, *People* ran a cover story.[151] Again, the magazine did not run a cover story when the three bodies were found, or when the murderer confessed. Of these girls, McCann is the only one to appear on more than one cover: *People* featured her three times in the space of six months.

In 1998, *Time* ran the only cover featuring kidnapped girls of color who had not been found.[152] The cover includes two pictures: one in the foreground of the girls' father, Indian American Bipin Shah, holding a (blonde) child's doll; and one in the background of the two girls, Sarah Lynn Shah and Genevieve Marie Shah.[153] Their mother (Bipin's ex-wife) had taken them, and he was offering a $2 million reward for their return while running a worldwide search.

Additionally, girls who died as a result of something other than kidnapping appeared on all three magazines during this twenty-two-and-a-half-year period—almost all featuring blonde-white girls under the age of ten. JonBenét Ramsey—the child beauty pageant participant whose murderer still has not been found—is, of course, the most famous of these girls; she appeared on five *People*[154] and two *Newsweek*[155] covers.[156] Caylee Anthony is a more recent example; she appeared on five *People* covers between 2008 and 2011, all of which included images of her mother who was arrested and then tried for her murder.[157] In addition, the following dead white girls appeared on the covers of these magazines: Jessica Steinberg, who died as a result of child abuse;[158] Adrianne Jones, who was killed by two other teens;[159] and Phoebe Prince, who committed suicide as a result of bullying by "mean girls."[160]

Only two girls who died as a result of something other than kidnapping stand out as distinct in this category. First, in 1995 *Time* ran a story on the only dead girl of color to appear on these covers: Cuban American/African American Elisa Izquierdo, who had been murdered by her mother (who was known to have been abusing her).[161] Second, only one girl to appear on these covers died because of her own actions rather than others' abuse: Jessica Dubroff, a seven-year-old pilot who died while trying to fly a plane across the country (in the company of her father and flight instructor). When the plane crashed as a result of bad weather in April 1996, both *Time*[162] and *People*[163] ran cover stories.

As with the teen celebrities, the thirty-five covers and twenty dead and/or kidnapped girls make close examination of each cover impossible in the space of one chapter, but I do want to mention several themes that emerge. First, as my descriptions above suggest, the girls are overwhelmingly not just white, but blonde-white. Their whiteness is definitive.[164] Only the two teens who fought back and avoided kidnapping (Jacqueline Marris and Tamara Brooks), one of the two girls kidnapped in Oregon, the two Shah girls, Jessica Steinberg, Elisa Izquierdo, Caylee Anthony, Polly Klaas, Phoebe Prince, and Jessica Dubroff are not blonde and/or blue-eyed; and, of those, only Tamara Brooks, Jacqueline Marris, the two Shah girls, and Elisa Izquierdo are not white. Second, the girls are primarily under the age of ten, profoundly innocent and vulnerable. Only eight are teenagers. Third, all but one of the girls faced assault; hence, they had no part in causing their own trauma. Only Jessica Dubroff died as a result (at least in part) of her own decisions and actions. Finally, almost all the girls are smiling in happy snapshots obviously taken before the abduction or death, or in posed photos taken after rescue (e.g., Elizabeth Smart).

Overall, these girls' racialization as hyper-white, their youth, their lack of agency in the face of violent assault, and their smiles (many from beyond the grave) mark them as particularly innocent, their death and/or abductions all the more tragic, their vulnerability all the more powerful, the need for protection all the more clear. Given the overwhelming whiteness and vulnerability of these girls, only a few stand out as alternative or exceptional. Here, then, I examine in more detail the girls of color in this group, as well as Jessica Dubroff, the only girl to die as a result of something other than assault.

The *Time* cover headline about Elisa Izquierdo claims that her death "symbolizes America's failure to protect its children," and the article inside the magazine continues this argument. She begins as a "princess," adored by her Cuban father, but when he dies, her African American[165] mother gains custody of her. A drug addict with five other children, she (and possibly Izquierdo's stepfather) abuses Izquierdo. Neighbors hear the girls' cries, schoolteachers notice injuries, but Child Welfare Administration (CWA) caseworkers ignore the signs. Eventually, Izquierdo's mother beats her to death. Blame, according to *Time*, lies with the mother, who abuses drugs and her daughter, and who is unwilling to face reason when others try to intervene on Izquierdo's behalf. But, as the article concludes, it is ultimately the "system" that fails the girl—the CWA not only did nothing, but it refuses to release any information about the case. Going further, *Time* uncovers a letter written by the CWA commissioner to the New York mayor, stating that cuts to the budget have made "it impossible for her to train child-abuse caseworkers or even measure their competence."[166] The arc of the story, then, depends on both the vilified mother and a critique of the lack of social service support for "the poor." While there is no direct discussion of race, and while social service statistics (not reported in the article) in fact show that "the poor" in the United States are predominantly white,[167] the lack of discussion of either race or class normalizes the poor as people of color and implicitly links the mother's abusive behavior to both her poverty and (by extension) her race.

I would argue that race is also an important dimension of the cover image itself. While it is likely that many other photos of Izquierdo existed (given her attendance at a Montessori preschool and her reportedly happy life with her father before his death), the cover photo not only shows her not smiling, but also is out of focus. While the many other cover girls lost or murdered smile out at the viewer—producing pathos—this cover produces a potentially un-crossable experiential rift between the viewer and the girl. She is not available to us; she is lost to the system and her mother's (supposed) pathology: she is out of focus. As Rebecca Wanzo argues in relation to the representation of African American children, rather than functioning as an individual for whom we feel sympathy, Izquierdo becomes "aligned with [a] universal idea,"[168] here the need to fix the broken CWA system. We are not meant to be moved by the death of this girl of color as an individual.[169]

Despite the boundary between the viewer and Izquierdo, if we read the article inside the magazine we at least learn a bit about her life; yet the *Time* story on Bipin Shah is not at all about his missing daughters. While the cover features their faces in close-up as a backdrop behind their father, the article inside reports first on Shah's search for them as well as his failed marriage and struggles with their mother, Ellen Devers; and then on Faye Yager's organization, Children of the Underground, which helped Devers take and hide the girls. There are no details in the story about the girls' lives, except through the lens of their parents. The article does end, however, with a focus on the girls, holding Shah, Devers, and Yager responsible for their victimization: "Everyone in this story is a little deluded. And the saddest part—the part Bipin and Ellen and, yes, Faye all have to answer for—is that the victims of those delusions, somewhere on the run with their mother, are those two little girls who never asked for any of this."[170] Despite this pathos-producing ending, however, the cover is much like the Izquierdo cover: slightly out of focus and, in this case, with the image of the father blocking a significant portion of the girls' faces. Again, these girls of color are less available to the viewer: lost, yes; victimized, yes; but not achingly present with bright eyes and smiling faces, as are most of the other (white or blonde-white) dead and/or lost girls on the covers of these magazines.

Elisa Izquierdo and Sarah Lynn and Genevieve Marie Shah are all children, hence innocent and without agency. Their racialization—caught in the system of poverty, or caught between their Indian American father and white American mother whose marital difficulties are coded as cultural as much as, if not more than, personal—depicts

them as different from the imagined reader and merges with the photos' literal lack of focus to decrease pathos. Nevertheless, they retain
the marks of childish innocence and vulnerability. The *People* cover
featuring teenagers Marris and Brooks, however, gives the girls a fair
amount of agency, implying that they rescued themselves: "Surviving
a Kidnapping: How We Fought Back: In their own words, two courageous California teens tell how they attacked their captor and lived."
The cover features them together in close-up, looking directly into the
camera but not smiling: the shot seems to support the claim of courage and implied toughness. The story inside builds the same argument,
reporting on how they immediately bonded during the kidnapping,
even though they did not know each other previously. They sang to
each other, gently touched each other, communicated by tracing letters
on each other's hands, and decided not to take an opportunity to escape
if it meant leaving the other behind. When they had an opportunity,
they attacked the kidnapper with a knife and a bottle, but they were not
able to escape because he still had control of his gun. In the end, they
did not rescue themselves. Instead, police spotted and rescued them,
killing the kidnapper in the process. Thus the cover headline is accurate
but misleading: they were courageous and they did attack their captor,
but they likely lived because the police were able to intervene.

This representation of Marris and Brooks as fighting back can be
read in at least two ways. First, as girls of color, Marris and Brooks
more easily connect to a "tough" or "brave" stereotype; whereas, for
example, the covers featuring Elizabeth Smart, who also fought back
against her kidnapper, emphasize that she was rescued, and the smiling images of her suggest vulnerability and innocence. From this perspective, the Marris and Brooks cover is problematic, drawing on and
contributing to stereotypes of girls of color as able to protect themselves and therefore not in need of society's protection.[171] This reading
is analogous to the way the covers distance the viewer from both the
Shah girls and Izquierdo. Second, though, it is a relief, when looking
at all these covers, to see at least one on which the girls have a certain amount of agency, have the right not to smile, have the capacity to
think and act for themselves. From this perspective, these girls of color,
while stereotyped, also intervene in the overwhelming representation
of girls as vulnerable and victimized. Like Venus and Serena Williams's

Figure 2.5. Kidnapping survivors Jacqueline Marris and Tamara Brooks do not smile for the camera/viewer on the cover of *People*, August 19, 2002.

relation to patriotic nationalism, the presence of Marris and Brooks is at least a disruption of the overwhelming white vulnerability of the vast majority of these girls in peril.

Elsewhere, I have made a similar argument about Jessica Dubroff.[172] The only dead or missing girl to appear on these covers in twenty-two and a half years and not be a victim of abuse, kidnapping, and/or murder, she offers another version of girlhood. While her death is tragic, she nonetheless appears on the cover of *Time* looking like a miniature and queer Amelia Earhart:[173] she wears a "Women Fly" cap[174] and a bomber jacket as she looks to the side and up—as though at the sky where she wants to be, rather than out at the viewer for help.[175] On *People* she also wears a masculinizing cap and bomber jacket, with messy hair whipping in the wind.[176] In short, she looks not like a beauty contestant, not like a posed little girl, not like a blurred-out victim, but like a pilot and a masculinized queer girl, what Judith Halberstam might call a "rogue tomboy." As Emma Renold argues about tomboyism in general, here Dubroff "destabilize[s] and reconfigure[s] gender/sexual norms."[177]

The magazine does not explicitly invite this reading, of course. Instead, the *Time* headline asks "Who Killed Jessica? Her shocking death raises questions about how far we push our kids," making her a victim of (presumably) her parents and hence folding her into the innocent, vulnerable girl narrative. The *People* cover allows her a little more autonomy, but also blames her mother explicitly: "Jessica's Joy—and Tragedy: Raised in a unconventional style—no school, no TV, no toys—Jessica Dubroff was a delight to all. Her mother, Lisa, now under fire, finds only happiness in her memory." This tension between Dubroff as a seven-year-old queer pilot with self-determination and Dubroff as a victim of esoteric parenting/mothering continues in the articles inside the magazines. *Time* writes, "Jessica was urged on [to attempt a transcontinental flight] by overzealous parents, by a media drawn to a natural human-interest story, and by a willfully blind Federal Aviation Administration."[178] Yet it also sets off in large print a quotation from Dubroff saying "I just like to fly. It's like floating." The *People* article offers a similar tension. Amid various details about her father conceiving of and hyping the trip, the article also includes quotations from several people who knew Dubroff, painting her as a self-possessed and

Figure 2.6. Jessica Dubroff, aviator, on the cover of *Time*, April 22, 1996.

self-directed child: "Reid [her flight instructor] quickly bonded with Jessica, his youngest pupil ever. 'They both loved flying and they had a love of life and people,' says Auld [part owner with Reid of the plane]. 'It was amazing when you watched them together. Joe was always happy and smiles.' Though Joshua [Jessica's brother] dropped out, 'Jessica was looking forward to every lesson they had,' says Ana Reid . . . Joe's wife."[179]

Certainly, overall, both Dubroff covers/articles activate the dominant narrative of white girl as tragic victim; yet they also leave space for an alternative reading, one that acknowledges Dubroff's engagement with the world and her interest in learning and doing new things. As with the Marris and Brooks cover and the Venus and Serena cover—given the larger context of cover girls as victims, as impossibly can-do, or as squeaky-clean teen celebrities—I employ a critical perspective in relation to Dubroff that looks for and pauses over the potential for different and varied girlhoods; I seek a moment of respite that values a girlhood with agency and complexity.

Conclusion

This chapter makes two interrelated arguments. First, based on an empirical review of the covers of *Time*, *Newsweek*, and *People* from January 1990 to July 2012, it is clear that the overwhelming majority of girls who capture national attention are white. They are *innocent and vulnerable*, like the kidnapped/murdered girls; or they are phenomenal *can-do* symbols of national achievement, like the athletes who seem to leap effortlessly across the sky and the teen celebrities who appear to be happy-go-lucky; or they are *can-do/at-risk*, slipping between their status as high-profile (daughters of) political figures or as world-class athletes and their decisions to engage in "bad" behavior like premarital sex and drug use, leading to pregnancy (Bristol Palin) or arrest (Jennifer Capriati). These girls mark the larger context, the dominant representational field, in which girls of color and girls who make alternative choices rarely—but nevertheless do—appear. Hence, my second argument depends on acknowledgment of the first: these alternative girls are powerful in large part because they directly counter what I have identified as the dominant versions of girlhood on these magazines.

That said, I would suggest my analysis brings out three possible alternative girlhoods, two of which I want to claim as potentially disruptive. The first alternative girl is not one I would want to recuperate: she is a girl of color, but—compared to other girls in her category—she is relatively less available to the viewer/reader, less vibrant, less present:

Michelle Kwan is American, but not quite as much as the other athletes; she is beautiful, but does not seem to have an athletic super body; and Elisa Izquierdo, Sarah Lynn, and Genevieve Marie Shah are sadly lost, but still out of focus, not quite as urgently of concern as are the white kidnapped/lost girls such as Elizabeth Smart and JonBenét Ramsey. I simply cannot find a way to recuperate the depictions of these girls for a feminist reading, or even for a reading simply in pursuit of variation in U.S. girlhood.

Two other alternative girlhoods do seem to offer a potential interruption, however: (1) the racialized, super can-do girl (Sasha and Malia Obama, Vanessa Hudgens, and Selena Gomez), and, more powerfully, (2) a (usually) racialized girl with agency who confronts and refuses the standard anxious adoration set up by the larger field of girlhood in U.S. media culture (Venus and Serena Williams, Tamara Brooks and Jacqueline Marris, and Jessica Dubroff). Both these types of girls are potentially awe-inspiring. While Sasha and Malia function as an impossible ideal, a symbol of bootstrapping determination that no one could ever actually achieve, they nevertheless displace whiteness at the center of the ubiquitous can-do girlhood. They are *present*. And while depictions of Selena Gomez and Vanessa Hudgens either completely mask their racial identities or transform them into vague markers of ambiguous ethnicity, their status as girl celebrities of color who actually make it to the covers of these magazines potentially opens up reflection on mixed identities and provides a potential point of identification for mixed audiences. Again, they are *available* as girl celebrities of color, even if they are only a small fraction of the many potential girl celebrities of color who could have appeared on these covers during these two decades.

The active and arguably confrontational girlhoods offered by Venus and Serena Williams, Tamara Brooks and Jacqueline Marris, and Jessica Dubroff read as the most alternative to me. While, as I discuss above, many aspects of the covers and the inside stories contradict this reading, it is possible to see Venus and Serena as defeating the world, Brooks and Marris as thwarting a kidnapper, and Dubroff—a girl who flies—as determinedly entering a world that is simultaneously one of the remaining areas of masculine dominance in U.S. culture and functions as a potent symbol of feminism and queerness. This chapter, then, insists on an analytical strategy that recognizes the dominance of the can-do/at-risk dichotomy for a vulnerable and relatively passive white girlhood, but also turns away from this version of girlhood in search of alternatives that open up space for happy African American girls who succeed, mixed race teen celebrities, athletes who take on the world (and win), girls who work together to protect themselves, and girls who choose to fly. In short, I argue that not only is it possible, but it is crucial to see alternative girls in the heart of media culture.

3

What Is There to Talk About?

Twenty-First-Century Girl Films

As part of the turn-of-the-twenty-first-century media obsession with girls, between 2000 and 2009 literally hundreds of films featuring girls as central characters appeared in U.S. movie theaters: a group of films I define here as "girl films."[1] Some of them were obscure, lasting only a few weeks in art house and specialty theaters (e.g., *Quinceañera* [2006], *Gracie* [2007]); others enjoyed long runs and extensive public discussion (e.g., *Mean Girls*, [2004], *Juno* [2007]). Some had large budgets, generated lots of hype, and/or featured major stars (e.g., *The Sisterhood of the Traveling Pants* [2005], *Twilight* [2008]); others were lower-budget, surprise crossover hits (e.g., *Bring It On* [2000], *Precious* [2009]). Most were U.S. films; a few were international (e.g., *Spirited Away* [2001/2002 U.S. release], *Bend It Like Beckham* [2002]). Some were aimed at children, tweens, or teens (e.g., *Lilo and Stitch* [2002], *Bratz* [2007]); others were R-rated and marketed to adults (e.g., *Thirteen* [2003], *Little Miss Sunshine* [2006]). All, however, drew on and contributed to public definitions of girls.

This chapter explores this decade of girl films as another site through which to engage contemporary U.S. media culture depictions of girls. As in the previous chapter on mass-magazine cover girls, here I address dominant trends within this time frame, but I am most interested in

contentious or alternative moments that allow for a complex understanding of girlhood. While the last chapter challenges the marginalization of alternative girls on magazine covers by focusing the most critical
attention on the few alternative girls who fleetingly appear, this chapter
examines alternative girls within the *most spectacularized films*, those
that led to seemingly endless public debate about girls, girl films, and/
or girl stars. In this context, I am interested in the relationships and
tensions between and among the films and the public discussion of the
films. What kinds of films lead to pervasive attention to girls and girlhood? What anxieties and assumptions seem to be the basis for these
public discussions? When comparing the public discussion to the films
themselves, what contradictions or tensions emerge? And what versions of girlhood are available when reading the films from an antiracist, queer feminist perspective?

In order to identify the most talked about girl films of the decade, I
began by building a list of girl films from 2000 to 2009 based on films I
knew of, films that colleagues and both adult and child friends recommended to me, multiple searches of IMDb.com,[2] indexes and appen-
dixes in books about girls and film,[3] and scholarly articles and book
chapters about girls and film. I also identified the girl star(s) of each
film in my database and included any additional films in which they/
she portrayed narratively significant girl characters. This list is still
growing as I come across additional films, but as of this writing there
are approximately 450 films on the list.[4] Then, because of my interest
in public discussion about girls in relation to the films, I searched each
title in three different sets of databases: (1) LexisNexis "U.S. News," to
capture national and mainstream conversations; (2) LexisNexis "Broadcast Transcripts," to capture national and mainstream discussions in an
entertainment medium; and (3) a combination of three ProQuest databases—"Alternative News Watch," "Gender Watch," and "Ethnic News
Watch"—to capture discussion and debate in sources explicitly concerned with issues of gender, race, sexuality, and class and often explicitly committed to a leftist or at least liberal response to media culture.
Chart 3.1 lists the top five films in each of the three sets of databases,
plus any additional films that fell within ten hits of the top five.

In order to address multiple types of film as well as the breadth of
public discussion, while still allowing enough space for a careful analysis

Chart 3.1. The Eleven Most Discussed Girl Films, 2000–2009

Film title	LexisNexis news rank	LexisNexis TV and radio transcripts rank	Alternative press indexes rank
Precious (2009)	1	1	1
Juno (2007)	3	3	2
Mean Girls (2004)	5	2	
Little Miss Sunshine (2006)		4	6
Twilight (2008)	2		
Akeelah and the Bee (2006)			3
Hairspray (2007)	4		
The Secret Life of Bees (2008)			4
Lilo and Stitch (2002)		5	
Whale Rider (2002)			5
Coraline (2009)	6		

of the substantial public discussion, I set the criterion of a film appearing in the top 5–6 of at least two of the three categories. With this in place, I ended up with four films that come close to spanning the decade: *Mean Girls* (2004), *Little Miss Sunshine* (2006), *Juno* (2007), and *Precious* (2009). Thus, this chapter discusses these four films, offers close analyses of the public discussion of them—not only in the three sets of indexes I used to build the list but also in all the relevant indexes available to me—and considers the relationships among all this material.

I organize the analysis that follows in three main sections. I start with a discussion of the public conversation surrounding the films, identifying one dominant theme across all four films—the simultaneous adoration and denigration of girls—a theme that is rampant not only in coverage of these films but also in most of the representations of girls I address throughout the book. Here, adoration of these films, their girl characters, and their girl stars depends on the denigration of other kinds of girls. Hence, I argue that the extensive coverage and celebration of these unique girls is shadowed by a more diffuse distrust of girls. In particular, this simultaneous adoration/disdain emerges in anxiety about girl stars, specifically Abigail Breslin and Lindsay Lohan, who (unlike Ellen Page in *Juno* and Gabourey Sidibe in *Precious*) were under the age of eighteen when they made *Little Miss Sunshine* and *Mean Girls*, respectively. Overall, this is an ambivalent representation that contains both (1) an affectionate but nevertheless objectifying gaze at a "special" or "unique" girl, and (2) a Foucauldian surveillance and disciplining of what is figured as a much more common girl: one that—because it is empty-headed or unhealthy—serves as a negative example. Hence, I argue that two linked girlhoods emerge in the discussion of these films: (1) a special girlhood, made all the more fabulous by its difference from (2) an everyday girlhood that is just "wrong."

Second, I look specifically at debates in the coverage over whether the films are "good for" girls or, in fact, for the rest of us. In the coverage of all but *Little Miss Sunshine*, the films are often understood to be pedagogical, to be useful for girls in the audience who are presumably confronting difficulties in their own lives or who simply could benefit from a powerful girl hero. In this context, some of the media coverage asks whether the films offer "good" feminism, including discussion of feminist issues such as abortion, domestic violence, and stereotypes. My goal here is to draw attention to the fact that public discussion of the highest-profile girl films of the decade is invested in feminism. While more of this debate appears in the alternative press, it is by no means limited to these sources; questions of feminism are part of debate about these films across all three types of sources I examine. Hence, not only do these films contribute to the public understanding of feminism, but they also serve as vehicles for the discursive production of (particular kinds of) feminist girlhoods.

Lastly, I shift to a feminist film studies methodology that pushes back against the coverage of the films, moving even further toward optimistic readings of the films. Specifically, I analyze a theme that is central to the coverage of each individual film and then read the film through the same theme, but in a different way—in a way that asks how the films can be understood to offer girlhoods that escape the ambivalent oscillation between adoration and disdain. In particular, I argue that reading in this way produces a critique of heteronormativity—as well as the presence of girls' autoeroticism, girls' choice and agency, and the specificity of an African American girlhood—in and through these films. Thus, in the last section I take my lead from the public discussion, but I focus on my own investment in alternative girls. Throughout, my methodology is to imagine as many different versions of girlhood as possible, while remaining both critical of the denigration of girls and open to—in fact, insisting on—finding queer, antiracist, feminist girls amid U.S. media culture.

Adoration and Denigration

Commentators often place *Mean Girls* in the context of a teen girl film genre, including *Heathers* (1989)[5] and *Clueless* (1995),[6] as well as Lohan's prior films: *The Parent Trap* (1998), *Freaky Friday* (2003), and *Confessions of a Teenage Drama Queen* (2004).[7] Many reviews point out that most girl films from 2003–2004 did not do as well as had been hoped at the box office.[8] In comparison, they say *Mean Girls* did unexpectedly well and suggest this is because "it is a much harder-edged film."[9] *Mean Girls* is unique in relation to those other films: *Mean Girls* is actually a good film, unlike girl films in general, which are implicitly bad. And not only are these other girl films bad, but also their girl audiences are abject. Sometimes commentators define girls as ignorant: "*Mean Girls* even contains some wisdom, although I hesitate to mention that lest I scare off its target audience."[10] Other girl fans are just silly: "At a recent opening-night screening of *Mean Girls* . . . we [saw] an ocean of . . . 13-year-olds in *Apprentice*-short skirts. A phalanx of about a dozen of these odd creatures sat directly in front of us and spent the 15 minutes before the movie playing musical chairs."[11] Thus, commentators' praise of *Mean Girls* for offering a harder-edged girlhood depends on the denigration of both other girl films and their girl audiences.

Regarding *Little Miss Sunshine*, within a family almost every review and commentary calls "dysfunctional," Olive is the "one shining hope."[12] She is "a perpetually gushing fountain of optimism" and is "sweet," "sensitive,"[13] and "innocent."[14] Yet, despite their affection for Olive, commentators also read her obsession with beauty pageants as misguided, specifically because of her looks. Articles call her a "dumpling with oversized glasses"[15] and describe her as "overweight,"[16] "frumpy,"[17] "lumpy,"[18] "ungainly,"[19] "chubby, awkward, and unself-consciously weird."[20] Clearly, she could not possibly win a beauty contest. As I discuss in more detail below, commentators have a disdain for girl beauty pageants, and thus Olive's difference from typical beauty pageant girls— her "tiny potbelly"[21]—arguably is part of her appeal for them. Yet this affection for Olive, for her "sweet curve of baby fat,"[22] depends on denigration of other forms of girlhood, in this case pageant girls.

The adoration in commentary on *Juno* is quite explicit, with commentators expressing love for both the character Juno and the actor Page. For example, *Juno* "offers . . . a heroine who's a smarter and more admirable role model than the common sort of movie teen who, say, discovers her inner beauty with the help of a lot of makeup or becomes self-confident after tripping into a dreamboat's arms."[23] Juno is "brainy,"[24] "preternaturally precocious," "quick-witted,"[25] "sharp-tongued,"[26] and "whip-smart."[27] She is "hip,"[28] "independent,"[29] and "spunky."[30] And, about Page, *Entertainment Weekly* quotes screenwriter Diablo Cody saying "It would have been really heartbreaking to meet Ellen if she was like, 'Oh, hey, wassup?' while talking on a rhinestone-encrusted cell phone. . . . But she's so cool, she scares the s— out of me."[31] Page and Juno are cool and hip—with depth, wisdom, and complexity—unlike other teen girls and other teen stars. Page and Juno are thus exceptional by comparison. As in the *Mean Girls* and *Little Miss Sunshine* commentary, this difference from other girls (1) defines most girls as frivolous and empty-headed, (2) articulates a disdain for those more typical girls, and (3) produces an alternative version of edgy, hip girlhood, one we can celebrate as unique.

The Problem of the Large African American Girl/Body (Precious and Sidibe)

The tension between adoration and disdain for girls appears in the coverage of *Precious* in at least four different ways, all of which produce two versions of a large African American girl or girl body—one loveable, one detestable. First, coverage often insists Precious is lovable, but only because she is actually different from what she appears to be on the surface (inarticulate and sullen): a version of girlhood for which commentators express only disgust. Again, adoration of one version of girlhood is built on simultaneous differentiation from and disdain for another. The following example from the *New Pittsburgh Courier* sums up this tension: "If you've heard any 'buzz words' about the character, 'Precious,' the words 'overweight,' 'illiterate,' and 'victim' have likely been part of your orientation. But to pigeonhole 'Precious' in this way is to deny her wit, humor, intelligence, and most importantly, her boldness to believe she deserves a more fruitful life than the damaging, dysfunctional circle of abuse at the hands of her parents."[32] Here, the illiterate and victim version of Precious is unlovable, but, because contrary to appearances she is actually witty and curious, we can—and should—love her.

Second, the story of how director Lee Daniels cast Sidibe does similar work, differentiating between loveable Sidibe and the other abject women and girls who auditioned to play Precious but—counterintuitively—were just too much like the character to portray her successfully. Most commentaries mention that Precious weighs "300 pounds,"[33] and some report that Daniels and his casting director looked for potential actors at "McDonald's," "RadioShack," and a "popcorn counter"[34] by approaching young African American women[35] who, presumably, looked like they weighed three hundred pounds.[36] When Daniels met Sidibe, however, he realized she was smart and happy, unlike Precious and the other women who had auditioned. As the story goes, he decided that if he were to hire someone too much like Precious he would be "exploiting" her and putting her in situations for which she was unprepared.[37] About Sidibe, Daniels realized, "she would be able to be a mouthpiece for my film in a very articulate way."[38] Overall, Precious is inarticulate, abused, and fat, but that depiction is just a little bit easier to take because Sidibe, as an actor, has the capacity both to distinguish herself from Precious and to portray Precious in a compassionate and meaningful way. Thus the discourse simultaneously expresses love and hate for girls, love for wit (Sidibe, an exceptional black woman/girl) and hate for victimhood (the other normative black girls/women who auditioned).

Third, sometimes the commentary produces a split between Sidibe and Precious. Here, commentators seem to feel free to express disgust for Precious because they are expressing love for Sidibe. In these examples, Precious becomes only her overweight victim self, while

Sidibe becomes anything but a victim. Many commentators report that they have talked to Sidibe in person and "found her quite unlike her screen image."[39] They call her "bubbly,"[40] "friendly,"[41] "chirpy and giggly,"[42] "funny," "confident,"[43] "engaging and outgoing,"[44] "refreshingly honest," "personable,"[45] "a total charmer,"[46] "sunny,"[47] and "cheerful."[48] During awards season, some suggest she is a serious contender for the Best Actress Oscar because "when you listen to her normal speech pattern you realize that she really did transform to play that lead role of Precious."[49]

Finally, the fourth way the commentary on *Precious* combines adoration and disdain for girls is through a shift—over time—in the discussion of Sidibe's weight. At first, commentators seem to congratulate themselves for being able to adore Sidibe's large body. Several articles quote Sidibe saying something like, "I learned to love myself, because I sleep with myself every night and I wake up with myself every morning, and if I don't like myself, there's no reason to even live life. I love the way I look. I'm fine with it. And if my body changes, I'll be fine with that."[50] The *New York Amsterdam News* makes the issue of race and body size explicit, saying that it is "truly remarkable" to see a woman of her size celebrated and centered in Hollywood: "In an entertainment industry of size zeros, colored contacts, and an emphasis on 'exotic' or racially ambiguous beauty, Gabby is definitely a stand out."[51] During award season, commentators strive to treat Sidibe like any other nominee. On CBS's *The Early Show,* Maggie Rodriguez tells her "I love the color that you're wearing right now" and asks if she has "the dress, the shoes, and all that stuff" for the Academy Awards.[52] Overall, then, there is a celebration of Sidibe's success, almost a relief that it is OK to look at and take pleasure in a nontypical, large black body.

Only one day after the Academy Awards, however, Howard Stern commented negatively on Sidibe's size, and Whoopi Goldberg and her cohosts on *The View* blasted him for sexism.[53] CNN then picked up and perpetuated the story by discussing it at length and often quoting or even replaying Stern's words,[54] and occasionally the critique of him made on *The View*. In fact, *Showbiz Tonight* named Stern's comments (and their discussion of them) the "Great Gabourey weight debate." Commentators, of course, distance themselves from Stern's hostility, but go on to suggest that he might have a point, especially in terms of concern about health. *Showbiz Tonight*, in fact, carried the story for at least five days,[55] and it arose again on CNN on *Issues with Jane Velez-Mitchell* on March 24, 2010.[56] In each case, commentators cover the same ground and simultaneously give Stern and his comments more airtime. Thus the earlier tone of relief at being able to gaze at and love a large young black woman turns into concern for her, a concern that depends on both (1) repeatedly (re)playing vitriolic racist and sexist comments and (2) making unsupported assumptions that her size necessarily means she is unhealthy and that if she were smaller she somehow would not be typecast, even as a dark-skinned African American woman.

The Trouble with the Girl Star (Breslin and Lohan)

The simultaneous affection for and rejection of girls in the coverage of these four films functions as a moral panic about girls. Because both ideal and problematic versions of girlhood run throughout the coverage, panic about the potential loss of the more unusual ideal girlhood leads to protectionist discourse. This emerges most strongly in relation to the two actual girl stars among these four films: Breslin and Lohan. Specifically, in the discussion of both *Little Miss Sunshine* and *Mean Girls*, there is some concern about the idea of the girl-on-display and the potential threat of stardom to Breslin and Lohan's previously unsullied girlhood. Here, the coverage adores the girl star—as long as she is young and pre-sexual—but film itself threatens her hold on her status as innocent and adorable.

Commentators gush over Breslin as a girl star, claiming that she "is shaping up to be the next It Kid in American movies."[57] Other commentaries acknowledge the potential loss of innocence for the child actor that It Kid status represents, while nevertheless insisting strenuously on Breslin's continuing unsullied innocence. For example, *Entertainment Weekly* quotes Breslin talking about her lack of understanding of some of the adult themes in the film: "A lot of times, people were laughing and I'm like 'I don't get it.' Sometimes when there's bad language in a movie, my mom covers my ears."[58] When Breslin receives the Oscar nomination for Best Supporting Actress, the inevitable comparison to Tatum O'Neal, Jodie Foster, and Anna Paquin as three other young Academy Award nominees emerge.[59] In comparisons to O'Neal,

Breslin seems all the more normal as a child, "in her age-appropriate [and, of course, gender-appropriate] evening attire and accompanied by a stuffed Curious George."[60] In short, not to worry, as Ben Lyons puts it on *Good Morning America* (seemingly unaware of his own irony): "It's very difficult to live a normal life. But she's got it down perfect. Like a pro."[61]

This innocence—Breslin's ability to use childish things like covering her ears to separate herself from the film world—assures readers that, while many child actors face innumerable moments of stress in their lives, Breslin is safe from that. As Kerry H. Robinson and Cristyn Davies point out in their discussion of *Little Miss Sunshine*, "Within hegemonic discourses of childhood, innocence is viewed as natural, and moral panic is often associated with a perceived risk of the child's innocence being compromised."[62] In this case, the commentary acknowledges the threat but maintains Breslin's innocence. Panic is alluded to, but avoided. Nevertheless, the process of discussing child stars and of assuaging any anxiety about Breslin's potential loss of innocence simultaneously reinforces anxiety about girl actors in general—most of whom, the discussion implies, lose their innocence too soon. Further, the celebration of Breslin's supposed innocence paradoxically revels in the pleasure of gazing at Breslin as an adorable, innocent girl. In other words, by heightening the gaze at Breslin, the commentary contributes to the circumstances that it claims could lead to her downfall.

While Breslin maintained her hold on innocence during the coverage of her film, Lohan did not. In fact, *Mean Girls* was the last movie Lohan made without the cloud of the crash-and-burn girl surrounding her. Even before discussion of her personal troubles emerged in the press, commentary on her hyper-sexualization in the film had already moved her into the category of fraught teen star. For example, at the time of the film's release there was much discussion of her breasts,[63] including speculation about whether she had had breast-augmentation surgery, as well as comments on her ultra-tight and revealing wardrobe in the film. As one commentator put it, "Her character is supposed to represent this triumph of substance over style, but she's so voluptuously rendered, so provocatively dressed."[64] This commentary makes explicit the very moment at which Lohan changed from innocent child star to sexualized teen star. The category "teen star," which Lohan comes to embody in *Mean Girls*, then, contains a tension between innocent child and sexualized adult. In fact, I would argue the teen star makes explicit the fact that all girl stars embody the sexualized scandal at the heart of the star (as I argue in chapter 1), because the teen star who has entered puberty/adolescence but who is not yet adult brings together child and sexuality: a cause for panic. For the commentary on Breslin, the tension is split between Breslin (who still remains unsullied) and other stars (who do not). Coverage of Lohan surrounding the release of *Mean Girls*, however, depicts teen star Lohan as embodying that tension.

The August 19, 2004, issue of *Rolling Stone*, which features Lohan on the cover, embraces her new behavior as "real," calling her a "bad girl" and celebrating her because "she has been willing to talk shit about rival teen star Hilary Duff and didn't hide the fact that she liked to party."[65] While *Rolling Stone* is appreciative of this "new, adult image," it also claims that it "has her handlers worried." This article also spends some time discussing her father's troubles and questions her sincerity for being "relentlessly positive" about not "doing drugs." By October, approximately four months after the film's release, the dominant context in which commentary references *Mean Girls* is titillating anxiety. CNN's *Live From . . .* reports that Lohan was hospitalized during the shooting of *Herbie: Fully Loaded* (2005).[66] In December, NBC's *Today Show* reports on Lohan's family troubles,[67] as does ABC's *Primetime Live* in February 2005.[68] In May 2005, Lohan is in the news again for having lost a large amount of weight, with many speculating that she has an eating disorder.[69] Some commentators simply say she is no longer beautiful, because she lost too much weight and died her hair.[70] Paula Zahn says, "I barely recognized her in that photo," and wonders, "Where did all those freckles go?" implicitly mourning the loss of Lohan's childish innocence. This same show, in fact, summarizes Lohan's troubles since the release of *Mean Girls*, mentioning all the issues together: rumored breast augmentation, partying, her father, an eating disorder, a public breakup with her boyfriend, and hospitalization while filming *Herbie: Fully Loaded*.[71]

In short, coverage of both Breslin and Lohan emphasizes anxiety about the girl star, although much more explicitly in relation to Lohan as a sexualized teen and a troubled celebrity. In fact, the crash-and-burn girl star is always lurking, either as worrisome potential (Breslin) or as outright spectacle (Lohan). In this way, the girl star is suffused with internal contradictions: love but also disgust, innocence but also sexualization, and evidence of unimaginable success but also anxiety about (seemingly inevitable) catastrophe.

* * *

In all the examples in this section, adoration of the unique girl depends on the denigration of the typical girl: *Mean Girls* is a genre film that defies its genre because it is smart and hard-edged; Olive is pleasingly plump in contrast to misguided child beauty pageant contestants; Juno and Page are hip rather than obsessed with boys and glamour; Precious is different (thoughtful) from how she seems on the surface (depressed); and Sidibe remains a loveable large black woman for only a few months before anxiety about her health and capacity to succeed as an atypi-cal actor take over. Thus coverage offers smart, hip, thoughtful, and embodied alternative girls, but celebrates them only as unique exam-ples, exceptions that prove the rule that girl films, girls stars, everyday girls, pageant girls, and poor, abused, sullen, overweight black girls are unlovable, silly, and/or empty-headed.

It is noteworthy that this commentary—across all four of the most discussed girl films and therefore arguably across the girl film as genre during this decade—gravitates toward and embraces smart girls who eschew romance and beauty culture. Celebrating girls in this way as smart and anti–beauty culture is something worth appreciating. Yet to accept this particular celebration of girlhood requires a disciplining and derogatory denigration of girls in general, as well as the spectaculariza-tion of the teen star as an object on display, either on the precipice or already tumbling down the side of inevitable sexualized catastrophe. In short, the love of *Mean Girls*, Olive, Juno, Page, and (some versions of) Precious and Sidibe comes at a cost. Thus, I am arguing that we cannot appreciate the cultural celebration of these girl films, characters, and stars without acknowledging that that celebration is not of all girls. In fact, it requires the belittling of girls more generally.

These Films Are Good for Us! *Mean Girls*, *Juno*, and *Precious*

For many commentators, the exceptionalism of these films comes from their ability to transform audiences, and in the case of *Mean Girls* and *Juno*, girl audiences in particular.[72] For example, for Katie Couric, Lohan stars in movies Couric feels comfortable watching over and over again with her own daughters. She ends her *Today Show* interview with Lohan by saying "I know a lot of girls are very upset they are in school right now and aren't able to watch this interview. So I hope that they TiVo-ed it or have their VCRs set."[73] Other commentators call Lohan "an empowering mascot for young girls."[74] This perspective on the film continues for years after its first run (despite Lohan's ongoing personal troubles), with many articles on "mean girls" or "cliques" continuing to mention both *Mean Girls* and *Queen Bees and Wannabes* (Roselind Wiseman's moral panic book on which the film is based) as useful resources, at least in passing, as late as December 2007. For example, *Girls' Life* says: "Being bullied by the popular crowd? Sounds like a *Mean Girls* rental is in order."[75] Another article reports on a film festival organized by a leadership program for girls, "Girls for Change," and mentions that *Mean Girls* will be screened.[76] Thus, not only when it was released but also for many years after, *Mean Girls* is understood to provide useful pedagogical material to help girls understand their lives. It can function as a self-help film.[77]

Coverage of *Juno* also often assumes it is good for girls, in this case because it acknowledges their fantasies and pleasures and offers them an alternative girl hero. Drawing on the pervasive adoration/denigration discourse, the *San Francisco Chronicle* quotes Page as follows: "I really hope that [*Juno*] just broadens the horizons for what a young woman is allowed to be. . . . We're so used to popular media putting so much pressure on young individuals to be a certain way. . . . But it's so nice that a film can come out that has a sense of honesty and looks at some other possibilities."[78] And Page isn't the only one making this argument. For example, *Entertainment Weekly* claims, "After years of being served mostly bland good girls and ciphers—from Molly Ringwald in the '80s to Lindsay Lohan in the '00s—teenage girls are clearly starving for a female antihero."[79] Importantly, this girl hero is powerful because viewers can already connect with her—rather than perpetually aspire to be her. For example, *Entertainment Weekly* reports, "Log on to YouTube and you'll find scads of homemade videos with girls (and guys) singing songs they've written about the film. . . . Others are stenciling their favorite Junoisms onto T-shirts ('They call me the cautionary whale'), while Facebook and other websites are quickly filing up with breathless declarations of Juno love: '[Juno] is everything a girl like me wishes she could be,' writes one. 'Blunt, brave, chill, caring, hilarious, ingenious, mirthful . . . totally boss . . . alive, sparkling . . . retro . . .and nonchalantly kick-ass.'"[80] In short, *Juno* offers viewers not only an alternative girl hero but also one who (despite her teen pregnancy) is both healthy for and attainable by ordinary girls in the audience.

Coverage of *Precious* understands the audience as perhaps more deeply affected than the *Mean Girls* and *Juno* audiences: *Precious* transforms audience members' lives. It can *cure*. For example, Richard Knight Jr. claims audiences will have "an emotionally cathartic experience rare in cinema,"[81] while *Ebony* calls it "gut-wrenching"[82] and claims it "will pierce the soul of an audience."[83] More specifically, for those in the audience who share some of Precious's experiences, commentators suggest the film sees them, acknowledges and validates their feelings, and may just provide a path out. This version of the audience begins with very personal stories from the filmmakers, which then serve as guides for living. Five of the filmmakers explicitly come out as survivors of domestic abuse, and explain that they connect with Precious on that very specific level. Mariah Carey, who plays Precious's social worker, implies on *Larry King Live* that she, too, has faced "emotional" and "mental" abuse, although she refuses to elaborate, promising instead, "I will eventually talk about [it] when I write my book."[84] Director Lee Daniels, actor Mo'Nique, and executive producers Oprah Winfrey and Tyler Perry had all previously gone public about the abuse they faced as children, and they repeat their stories for the press.[85] They all claim that, through their own experience, they came to understand the character of Precious and, more importantly, felt this story must be told in order to "help," as the film's dedication declares at the end, "precious girls everywhere." In fact, as I discuss in more detail below, the filmmakers often tell stories of audience members reporting their own experiences with abuse and then thanking the filmmakers for the film. For example, on *Good Morning America* Sidibe says, "It seems to be helping people. So many people approach me and tell me that it's changed their lives. And it makes them feel less alone in the world. And so like that, that's so much more than an award."[86] In short, *Precious* has the power to change lives.

But Is the Feminism in These Films
Good for Us? *Juno* and *Precious*

While commentators are generally in agreement that these films are good for us, some explicitly ask whether the films offer a version of feminism that is good for us. More specifically, they debate the value in the ways *Juno* and *Precious* represent feminist issues such as abortion, child abuse, and racial stereotypes. Hence, feminism—or at least questions relevant to or about feminism—is part of these particular girl-hoods and part of what is assumed to be good for girls in the audience.

Most of the debate about *Juno*'s feminism addresses its representation of unplanned pregnancy and abortion, asking "Is this a feminist representation of abortion or not?" Some commentators appreciate that Juno seriously considers abortion as an option, going so far as to visit an abortion clinic. In *People*, Curly Cohen writes, "Just under the cute tenderness of Juno, we're watching a movie about a woman's right to decide, even if she's sixteen, and the right to trust our children and the decisions they make."[87] Many critics, however, are not persuaded that the film is feminist. For example, Lisa Schwarzbaum, in an otherwise generally positive *Entertainment Weekly* review, says, "The old-school feminist in me wishes *Juno* spent more time, even a tart sentence or two, acknowledging that the options taken for granted by this one attractive, articulate teen are in fact hard-won, precious rights, and need to be guarded by a new-generation army of Junos and Bleekers."[88] Explicitly setting up a debate about the film, the feminist newspaper *off our backs* hosts a forum asking "*Juno*: Feminist or Not?" In the forum, commentators praise the film for giving Juno "agency," and point out that "she decided to have sex" but "didn't have a 'natural' maternal instinct for her baby." Yet they also critique the film for depicting the abortion clinic receptionist as "unfriendly" and for "the plot's pronatalist message." Perhaps the most optimistic commentator says:

I do think it's a baby step in the right direction. Why, you ask? Because we finally have a film that's based on a strong-willed teenage girl (a female lead character!) who knows the consequences of unprotected sex (pregnancy!), considers abortion (and even attempts to have one . . . a true rarity in mainstream cinema!), doesn't miscarry (a convenient way most television shows and movies choose to end an unwanted pregnancy), chooses a single woman to adopt the baby (unheard of!), and grieves over the difficulty of her decision (acknowledging that adoption isn't easily forgettable or painless as many right-to-lifers would have us believe).

And perhaps the least optimistic commentator critiques the film for reproducing a feminism she does not support: "It is emblematic of so much of what passes for feminism these days—women who define themselves as 'alternative' end up making the exact same 'choices' that anitfeminists do or that feed into longstanding patriarchal roles for women."[89]

Even before the film's wide release, commentators report that there is a debate about the representation of abortion and pregnancy in the film. Hence, disagreement about the film itself becomes a noteworthy topic. For example, *Solares Hill* mentions op-ed pages, online movie discussions, and Slate.com as locations for dispute about the film's representation of abortion and teen pregnancy.[90] One commentator reports that "conservative bloggers and film critics are applauding what they interpret as the film's pro-life message,"[91] while other commentaries imply that conservatives critique the film for representing abortion as an option at all. *Entertainment Weekly* says, "To those on the right, it's a movie about the sanctity of human life. To those on the left, it's a movie about the reality of teenage pregnancy. And to those vocal Internet bloggers, *Juno* is everything from 'the movie pro-aborts will hate' to a message film that's 'all about choice.' However you interpret it, *Juno* has hit a nerve—and it's helped renew the cultural debate about teenage pregnancy."[92]

In short, whether critiquing the film for not being feminist enough, praising the film for its feminism, or simply noting that there is a public debate about the film, the coverage connects *Juno* to feminism and often takes at least an implicitly feminist stance. Importantly, commentators' commitment to feminism appears not only in alternative publications such as *off our backs* and *Solares Hill*, but also in mainstream outlets such as *People* and *Entertainment Weekly*. Hence, coverage of

Juno brings feminism and abortion to the forefront and into the mainstream, defining a feminist version of girlhood that considers abortion to be a legitimate choice.

While Precious is also pregnant, abortion never comes up in either the film or the coverage. Arguably, stereotypes of African American teen moms make an abortion narrative unlikely (if not impossible). In other words, together the coverage of these two films defines abortion as a white girl's option and teen motherhood as an African American girl's burden but also right. Thus, while teen motherhood is a feminist issue raised by *Precious*, the public discussion does not address it except in passing.

The coverage of *Precious* does, however, address another feminist issue: domestic violence. For example, some reviews address the feminist concept of a "cycle of abuse" and understand Precious to have made a huge change by leaving her "toxically cruel"[93] mother's home. On PBS's *Fresh Air*, Daniels tells host Terry Gross that "the genius of *Precious* is that . . . the cycle is broken. When she walks out of there with her kids, you know from the way she says to her mother, 'I never want to see you again.'"[94] For Mo'Nique, who thought of her brother (who she reports abused her for several years) in order to portray Precious's mother, the film makes an intervention by reaching out to abusers. A *Washington Post* article quotes her as saying "This story's going to save somebody's life. It'll save the life of the person who is the molester, and it will save the life of the person being molested. It's going to do so much."[95] Most of this discussion is not race-specific, but at least one article in the African American newspaper the *Washington Informer* uses *Precious* as an opportunity to talk about "sexual abuse of children" as "one of Black America's most troubling secrets," and it provides relevant statistics.[96]

While the bulk of the public commentary lauds the film for the role it can play in drawing attention to and even preventing domestic and sexual violence, some commentary critiques the film for reinforcing racial stereotypes.[97] Further, as with *Juno*, discussion of the fact that there is a "debate" amplifies and reinforces the question of whether the film trades in stereotypes.[98] For example, on November 1, 2009, even before the film was in wide release, Katie Couric reports that "some critics have charged that *Precious* does precious little to challenge stereotypes."[99] And, on November 21, 2009, the week the film opened nationwide, the *New York Times* published an article on the front page of the Arts section titled "*Precious* Spawns Racial Debate: She's 'Demeaned' or 'Angelic.'" Quoting African American cultural critics such as Mark Anthony Neal, the article pits the critics against one another, with some seeing the film as "demean[ing]" and others, such as Latoya Peterson, arguing that the film "tackled many issues affecting young girls: 'sexual abuse, poverty, violence, and failing schools.'"[100] The African American newspaper the *Call and Post* also reports on controversy, quoting critics ("one of the worst images of a Black woman onscreen that I have ever seen"), but also mentioning the fact that African Americans Oprah Winfrey and Tyler Perry support the film, and thereby presumably do not consider it racist. The article then ends with a relatively positive claim: "[*Precious*] has undoubtedly opened conversation about issues that were once taboo not only in the African American community, but among people of all backgrounds."[101]

While I am claiming that the topics of domestic violence and African American stereotyping are feminist, the coverage of *Precious*, unlike in the discussion of *Juno*, does not use the term "feminism." Hence I could argue that the public discussion of *Precious* does not address feminism. Yet when reading both the commentary and the film from a perspective that understands domestic violence, sexual violence, and racial stereotyping to be feminist issues, both the film and the commentary confront feminism and either laud or debate how feminist the film is. As with *Juno*, not all commentators agree on the value of the film from a progressive and feminist perspective. Nevertheless, the commentary on both films brings these issues forward and makes them part of the girlhoods the films offer. Thus these films and the discussions of them define pregnancy, abortion, domestic abuse, and racism as aspects of girls' lives that they must—and (in the films) successfully do—confront and manage.

Pushing Back against the Commentary

Thus far, I have argued that media coverage of these films trades in and supports a widespread adoration/denigration of girls, but also offers potentially (but not definitively) feminist girlhoods as one piece of the celebrations of the films. And yet there is much more to these films. Here in this chapter's third and final section, I shift my critical method to emphasize this point. Rather than simply describe and challenge the depictions of girls in the coverage as I do in the previous two sections, I take the focus of the coverage back to the films, seeking additional ways to understand the films' girls. For each film, I first analyze a key focus of the public discussion: for *Mean Girls*, the meaning of "mean girl"; for *Little Miss Sunshine*, the child beauty pageant; for *Juno*, the question of choice; and for *Precious*, a tension between universal humanity and the particularity of black girlhood. I then place these issues in relation to specific aspects of the films themselves—I "defamiliarize [their] every-dayness"[102]—arguing for a reinterpretation of the relationships between girls and meanness, autoeroticism, choice, and universality, respectively.

Mean Girls Are Queer

In an essay on the concept of "mean girls," Marina Gonick argues that at the beginning of the twenty-first century the "mean girl" is "a cultural symbol of disorder, moral decay, and social instability. . . . Yet at the same time, the treatment and resolution of the [mean girl] problem is almost always articulated in individualized and individualizing terms," rather than in social ones.[103] The commentary on the film *Mean Girls* illustrates Gonick's argument perfectly. It defines the mean girl as a "real" and unavoidable problem in society—girls by definition are going to be mean—and then imagines how individual girls can nevertheless escape meanness.

The reported response of girl audiences proves just how mean girls can be: "The minute the film was over, the mean tween behind me rang up her friend on her cell phone and under the guise of 'sharing,' purposefully gave away the film's big surprise ending."[104] Yet individual girls can avoid becoming mean. In fact, Lohan, as the film's star, is adored in part because, despite her character Cady's moments of weakness, Lohan is not actually mean at all. For example, when *Today Show* host Matt Lauer says, "Up next, actress Lindsay Lohan tells us about being a mean girl" as a hook before a commercial break, he then follows the comment with "She doesn't look that mean. But, first, these messages."[105] Thus he uses the sensationalism of the "mean girl" concept, while also promising that Lohan will not be mean to us (or, presumably, he hopes to him) if we stick around to watch the interview.

If individual girls (such as Lohan) can avoid meanness, and (as I argue above) if the film and commentators' interpretation of it as peda-gogical show how damaging meanness can be, and if watching the film can help girls deal with meanness in their own lives, why does mean-ness persist? The commentary does not address this question other than to assume "girls will be girls," but I want to argue here that critical attention to the representation of heteronormativity in both the cover-age and the film can illustrate another way to understand meanness. In other words, I am going to queer the text.

The only time there is a hint of meanness to Lohan in the public commentary is when she repeatedly says in interviews that she and her friends only ever were mean to one another when they were fight-ing over guys.[106] This claim, in fact, parallels the movie, since it is not until Regina takes her ex-boyfriend back to get him away from Cady that Cady fully crosses over into being a mean girl. Here, heteronor-mativity and a heterosexual narrative imperative are preconditions for meanness: heteronormativity causes meanness. In other words, even nice girls who would ordinarily resist doing things like calling up their friends to give away the ending of a film cannot help but fall into mean-ness when boys are involved.[107] One way to think about the narrative structure in which heterosexual desire causes meanness would be to read the figure of the mean girl as queer, in that her very existence—which is always a subject of critique—depends on heteronormativity: without the heterosexual imperative, she might not exist.[108] By queering the mean girl here, I mean to heighten the critique of heteronormativity that her characterization and role in the narrative progression at least implicitly initiates.

There are other potential queer readings of the film, as well, par-ticularly in the film's ending when Cady rejects meanness and returns to her platonic yet queer-positive friendships with Damien and Janis. Here, the film takes on the question of Janis's sexuality. Despite both the claim of the Plastics (the mean girls in the film) that Janis is a lesbian and her own willingness to embrace a queer self-presentation (e.g., she wears a tuxedo to the Spring Fling dance), in this scene she has a boy-friend: Indian American Kevin, who declares earlier in the film that he only dates women of color and therefore is delighted that she is "Leba-nese" and thus an appropriate partner of color for him. Heterosexuality

Figure 3.1. Cady with her queer-positive friends, Janis and Damien. Courtesy of Photofest.

is reaffirmed, but it plays a very different role than it does throughout the rest of the film. Here, heterosexuality is linked to racial conscious-ness in a way that evokes Kimberly Springer's use of queer theory to argue that to affirm black female heterosexuality as neither excessively to-be-looked-at nor as an aspect of one's life that must be set aside in the interest of decorum, is to queer heterosexuality, to insist on a black female sexual subjectivity.[109] Admittedly, the romance between Janis and Kevin is fleeting and played for laughs because of Kevin's over-the-top racial stridency; and, as Tanya Ann Kennedy argues, the film engages a "*National Geographic* subtext" through its "juxtaposition of girl nature with the jungle cats of stereotypically imagined Africa."[110] Certainly, I do not want to argue the film is overall an antiracist film. Nevertheless, by drawing on Springer's theory of a queer racialized het-erosexuality and focusing on Janis, I do want to argue that her racial-ized queerness remains available and is part of her heterosexuality. Through Janis, *Mean Girls* recuperates a heterosexuality unattached to meanness, significantly displacing that heterosexuality from whiteness and from the dominant narrative trajectory of the film in which Cady's white femininity is recuperated.

While queer girls do emerge in provocative ways in *Mean Girls*, the film does not explicitly articulate queer sexuality, only a queer sensibility. Janis does not get a girlfriend after all, nor does Damien get a boyfriend. In the context of this film and public discussion of it, then, heterosexuality remains the only option. Nevertheless, through my queer readings of the text, I want to emphasize that *Mean Girls* can be understood both to displace heteronormativity and to take it to task.

Little Miss Sunshine *and the Autoerotic Child*

When commentators mention the beauty pageant sequence at the end of *Little Miss Sunshine*, they invariably express disgust with the whole concept of child (read: girl) beauty pageants and celebrate the film for critiquing "creepy prepubescent beauty contests."[111] Reviews call the beauty pageant "misbegotten,"[112] "surreally sexualized,"[113] "ultra-weird,"[114] and "garishly oversexualized,"[115] and describe in horrified terms "a gaggle of seven-year-olds tarted up to look like midget prostitutes."[116] Some commentators seem to be shocked to discover that such things exist, suggesting "the surreal sight of little girls with giant bouffant hair and gobs of makeup caked on their faces is just thoroughly creepy."[117] Other commentators are unaware that the filmmakers used actual contestants, and critique the film for exaggerating: "To engineer a happy ending— the heroes mustn't look like losers—the movie has to make everyone else look worse. Thus the contestants are made up into grotesque little kewpie whores. . . . It goes past comic exaggeration into cruelty."[118]

What is the disgust and concern about here? In large part, it is about the sexualization of girl/childhood. The girls are described as looking like kewpie whores/dolls, tarts, prostitutes, sex objects, and "hookers."[119] Yet none of these commentators actually finds the girls to be erotic or desirable. Rather, they find them to be repulsive. This repulsion can be understood not only to be for the beauty pageants, but also for the girls themselves, as one commentator's odd choice of words in describing the pageant girls as "predators" makes clear. Matt Brunson writes that the film depicts "prepubescent beauty pageants as grotesque spectacles in which tiny girls are encouraged by their parents to pose as sexual predators experienced at shaking their butts, lasciviously licking their lips, and applying more makeup than even a 60-year-old trollop trying to conceal her age."[120] When we "hate" beauty pageants, it is supposed to be because they make girls sexually available in an inappropriate way to adult men on the visual level and therefore—based on a common-sense (but unsupported) assumption—potentially on the physical level as well. But what Brunson's slip of the pen provocatively suggests is that the hatred, sometimes vitriolic, is often really for the girls themselves. Here, the implicitly feminist critique of beauty pageants for putting girls on display authorizes what is in fact a misogynous hatred of girls.

And yet commentators harbor no hatred for Olive as beauty pageant contestant. In fact, ironically, none of the commentators I found was offended by Olive's striptease dance routine, despite the fact that it explic-itly represents the idea of "girl as sex worker" to which the makeup, hair, and costumes of the other girls only implicitly refer. As Myke Bartlett puts it, "There is nothing sexual to [Olive/Breslin's] performance, only in the audience's recognition of its connotations."[121] As a result, the arti-fice and constructed nature of the other pageant contestants' feminine sexuality comes to the fore, making it suddenly not just undesirable but also repulsive. But what about the fact that Olive is, nevertheless, a child beauty pageant contestant? How do commentators deal with this aspect of the film, and how might a feminist media critic respond?

Commentators interpret Olive as deeply invested in beauty contests, and this reading is certainly supported by the opening shot of Olive practicing a Miss America wave while watching the pageant on tele-vision, as well as by her visible and verbal excitement about getting a chance to participate in the Little Miss Sunshine contest. Yet reviews read beyond the depiction of her pleasure in performance and her excitement about participating, suggesting she is "besotted,"[122] "pageant-obsessed,"[123] and "dying to win."[124] One review claims that the image of "Miss America accepting her tiara [that] flickers in [Olive's] eyeglasses [in the film's opening scene] . . . might as well be projected on her fron-tal lobe."[125] Not one commentary I found mentions one of the many iro-nies in the film: Olive had only just begun participating in beauty pag-eants when she was visiting her aunt. Admittedly, this information flies by in a brief telephone conversation between Olive's mother and her sis-ter, but it seems fair to imagine that Olive has participated in only one beauty contest prior to the Little Miss Sunshine event. Nevertheless, on the *Today Show*, for example, Matt Lauer describes Olive as having a "lifelong dream of competing."[126] And one of the most frequently used clips on television programs discussing the film is of Olive screaming and running for joy when she finds out she will get to participate in the Little Miss Sunshine contest. In short, commentaries understand Olive to be like any other child beauty pageant contestant, as completely "into it." It should not be a surprise, then, that some of the reviews suggest that the audience will anticipate Olive's "humiliation" in the Little Miss Sunshine contest, because she so clearly does not look like the other contestants and therefore could not possibly win. In short, "she clearly doesn't have a prayer."[127]

This reading of Olive's relationship to beauty pageants, however, does not embrace her desire to compete in the pageant as a desire—perhaps—to perform in, as opposed to look like a contestant in, a beauty pageant. The collective reading assumes the narrative will tell the story of Olive's journey toward a rude awakening, as opposed to the story of Olive's journey toward achieving her dream. To end with a rude awakening, Olive's dream must be to win the pageant. But to end with the pleasure of performance, Olive's dream could be to participate, to dance, to

Figure 3.2. One of Olive's many engagements with pleasure and performance. Courtesy of Photofest.

move her body, to take erotic pleasure in her own body, and to take up space in the social world. Robinson and Davies read her performance at the pageant as a mark of "self-possession" and as "Olive's ability to distance and detach herself from the audience's negative affect."[128] And, if I reread from this perspective, the opening of the film, when Olive practices her wave while watching a videotape of Miss America, can be understood as pleasure not in traditional, hyper-sexualized femininity on display (as some of the commentary would have it), but rather in the process of performance itself. Similarly, from this perspective, when she goes on stage at the end to perform her dance routine, she shifts from the discomfort she has begun to feel with the entire pageant to her typical smile as she moves further into her erotic dance performance.

It is not that I want to recuperate the girl beauty pageant as somehow feminist (although this argument can be made). Rather, I want to see if I can understand *Little Miss Sunshine* and Olive's participation in the pageant to be offering a version of girlhood that is about the possibility of taking up social space—both in the family and beyond. For girls to inhabit and take pleasure in social space, I would argue, is feminist. Further, my reading of Olive as taking pleasure in public performance and the autoerotic feel of her own body in motion pushes past the implicitly feminist abhorrence of child beauty pageants in much of the commentary to a different feminism, one invested in the possibility of a sexual child, not as an object for consumption by an adult gaze but simply as a potential and possible version of her own childhood.

Juno *and a Plethora of Girls' Choices*

A large portion of the commentary on *Juno* focuses specifically on the issue of teen pregnancy,[129] and references to *Juno* in public discussion of teen pregnancy continue years after its release (e.g., in relation to MTV's *Teen Mom* [2009–present]).[130] Most of this discussion uses a critique of the film to help build a moral panic about a seemingly unprecedented escalation in teen pregnancy, despite statistics—available in the very same commentaries—that show the contrary. For example, some commentaries report December 2007 National Center for Health Statistics: Between 2005 and 2006 for girls between the ages of fifteen and nineteen, pregnancy was up 3 percent. Between 1991 and 2005, however, there had been a 34 percent overall decline in teen pregnancy.[131] Nevertheless, CNN claims the 3 percent increase between 2005 and 2006 represents a "big surge in teen pregnancy."[132] An op-ed piece in the *San Francisco Chronicle* suggests that *Juno* might even cause an increase in teen pregnancy: "It'll be interesting to see the teen birthrate figures for 2008 and beyond, in the post-*Juno* era. . . . I'm a card-carrying Berkeley liberal, but I found the blasé attitude toward teen pregnancy among the film's characters disturbing. . . . [The film has] a powerful anti-abortion, pro–teen pregnancy message."[133]

Given that *Juno* did not even have a limited release until December 2007, this author's suggestion that the film could somehow lead to an increase in teen pregnancy as soon as 2008 may seem far-fetched; yet, in late December 2007, Jamie Lynn Spears became the first of several high-profile real-life teen pregnancies—followed by the supposed Gloucester, Massachusetts, pregnancy pact, Bristol Palin, and MTV's *16 and Pregnant* (2009–present) and *Teen Mom*—to generate substantial media coverage soon after *Juno's* release. In this context, media anxiety about an increase in teen pregnancy—presumably spurred on by *Juno* and real-life celebrities—escalated, with claims such as "there is a little bit of fear that a baby could become the new teenage accessory in Hollywood."[134] Regardless of whether a reader/listener/viewer of all this coverage takes seriously the idea that teen girls would choose to get pregnant because Juno and Jamie Lynn Spears did, the particular version of girlhood on offer here is reckless and brainless. These imaginary pregnant girls make a mistake—a choice—that is understood to ruin their lives, just to be like high-profile celebrity girls. To make this choice is to make the wrong choice. This is a girl in desperate need of disciplining, a girl who cannot be trusted with choice.

Choice, of course, is a key issue in media representations of feminism. For example, media coverage consistently defines feminist activists simply as "pro-choice," even when many activists actually define abortion as only one of many aspects of reproductive health and women's human rights.[135] And postfeminist discourse about women's supposed desire and struggle to have it all—work, romance, family—produces what Elspeth Probyn calls "choiceoisie": the idea that women have an equivalent free choice between a liberated career or a new traditionalist life as a wife and mother.[136] In other words, "choice" is a fraught concept within public understandings of feminism. With the concepts of pro-choice and choiceoisie, however, women are at least understood not only to make choices, but also to have a right to do so. In the discussion of *Juno* and teen pregnancy, girls have no such right and no such capacity. And so I turn to the film to ask it to produce a girlhood with choice, even if other scholars who have written on the film argue persuasively that Juno's choices are "constrained."[137]

First, most obviously, Juno considers an abortion, speaks the actual word "abortion," and visits an abortion clinic. Gabrielle Hine argues persuasively that the film "frame[s] . . . every aspect of the abortion process as . . . hostile" and thereby naturalizes Juno's choice not to have an abortion,[138] but the film does take Juno through the process of choosing, rather than leaving abortion unspoken. Second, Juno chooses the adoptive parent(s)—not once, but twice. At the beginning of the film, her choice is quick and relatively unreflective: as many commentaries point out, she finds the adoptive parents in the *Penny Saver*. Yet a key narrative turn in the film is when Juno, Vanessa, and Mark all must confront the fact that Mark does not want to be a father, nor do Vanessa and Mark want to remain a couple. Vanessa and Mark choose to separate; Juno then (re)chooses Vanessa as the baby's now-single mother. Late in the film, we see Juno write something (what turns out to be her

Figure 3.3. The moment at which Juno makes the decision to choose Vanessa as the baby's mother, in *Juno*.

decision) on a scrap of paper and deliver it to Vanessa, but Vanessa is privy to the decision before the audience is. This structure makes the audience wait for, anticipate, and care about Juno's choice, and a closing scene of the film shows just how crucial that choice is to Vanessa's life and the "happy ending" of the film: we see Vanessa with her baby in the nursery, Juno's note—her choice—framed and hanging on the wall above her head. Finally, Juno chooses her friend Bleeker—like her choice of Vanessa—twice. First, the film makes clear, she chooses to have sex with him: she initiates the encounter, and when he says "I've wanted this for a really long time," she says, "I know." She is the one to make the choice at that moment to have sex. Second, she chooses to return to her relationship with him late in her pregnancy and after the birth, securing a happy ending not only for Vanessa but also for herself (and for Bleeker).

In short, *Juno* depicts a girl who can and does make choices. Further, the narrative depends on those choices: she chooses first to have sex and then not to have an abortion, allowing the story to progress; she chooses Vanessa as a single mother in order for Vanessa and the baby to have a happy ending; and she chooses to return to Bleeker in order for her own story (and Bleeker's) to provide a feel-good ending. Certainly, these choices are tied to aspects of the narrative that are relatively typical: motherhood and heterosexual romance remain the source of the happy endings, and abortion remains the choice inevitably not taken.[139] Yet the film and Juno's choices clearly separate motherhood from romance—Vanessa gets one, while Juno gets the other. Thus, not only does Juno make choices, but also—if only in part—the choices she makes rewrite media narratives, both those of typical postfeminist choiceoisie discourse and those in the media coverage of *Juno* that define girls as incapable of choosing choices worth making.

Precious's Specificity

As if predicting *Precious*, J. Hoberman writes, "Had the protagonists [of *Juno, Knocked Up* (2007), and *Waitress* (2007)] been poor, black, illegal, or Jamie Lynn Spears, the movies necessarily would have been more serious and scarcely as much fun."[140] This is as close as I can get to a connection in the media between *Juno* and *Precious*, despite the fact that both are high-profile surprise indie hits about pregnant teenagers released within two years of each other. Of the hundreds of articles about both films I read, not a single one made a connection between Precious and Juno or other high-profile pregnant teens or teen moms.[141] Certainly, race is at issue here. The figure of an African American pregnant teen often stands for "dependence on welfare," the "irresponsibility of black men," or the "hyper-sexuality" of black women and girls.[142] Hence, Precious is a different kind of girl from other pregnant (white) girls. Further, Precious's pregnancy is a result of child abuse and rape, not sexual agency as is the case for all these other girls (one wants to assume). If part of the anxiety about *Juno* and teen pregnancy is concern not only about pregnancy but also about girls' sexual agency, *Precious* does not fit here either.

If Precious does not get to participate in the new Hollywood trend of young pregnancy, and if she does not get at least implicitly to stand for girls' sexual agency, then what does she get? In much of the coverage, Precious becomes a universal symbol first of suffering, and then of hope. For example, the filmmakers generally defend *Precious* against the charge of racial stereotyping by insisting that it tells a universal story and is not really about African Americans at all. In an interview published in the African American newspaper the *Sacramento Observer*, Sandra Varner asks the film's director, Lee Daniels, "Is this story primarily about race or is it primarily about poverty and do [you] have any concern about how this story may stigmatize the Black community?" Daniels responds by denying that race matters to the film: "It's a universal story. I am a Black filmmaker so the film is from a Black perspective and it happens to a Black girl, but this story is universal. I've been around the world with the film and I'm continually shocked and surprised at little women from Japan and Australia that are sixty and seventy and eighty years old feeling like they are Precious."[143]

Of the four film girls in this chapter (Cady, Olive, Juno, and Precious), ironically, the coverage makes Precious—despite her relative uniqueness in the history of U.S. cinema as a poor African American girl at the very center of a film—the most universal, the best stand-in for the rest of us. But, importantly, "the rest of us" are generally not imagined as girls—in fact, in the coverage of *Precious* "we" are often sixty, seventy, or eighty years old. Thus the universal figure is not a girl, but an adult who faces generic pain and difficulty in her or his life. Hence, at least in this aspect of the coverage, Precious not only does not get to be a Hollywood pregnant teen, does not get to have sexual agency, but she does not even get to be a girl.

In response, then, can I read Precious as a girl? Given that, as many African American feminist scholars point out, black girls are systematically denied girlhood, this is a question that must be asked of the film. I would argue, in fact, that this film can be read to challenge the denial of black girlhood.[144] First, the film acknowledges the way, as an underage girl, Precious is beholden to her mother, trapped in her mother's home not only because she lacks her own resources but also because she is young and therefore has never had any other choice or resources. For example, an image of her standing at the sink doing dishes while her mother prepares to yell at her in the background, dark and fuzzy because it is shot through a dirty window, emphasizes a feeling of entrapment in this space. She is a child, without recourse. Second, more pleasurably, Precious finds childlike pleasure in her fantasies, shot in vibrant colors, and in her friendships with her classmates at an alternative school and with Nurse John at the hospital where she gives birth to her son. Scenes including Nurse John and her friends depict the characters as playful, both teasing one another and showing affection.

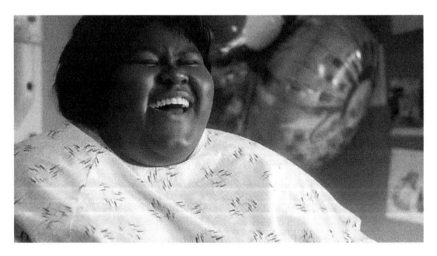

Figure 3.4. Precious laughs with her friends in the hospital after giving birth to her son, in *Precious*.

Thus, as a girl, and specifically as a poor African American girl, Precious faces abuse of power, but she also accesses fantasy and play. While, at the end of the film, as an HIV-positive teen mother on her own she certainly faces adult responsibilities and situations, throughout the film she also faces situations unique to girls: parents, school, and social workers who exercise and/or abuse power in ways that affect her life. And she engages the world as a girl, through fantasy and play. My goal, then, is to reclaim Precious from her status as "universal" victim who overcomes and instead to understand her specifically as a girl, navigating a girl's life.

Conclusion

Mean Girls, Little Miss Sunshine, Juno, and *Precious* are very different films, telling very different stories. Yet, across the four sizeable public discussions, several themes emerge that are typical of turn-of-the-twenty-first-century U.S. media culture depictions of girls. First, the coverage both adores and denigrates girls: it claims all four of these film girls as unique and loveable, but only over-and-against other generic unlovable girls who engage in mean behavior; enjoy empty, formulaic narratives; or are depressed, unhealthy, or sullen. Second, the coverage draws on and contributes to public anxiety about girls, in particular in relation to the threat of the crash-and-burn girl star, the supposed inevitability of girl meanness, and the supposed exponential growth in girls who make bad choices and end up pregnant. From this perspective, the massive cultural attention paid to these films is troubling in that a key version of "girl" it offers is abject, without agency, worthy only of disdain, and in need of disciplining.

Alongside and running through these themes, however, is a crowd of other girls: mean girls, queer girls, girls of color and very young girls with healthy sexuality, feminist girls, pregnant girls, teen moms, girls who seriously consider abortion, girls who make choices and thereby drive the narrative of their own lives, sexually active girls, girls who speak back to power, poor girls, girls who face and survive abuse, girls who fantasize, girls who play, and girls who remain girls even though they are poor and black.

Importantly, the public discussion does not address all these girl-hoods, and, in fact, much of the commentary seems to disavow most of them. In this chapter, then, I respond to this coverage both by analyzing and critiquing its depiction of the films and their girls, and by turning a feminist critical eye away from the coverage and toward the most optimistic readings of the films I can imagine, asking what alternatives these films can offer both to the coverage's impossibly unique can-do celebrated girl and to its denigrated empty-headed girls. From that perspective and purposefully overstating the case in order to give it more traction, I argue that *Mean Girls* holds heterosexuality responsible for meanness and articulates queer girlhoods, *Little Miss Sunshine* acknowledges and celebrates autoeroticism and the pleasure of performance for young girls, *Juno* puts a girl's choices in the center of the story and lets her make them, and *Precious* insists on the existence of an African American girlhood that both faces power and engages in playful pleasure. In short, I argue for a feminist critical method that explicitly challenges media coverage by asking *Mean Girls, Little Miss Sunshine, Juno,* and *Precious*—films that have a sustained hold on public attention—to do feminist work in the heart of media culture: to articulate girlhood differently and heterogeneously.

4

"I'm Not Changing My Hair"

Venus Williams and Live TV's Racialized
Struggle over Athletic Girlhood

In 1997, teenage girls dominated women's professional tennis and its
U.S. media coverage. That year, African American Venus Williams
turned seventeen and began playing regularly. Starting the year ranked
216th and ending the year ranked twenty-second, she played three of
the four Grand Slam tournaments,[1] broke through at the U.S. Open
when she reached the finals as an unseeded player, and appeared on the
cover of *Sports Illustrated*.[2] The already-successful Swiss sixteen-year-
old Martina Hingis began 1997 ranked fourth in the world, reached the
finals of all four majors, won three of them, and ended the year ranked
first.[3] Another teen phenom broke through in 1997: Russian[4] Anna
Kournikova. Turning sixteen in June, she played all four majors, made
it to the semifinals of Wimbledon, and ended the year having moved
from fifty-eighth to thirty-second in the world.

Venus,[5] Hingis, and Kournikova all went on to high-profile careers as
adults, and Kournikova and Venus (along with Serena Williams) are still
well-known celebrities recognized well beyond tennis (and even sports).
This chapter, however, addresses 1997–1999, the three years during which
these players ruled tennis as teenage girls.[6] In contrast to the two previous chapters, which examine themes and possibilities in representations
of girls across at least a decade, this chapter offers a very focused case

study in order to highlight the significant role late 1990s women's tennis played in the production of and negotiation over turn-of-the-twenty-first-century girlhood.

This negotiation took place against the backdrop of the various media depictions of girls I explore in previous chapters, in particular anxious adoration and depictions of can-do girl power. For example, at the 1997 Wimbledon tournament Billie Jean King said, "I like that [the teen players] are haughtier. Girls [today] have higher self-esteem than they used to in my era. I like it." And Mary Carillo said, "We are going to have our hands full with these teenagers who are taking over our sport. They all have an awful lot of attitude, an awful lot of savvy and smarts for their young ages." By the end of 1997 at the U.S. Open, advertisers joined in, airing commercials that claimed a causal link between girls' sports participation and success as an adult woman. For example, one ad claimed that if you want a girl to be a scientist, you should give her tennis shoes instead of a tea set. And during Venus's U.S. Open semifinal match, Nike's "If You Let Me Play" ad promised all sorts of positive effects of sports, including "I will like myself more" and "I will learn what it means to be strong."[7]

Not all of the girl athlete hype was unadulterated girl power nirvana, however. Bud Collins's introduction to the 1997 French Open final, in which nineteen-year-old Iva Majoli beat sixteen-year-old Hingis for the title, makes explicit a particularly icky aspect of the media's obsession with these girls: "Remember [Maurice Chevalier] in *Gigi* [1958] singing 'Thank heaven for little girls'? Well, he would love this final. This is as young as it gets. With Martina Hingis, sweet sixteen, she joins some of the great sixteen-year-olds of the past. Like Maureen Connolly . . . Tracy Austin . . . Monica Seles . . . and . . . Chris Evert. . . . So, like Chevalier, I say, 'Thank heavens for these little girls.'" Collin's reference to Chevalier and *Gigi*'s sexualization of "little girls," his delight that "this is as young as it gets," and his suggestion that Chevalier "would love this" all implicitly define the teen girls more as objects for consumption than as athletes. And by using *Gigi* to revel in their youth, Collins authorizes a sexualized gaze without seeming to generate it himself.

The media were interested in these teenage girls not only because they played phenomenally well, not only because they were authorized by and concomitantly authorized girl power rhetoric, not only because they were available as delightful objects on display, but also because they brought intrigue, particularly around issues of race and, as Collins's comments foreground, sexuality. In terms of race, Venus was raised and coached by her father,[8] Richard Williams, primarily outside of what Richard explicitly identified as the monied and predominantly white U.S. tennis world. And Kournikova (whom Collins often explicitly called "the Lolita") looked and often acted like a model and had endorsements to match. In short, in 1997, teenage girls not only changed tennis but also contributed to public discussions about and media fascination with girls more generally, a fascination deeply invested in race and sexuality.

While Venus, Hingis, Kournikova, and the 1997 intrigue surrounding them were enough to mark the new reign of teenage girls, the next year two additional teenage players emerged: Venus's sister Serena Williams and Croatian Mirjana Lučić. At age sixteen, Serena played all four majors that year, ending the year ranked twentieth. Lučić turned sixteen in 1998, played three of the four majors, and ended the year ranked fifty-first. As early as the January 1998 Australian Open, television commentators were talking about "the five young ones,"[9] the "young guns,"[10] and the "teen queens,"[11] claiming that interest in women's tennis was way up: "The reason why [is] the young kids."[12] The 1998 press emphasized that all five already had major sponsorships, publishing articles with titles such as "The Dream Teens"[13] and—emphasizing girl power by implicitly referencing the British pop group the Spice Girls—"Teens Spice of Women's Tennis: New Flavor: Cocky and Coquettish, Upstarts Making Waves on, off Court."[14] These players, along with nineteen-year-old Swiss Patty Schnyder (who reached the quarterfinals of both the French Open and the U.S. Open and ended the year ranked eleventh) and French Amélie Mauresmo (who turned eighteen that year, played all four majors, and broke into the top one hundred), made up "the best crop of teenagers . . . ever."[15]

In 1999, media continued to focus on the players' youth, emphasizing rumor and intrigue. For example, in January nineteen-year-old Mauresmo confirmed the rumor that she was a lesbian and identified her then-partner, Sylvie Bourdon, when she came out to the French press after her semifinal win at the Australian Open. While former and current players were already out (most notably, Martina Navratilova), as a young, highly ranked player who came out so early in her career and spoke openly about her love not just for women but for Bourdon in particular, Mauresmo's media visibility soared.[16] Alexandra Stevenson also came to prominence in 1999 when she reached the semifinals of Wimbledon at age eighteen.[17] As a mixed race African American daughter of a white woman who would not identify Stevenson's birth father, Stevenson's athletic ability led to media speculation and, ultimately, the claim that former basketball player Julius Erving was her father.[18] Having initiated persistent discussion of race and sexuality in 1997 with teen players Venus and Kournikova, respectively, by 1999 media had naturalized the association of these topics with teen girls such that they were readily available for making sense of Mauresmo and Stevenson. By 2000, however, the most dominant players were moving out of their teens. Thus, coverage spent less and less time on youth, bringing to an end the moment of negotiation over girlhood that took place through the late 1990s teen tennis players.[19]

In this chapter, I focus on Venus Williams, first because she was an important teenage player from the beginning; hence, by tracing how media position her I can address the entire arc of the 1997–1999 teen girl narratives. Second, I choose Venus because I am most interested in how media coverage worked through questions of racism and African American identity in relation to girlhood. Third, I focus on Venus because the narratives about her were much more complex and contradictory than were those about Hingis (the Swiss Miss with a winning smile) and Kournikova (the Lolita). In short, of the three teens who played during the entire three-year period in which media highlighted the players' youth, Venus offers a possibility of finding the most challenging and alternative version of athletic girlhood, a girlhood that, I argue, can be read as independent, successful, self-possessed, sometimes unwilling to follow the rules of media narratives about racial assimilation and exceptionalism, and even on occasion explicitly critical of racism in both the tennis world and media coverage.

Importantly, this alternative girlhood is produced by and only available through media depictions. Thus, I do not argue that Venus is "actually" a resistant girl; rather, I argue that media depictions make Venus available as a resistant girl. In other words, media produce and provide the resistant girl, even when her resistance, paradoxically, is to the media themselves. Nevertheless, as David Andrews and Steven Jackson argue, the specificity of sports celebrity means that Venus is also a *"real* [individual] participating in unpredictable contexts."[20] By focusing on sports as my case study in this chapter, then, I emphasize this "unpredictability" both in terms of what might happen on court when athletes compete and in terms of the sports commentators' and producers' lack of experience covering an African American girl excelling at professional tennis.

In order to explore the mediated negotiations that took place over this unpredictability, I focus on a particular type of media coverage: television match coverage that is live or what I call "near-live"—produced to seem live, only slightly time-delayed (and therefore not able to be significantly re-packaged or re-narrativized), and/or called/ recorded live but aired later. Of course, as my definition of "near-live" implies and as many scholars have shown, "liveness" itself is constructed as a key aspect of television sports media; it is a "conceptual filter" and a "discursive practice."[21] Thus, again, I do not argue that live television makes it possible for us to know what "actually" happened; rather, I seek to demonstrate that liveness makes especially visible the process by which media both produce Venus-as-challenging-girl and work to contain her and her unpredictability within pre-established narratives about racial assimilation and postracial celebration of abstract "difference."

In particular, I focus on two kinds of live/near-live coverage. First, I emphasize play-by-play coverage during which announcers had to react in the moment without the aid of pre-written scripts[22] in order to discuss the racialized and gendered changes Venus was bringing to tennis and to public understandings of girlhood. In her comparison of live coverage to interviews with sportscasters about their goals during live coverage, Toni Bruce finds that "representations of natural black physicality continue to be reproduced in live sports television, despite a clear awareness among the commentators interviewed of what the stereotypes were and a stated desire to avoid their reinforcement."[23] Thus I focus on live/near-live play-by-play because, as Bruce shows, its unique qualities can make particularly visible the production of racialized girlhood. By highlighting moments at which announcers disagreed with each other, contradicted each other as well as other running narratives, and confronted the unprecedented presence of an African American girl not only succeeding at but also approaching tennis in a unique way—from her training, to her hair, to her father's public claims that the tennis tour was racist—I illustrate how the coverage worked through Venus's racialized girlhood, contributing to a complex field of girlhood in media culture.

Second, later in the chapter I address a few rare live television events that (at least initially) escape the various narratives of racialization commentators attempt to build around Venus. Because these unexpected events happened on live television, commentators and producers were unprepared for them. Thus, here, the liveness of television—in particular live sports television—means that explicit critique of the whiteness and racism in tennis can come to the fore. In short, this chapter is about live/near-live sports television because it is a particularly good vehicle through which to see the process of media producing and struggling over the meaning of girlhood, and because—even if rarely—it can offer moments of discord when unanticipated events directly contradict the narrative packaging of girlhood that comes before and then almost immediately after.

I break the chapter into two main sections. First, I focus on the representation of Venus as a racialized girl who brings difference to tennis. I compare the coverage of her to that of several of the other teen players, emphasizing distinctions between them. Here I argue that Venus is racialized in often stereotypical ways, but also that this racialization is not uniform and, further, that coverage includes moments in which Venus, her family, and occasionally commentators (especially Mary Carillo) articulate alternative and/or resistant perspectives on the disruption that Venus represents for the overwhelmingly white world of women's professional tennis as U.S. media had historically covered it. In the second section of the chapter, I focus on three particularly disruptive moments in the 1997–1999 coverage of Venus, when the actions of Venus, her family, and those around her cannot be folded into the racialized difference, assimilationist, and exceptionalist depictions of Venus I examine in the first section. As I move through the chapter, then, I ask more and more explicitly and insistently how much antiracism and independence one can find in media depictions of Venus's girlhood.

Defining Venus as Black: Racialized
Narratives and Resistant Openings

One way to understand the coverage of Venus as a teen player is as part of a process of media and other players producing and then trying to come to terms with Venus's (and Serena's) ascribed difference. Most commentators and players are unwilling to say explicitly "they are black."[24] Instead, they allude to race but displace it by claiming that the Williamses behave differently, in particular that they separate themselves from everyone else. Thus a generic "difference" stands in for blackness. And because difference has to be from something, whiteness remains the unspoken norm for the teen tennis players. Additionally, because commentators generally hold Venus responsible for taking actions that are different, she herself seems to be the source of her difference and (implicit) racialization. Further, when commentators make their own recognition of difference a talking point, they seem to authorize sustained surveillance of Venus's body and behavior, intensifying her difference. Collectively, by setting Venus apart, all this coverage reinforces implicit racialized systems of normalcy within both tennis and tennis broadcasting. Nevertheless, these regularities and systems are thrown into relief when Venus emerges as a top player and the television coverage has to find ways to depict her as not only part of but also central to tennis.

Venus versus the Other Players

During the 1997 U.S. Open, Venus broke through, making it to the finals, where she lost to Hingis. Throughout the tournament, announcers mention her age and marvel that she is going all the way to the finals. As Carillo puts it, "That's just unprecedented. I mean, no kid has ever come into a major for the first time [unseeded] and gotten to the semis." During the awards ceremony, Pat O'Brien says, "I feel like we've grown up with [Venus] here at the U.S. Open." Yet, even as they emphasize her youth and repeatedly draw connections between her and the other teen players, they also emphasize her maturity. Commentators mention her "composure"[25] and call her "mentally tough,"[26] regardless of whether she is winning the match. For example, in an early round match at the 1997

U.S. Open, Bill Macatee says, "The one thing that is really impressive, I think, about Venus is she rarely seems nervous. . . . She doesn't look uneasy no matter what her surroundings are." Tracy Austin responds, "She seems . . . very poised." They also comment that she doesn't show "much reaction":[27] "Venus Williams [is] very calm, methodical almost. The expression rarely changes."[28] Alluding to an ongoing public debate about Venus's supposedly fraught relationship with other players, O'Brien says, "Nothing seems to rattle [her]." Thus, not only is she mature and poised, but she is stoic, even at points inscrutable.

It is not unusual for announcers to marvel over a teenage player's maturity, Hingis in particular. For example, at the 1997 French Open, Dick Enberg says Hingis has "all the qualities emotionally you wouldn't expect from someone so young." And, later in the same tournament, he claims, "Precocious is almost too soft a word to describe the tremendous talent of this woman at sixteen." Yet, unlike for Venus, the commentators also continue to define Hingis as childlike and innocent, well beyond 1997. For example, as late as the 1999 Australian Open, when Hingis was eighteen, the commentators say her face "beams with childish happiness. . . . With the casual air of a schoolgirl, she's won four grand slam titles."[29] Venus, however, does not maintain her identity as a "kid." Although the announcers mention her age from time to time, by 1999 they no longer define her directly as a child in this way.

This comparison of Hingis's and Venus's relationship to girlishness illustrates a racialization of true and full girlhood as white. Hingis is the perpetual girl; Venus is an unusually stoic, adultlike girl. As Delia Douglas argues in her analysis of representations of Venus and Serena, the announcers seem to draw on stereotypical representations of African American girls and woman as able to shoulder any burden, as impervious to pain, as unflappable, and thus as lacking in ordinary human affect.[30] These types of representations not only distance Venus from girlness, but they do so in ways that define her in terms of preestablished cultural definitions of African American females.

Discussions of Venus's physicality also racialize her, contributing to "the construction of naturally Black sporting bodies."[31] At the 1997 French Open, Venus's first grand slam that year, Austin says, "I expect that serve to be a humungous weapon," and "She's a terrific athlete. Really quick out there." At the 1997 U.S. Open, commentators discuss her "power," "great athleticism," and "hustle." After one particularly strong point during the semifinal, Carillo says, "Williams continues to get herself out of trouble just from the sheer force of her physicality." And Ted Robinson states, "Talk about wingspan. Venus Williams got to that like a great condor," a reference Douglas also notices and critiques for the way it draws on a long tradition of associating African Americans (regardless of whether they are athletes) with animals.[32] Commentators also sometimes link Venus's physicality to masculine power. For example, at the 1997 U.S. Open when she jumps to hit a particularly high overhead winner, Carillo says she gets "the kind of airtime that Pete Sampras shows off with sometimes." They often discuss the speed of her serves—usually in the range of 115–120 miles per hour, which rivals most men's serves on the tour.

For the press to remark on an athlete's physicality is common, of course. However, a comparison to the specific ways commentators address Kournikova's and Mauresmo's physicality—both in relation to sexuality—makes clear the implicit racialization of Venus's body as animallike, as a physical force beyond the ordinary, but also as "unfeminine"[33] and asexual. Commentators call Kournikova a "blonde, rock star–type teenager"[34] and a "pin-up queen."[35] And they often perpetuate her eroticization by reporting on how other media eroticize her, such as commenting on how photographers' cameras are always and only trained on Kournikova during a match[36] and reporting on the tabloids' interest in her. During the 1997 Wimbledon, they claim the British tabloids call her "Baby Spice" while showing images of Kournikova in erotic poses (such as shots of her butt) or with her presumed boyfriend in those very tabloids. At the 1998 Australian Open, a shot of her bare legs pans up to reveal her on court playing, thus not only sexualizing her but also sexualizing her tennis. Tennis makes Kournikova sexy, and when Kournikova plays, tennis is sexy.

For some fans, tennis also makes Mauresmo sexy; and when Mauresmo plays, tennis is sexy. But this is a queer sexiness that commentators work to deflect, even as they must acknowledge it once Mauresmo speaks openly about her sexuality. While commentators seem unable to bring themselves to use words such as "lesbian" or "homosexual" or to mention Mauresmo's decision to come out, they manage to address her sexuality by talking at length about Davenport's faux pas after the 1999

Australian Open semifinal match when she said, "A couple of times I thought I was playing a guy, the girl was hitting it so hard and so strong. And I'd look over there and she's so strong and those shoulders." While Mauresmo said in an interview, "I'm a very solid player in all the areas of the game, so, yeah, I take [Davenport's comment] as a compliment," the press and Davenport herself (through an apology)[37] assumed that the comment had been hurtful to Mauresmo. It is not clear whether the assumption was that it was hurtful to call a woman manlike or hurtful to insult someone who has just come out as a lesbian by questioning her gender, but either way Mauresmo's sexuality is at stake.

Unlike for Kournikova and Mauresmo, however, there is no discussion of Venus's sexuality during her teen years: no mention or speculation about boyfriends, and very little discussion of her body as fashionable or sexualized, despite the fact that she often talked of her interest in fashion. In some ways, the representations of Venus's and Mauresmo's bodies are similar: they are both masculinized as powerful, strong, and dominating. For Venus, however, these terms refer to her tennis and implicitly racialize her, while for Mauresmo they relate to her sexuality (although, of course, also to her tennis).[38] In short, particularly in comparison to the coverage of Kournikova and Mauresmo, the coverage of Venus defines her physicality as asexual, masculine, and implicitly animallike. This depiction, in turn, sets her off as different from the typical girl tennis player. Certainly, neither Kournikova nor Mauresmo are typical—each presents an extreme version of (hetero/homo)sexuality within the media's world of tennis and thus stands apart from other girl players. Yet together they illustrate a collapse of the teen girl with sexuality, which heightens a long-standing, pre-established sexualization of girl tennis players.[39] Thus, for Venus to be distanced from sexuality just as depictions of Kournikova and Mauresmo emphasize sexuality makes even more clear how the depictions of Venus's physicality as animallike, as different, produce an implicitly racialized difference.

Admittedly, the coverage suggests that Venus succeeds not only because of her physicality, but also because of her intelligence—both on the court and off. For example, at the 1997 French Open, after Venus won an impressive point by hitting to her opponents' weak side, Austin says, "I think [Venus is] a smart player to know that's the side that is going to crack." She also calls her a "very intelligent young woman" during the 1997 U.S. Open. During the 1997 U.S. Open final Carillo says, "She's proven she can be a quick study." And, when discussing the Williams family's decision to keep Venus out of the junior tournaments, commentators often mention that (unlike most teen players) Venus used the time to finish high school and that, during 1997 at age seventeen and while playing professional tennis, she was taking two college classes.[40]

Hingis is also a smart girl. In fact, overwhelmingly coverage represents Hingis as intelligent, if not brilliant, even when she's losing. For example, Evert says, "You can see it in her face, she's trying to figure out 'What can I do? What can I change in my game? Why am I losing?'"[41] During Hingis's semifinal match with Kournikova at the 1997 Wimbledon, Evert says, "Martina just anticipates shots so well. . . . She almost has like a third eye." By the time she is making her way toward winning her third Australian Open in a row in 1999, Fred Stolle says she is "one of the best thinkers in women's tennis." In fact, Cliff Drysdale asks Mary Joe Fernández, "Is [Hingis] the most brilliant strategist that you have on the tour?" To which Fernández replies, "I definitely think so." During the final, Drysdale goes so far as to call her the smartest player—man or woman: "I want Hingis on my chess team. She uses the court better than anybody in, I think, men's or women's tennis."

Sometimes when I mention to colleagues that I am writing about Venus, they say something like, "Oh, I remember how racist the coverage was. You must be arguing that she's the 'strong one' while Hingis is the 'smart one.'" To which I respond, "Sort of." Above I illustrate, in fact, that commentators also sometimes define Venus as intelligent and do not entirely restrict her to physical strength and size. In other words, the commentary cannot be reduced to an anticipated stereotypical definition of "black athlete = body." Yet, in comparison to the definition of Hingis as the smartest tennis player in the world—male or female—it becomes clear that the representation of Venus as smart only goes so far. Further, as I discuss in more detail below, Venus's reported intelligence and investment in education contributes to a boot-strapping narrative that racializes her as an exceptional black girl, one who illustrates the possibility of assimilation and success, as long as she tries hard and values education.

For commentators, Venus's success comes not only from her maturity, physicality, and intelligence, but also from what they define as her confidence, a confidence that is often problematic for them. For example, announcers sometimes call her "cocky"[42] and suggest that her attitude is inappropriate, that as an unproven player who is different from typical teen players she is not showing enough (implicitly racialized) deference.[43] The media often report that, from the beginning, she said she and Serena would be number one and two in the world. During the 1997 Wimbledon coverage, NBC aired an interview in which she said, "It will definitely be myself, my sister Serena, and number three will have to be decided among everyone else." For Austin, this was just a little too much: She says, "I think that's very confident, but I also think you've got to show your fellow players some respect. Hingis is number one in the world right now. It's proven she can get there."[44]

In fact, throughout the second half of 1997, commentators spoke often of trouble on the tour for Venus. At Wimbledon, Frank Deford says, "She's something less than a success in the ladies' locker room. . . . Venus possess[es] an attitude that many of the other players consider rude, if not downright antagonistic." This comment precedes interviews with other players willing to speak on camera about Venus. For example, Brenda Schultz-McCarthy says, "After the match I said, 'Hey, well done.' And she was like, 'Don't touch me.'" During match coverage, Evert also mentions, "Some of the players have been critical of Venus and the close relationship with her sister, Serena: that they've closed off the rest of the world." This commentary continues at the 1997 U.S. Open, including quotations from Lindsay Davenport and Monica Seles about Venus not responding to them when they greeted her.[45]

The coverage does define both Venus and Hingis as "cocky." Yet for Venus, it creates almost a year of trouble on the tour, while for Hingis, it generally translates as "cute." For example, during the same match during which Austin critiques Venus for being cocky, she reports that after beating Venus in a previous match, "Hingis came into the press room afterwards. She picked up a couple of Venus's beads and threw them at a reporter and said, 'This is all that's left of Venus.'" While Austin might have pointed out that Hingis's actions were disrespectful to Venus, to the reporter at whom she threw the beads, and to the janitor who had to clean up the beads afterward, or that her actions were even violent and out of control, Austin follows it instead with the comment "So, I think the rivalry has begun already." And during Hingis's semifinal match at the 1997 U.S. Open, Carillo says, "All these phenoms have attitudes. But it really seems like the players in the locker room get a kick out of how Martina Hingis goes after them and has a good time." In short, in the coverage Venus is cocky, which leads to media interviewing other players regarding their dislike of her (something they are willing to discuss on-camera), while Hingis is cocky in a cute sort of way.[46]

Admittedly, at other times Carillo critiques Hingis for her attitude, reporting the same "toss[ing] a bead in the press conference" incident as inappropriate, and calling Hingis "haughty."[47] And at the 1997 Wimbledon, Evert says, "[Hingis] doesn't show much respect for Steffi Graf. It really is too bad." Further, by the beginning of 1998 at the Australian Open, commentators changed their approach to Venus, saying "[She and Serena have] sure turned things around here in Australia. They have been very friendly, very outgoing, very confident and cocky in a certain way, but in an endearing kind of way."[48] Thus two narratives operate in relation to the teen players' confidence, one that defines it as inappropriate and unproven—as "cocky"—and the other that defines it as cute. While both narratives adhere to both Hingis and Venus, overall Hingis is much more often understood as cute, while Venus is much more often understood as inappropriate, particularly in the 1997 coverage, which was much more skeptical of Venus overall.

Thus, as with depictions of her maturity, physicality, and intelligence, these depictions of Venus's cocky confidence draw on pre-established, racialized social categories and narratives, while also working through how to integrate Venus into definitions of previously (mostly) white women's tennis and thereby create a particularly circumscribed and racialized space for Venus in that world. As I explore next, however, Venus did not necessarily cooperate, allowing for reading her as resistant.

The Trouble with Blackness

The coverage of Venus's supposed unwillingness to interact with the other players illustrates a consistent pressure to socialize, but it also depicts resistance as part of Venus's difference. For example, announcers interview Venus about the locker room trouble at the 1997 U.S. Open, showing clips in which she says, "I go in, I go out. I don't hang around. I don't take naps in [the players' lounge]. . . . I don't dine in there. Lots of people do, but I have other things." And, in an interview aired during the 1997 Wimbledon tournament, Venus explains how she understands her own self-confidence: "I think my parents . . . taught us to believe in ourselves most of all because if you believe in yourself and you're proud of yourself and have self-confidence—not to the point that you're haughty—but you believe in yourself and that's a good thing." Similarly, when asked about the supposed trouble in the locker room, Venus's mother, Oracene says, "Well, I don't know what they're talking about. Any other questions? Players, I can't say what they are. But Venus is nice to everybody."[49] Thus, in various interviews, Venus and her mother deflect the critique of Venus's self-confidence, articulating an alternative perspective on why she believes in herself and why she might not talk to the other players all the time, a perspective that resists the "trouble in the locker room" narrative.

Here, coverage puts in Venus's and Oracene's voices a competing narrative about what it means to be black, to "behave black," although it is not articulated as such. In other words, in relation to cockiness and locker room trouble, to behave black is to be inappropriately above others, or it is to have other things to do, to disregard race altogether. This sidestepping of race, articulated through Venus's and Oracene's resistance, can be read as an investment in colorblindness, in the irrelevance of race. While, as I discuss below, there are moments when Venus can be understood to articulate a direct critique of racism, here the coverage seems to use her resistance in an effort to "move past" race. Through Venus and Oracene, race becomes irrelevant, which in turn authorizes the media coverage as non-racist.

This "race is not important" narrative is twin to a postracial affection for blackness, which seems to declare it is safe to speak of race, as long as it is with pleasure. Specifically, commentators articulate race most explicitly when expressing affectionate appreciation for Venus's exceptionalism and assimilation. For example, during the 1997 U.S. Open, a short special on Venus begins by defining her as a role model for African American kids who "need help." It starts with a shot of a street sign, "Malcolm X Boulevard," followed by shots of young African American children, one of which shows them behind a chain-link fence. During these images, we hear the lyrics "Make this a better place, if you can," from a Diana Ross recording.[50] Venus and her father then come into this space and greet a crowd of mostly African American adults and children, and then Venus (who looks to be fifteen or sixteen years old in the clip) reads a short motivational speech from a piece of paper she holds in her hand. Following this footage, Richard speaks to an off-camera interviewer, saying "Venus is extremely educated. And our job is not so much now to worry about what Venus's education is but to see that we can use Venus as an instrument to help other kids." Here, she is both exceptional and an instrument of assimilation for other African Americans.

Coincidentally, Venus made her breakthrough at the 1997 U.S. Open, the same year the Arthur Ashe Stadium opened in Flushing, New York. The announcers revel in this, claiming that Venus must be thrilled and honored to play in a stadium named for Ashe, and in at least one case claiming that "she's already spoken about what an honor it is to play in that stadium." While they do not actually say "because Ashe was also a black tennis player," given that they make no similar claims of honor for other players, one can assume they are engaging an assimilationist narrative celebrating the exceptionalism of both Ashe and Venus. Further, when Venus made the final, the announcers introduced the match by saying "Today Venus Williams covets the trophy in hopes of following in [African American] Althea [Gibson's] pioneering footsteps."[51] Venus, however, resists this assimilationist narrative. During a "beyond the baseline" special on her, Venus deflects the Ashe/race issue, saying "Arthur Ashe Stadium is great, but if I hadn't practiced and worked hard, whether I play in the stadium or not wouldn't have really mattered. So, that [presumably, race] has nothing to do with it. A lot of people say 'good luck' and things like that, but it's just nothing at all. I spent hours, a lot of time, when I could have been doing other things. But I put that time in." Like the commentators, Venus does not actually say the words "African American" or "black." Nevertheless, by shifting to a discussion of her hard work rather than the supposed honor of playing in Ashe Stadium, she resists the depiction of her as an exceptional African American, turning again to an argument that race has nothing to do with it.

Since race supposedly has nothing to do with it, it seems safe for the coverage to adore Venus's black body, to revel in marks of blackness represented as abstract difference, unmoored from social, cultural, and historical context. This happens most often in terms of Venus's beaded hair, which coverage represents as fun and playful, making her different but adorable. Commentators slip in reference to the beads when they seem to notice them or when the producer/editor includes an image of Venus that emphasizes her beads—for example, Austin says "beads flying" with a smile in her voice, before going on to discuss Venus's ability to move quickly on court.[52] In the introduction to the 1997 Wimbledon coverage, Bud Collins says Venus has "great hair and hair-raising strokes." During Venus's first round 1997 Wimbledon match, Enberg states, "That's a beautiful slow motion replay because of the beaded dreadlocks accentuating her every move." Then perhaps realizing he has veered rather far into adoration of Venus's body, he follows up with "three–all" with an official sound in his voice. At the 1998 Australian Open a commentator asks, "Can you hear the beads rattling there?" Later in the match, a shot shows Venus moving something off the court and Pam Shriver says, "I think a few beads must have fallen out there. Occasionally they do. Venus just swiped them away." After winning her quarterfinal match at the 1997 U.S. Open, Venus gave some spectators beads that had come out of her hair. Robinson commented on it as it happened, and then Jon Frankel asked Venus about it in the post-match interview, asking if they had fallen out or if she had extras for the fans, asking which color she was giving out, and then saying "Do you think that will be your trademark now, not only wearing them but perhaps handing them out after every win that you have?" As Venus often does when the media work hard to develop a racialized narrative around her—in this case one about how fun African American hair styles can be—she offers an alternative, deracialized perspective, downplaying the beads: "If they come out. Usually I give them to the ball kids."

The sound of the beads, however, is not only a point of adoration but also a fulcrum for media narratives about players' dislike of Venus and, later, Serena.[53] Thus, even as affectionate depictions of her beads define her as racialized in a way that makes no real difference, concerned depictions of the beads re-racialize her as just too different. For example, in a NBC piece during the 1997 Wimbledon, Deford claims Venus was asked "an innocuous question" about her beads, and then interview footage shows Venus saying "I don't think it's too loud of a sound. It's a pleasant sound, I would believe. If it bothered [other players,] I just think they have to get used to it. I'm not changing my hair." For Deford, this illustrates her cockiness, but one could read Venus's response as insisting that the question is not innocuous, that her beads are part of who she is and other players are going to have to get used to the role she is playing in tennis's desegregation. In fact, NBC's coverage of the 1997 Wimbledon tournament reported on official rules concerning Venus's beads: If they come out, a point will be replayed. If they come out a second time, she will receive a warning. If they come out a third time, she will lose a point. While this is, in fact, the rule about any on-court "involuntary hindrance," as reported by NBC it seems to be (but was not) a rule written just for Venus—just for her hair/fashion. Hence, as much as the commentators love her rattling, color-coded fashion statement, the beads are in no way innocuous. They are a symbol of her blackness, a specific point for public discussion. Further, not only must her beads be regulated, but—as I discuss in detail below—they also can get her into trouble.[54]

* * *

In sum, the coverage of Venus—especially in comparison to coverage of the other players—depicts her as a mature kid, defined by her intelligence, confidence, haughtiness, and masculine (but not sexual) physicality. Very early on, commentators are somewhat skeptical of her and her (unnamed) blackness, emphasizing her cockiness and playing up a narrative about "trouble in the locker room." Yet they also adore her and her (unnamed) blackness, specifically celebrating her exceptionalism and assimilation, and latching on to her beads as an excuse to gaze at and adore her black body. At times in the coverage, Venus explicitly counters both of these types of characterizations, insisting that her beads sound "nice," that she is friendly with everyone, and that there is no special connection between her and Ashe: in short, that racial difference (even when unnamed) does not—or at least should not—matter.

Nevertheless, occasionally, the coverage depicts her as claiming her own blackness, such as when she asserts that other players are going to have to get used to her (beads). In the next section, I turn to three specific issues/events that offer more sustained possibilities for reading Venus not only as resistant to the ways media racialize her but also as explicitly critical of racism on the tour.

Finding Antiracism on Live Television

In this section, I read the mediated Venus as explicitly antiracist. In order to make this move, I consider three different issues/events that led to complex and contradictory representations, particularly in the context of live television. Specifically, I look at media discussions of Richard as Venus's coach and the issue of Venus not playing junior tournaments, and then at two moments of live television when commentators quickly had to make sense of unanticipated events and actions: the infamous "bump" between Venus and Irina Spîrlea, and a moment when Venus lost a point because of her beads. No single or cohesive characterization of Venus emerges in these three examples. Rather, each instance opens up resistant and alternative possibilities that potentially challenge standard racialized and postracial narratives and that speak back to events that are in some cases racist and in all cases regulatory of Venus's girlhood.

Richard Williams, the Juniors, and Age Eligibility

Pre-existing anxieties about tennis parents come to the fore in narratives about Richard, but because he fits neither of the already established narrative roles (abusive and overbearing or doting and supportive) commentators had difficulty making sense of him. Further, the approach the Williams family took to tennis—Venus turning pro at fourteen but staying out of junior competitions and mostly staying out of the pro tour until age seventeen—puts some of the choices other parents made for/with their children in potentially negative relief. In general, television commentators work together to attempt to build a cohesive narrative around the teen players—both explicitly and presumably intentionally within individual matches, and also implicitly and presumably unintentionally across different matches, broadcasts, and television channels. This coordination was not the case with Richard and the Williams family's decision that Venus and Serena would stay out of both the juniors and the pro tour until the year they turned seventeen, as well as Richard and Oracene's reported choice to let Venus and Serena make their own decisions. In fact, the media went in multiple directions regarding Venus's family, with commentators sometimes explicitly disagreeing with one another.

Both the press and television commentators report that "[Richard] doesn't want [Venus] to get burned out, he wants to focus on education."[55] Austin, in particular, often talks about how Venus and Serena have "a terrific relationship" with their dad; he "really loves them."[56] During the 1997 U.S. Open finals, Oracene reiterates that Venus makes her own decisions about tennis, and that those decisions emerge in the context of a healthy and balanced life, telling Andrea Joyce that whether Venus starts playing more "depends on Venus, because she loves the game. . . . I always ask her the question, if she loves what she's doing, do it. But if she doesn't, anytime she doesn't have to do anything, anytime she wants to stop, that's fine with me. And she knows that. She's loving it. She's enjoying it. And she's happy." For Robinson, who is calling the match, that's "a great perspective."

At other times, however, commentators say that Richard has raised Venus in an "isolated fashion"[57] and that he "dominates the family."[58] Here, the tennis father who verbally or physically abuses his daughter haunts the depiction of Richard. In other words, ironically, the commentators evoke the abusive father when describing Richard's choice to decrease (not increase) tennis pressure on his daughters. For Austin, Navratilova, and King, his choice is a horrible "experiment."[59] During HBO coverage of the quarterfinal match between Kournikova and Majoli at the 1997 Wimbledon, even after Venus had already lost in the first round, Billie Jean King, Mary Carillo, and Martina Navratilova have a long conversation about Venus as a "laboratory experiment":

BJK: It's very important to play juniors. . . .

MC: So, you're saying Kournikova has been facing pressure situations her whole life?

BJK: Yes, absolutely. She did the appropriate thing. You have to compete to find out what you need to do to get better.

MC: Does that mean that Venus Williams has lost an awful lot of ground or can perhaps the way the Williams family has done it with Venus and her sister end up working?

MN: She's a year behind, if not more.

BJK: I think she's more than a year behind. . . .

MC: Is that make-up-able any time soon?

BJK: . . . From her schedule this year it looks like she's not going to play many more tournaments. I think that's a mistake. Get right in the fire and go for it.

[THEY CONTINUE TO RETURN TO THE TOPIC THROUGHOUT THE MATCH, CRITIQUING SERENA FOR HAVING SAID "I'M TOO GOOD FOR THE JUNIORS."]

MN: You can't live on potential.

BJK: . . . You've got to get out and play.

This extended and highly opinionated exchange among the commentators is not unprecedented, but it is not typical of television tennis coverage. Thus, at this moment, Venus's difference puts pressure on the coverage, and in a moment of live television, the commentators move relatively far into their own opinions, implying an almost personal stake in Venus's career and an unwavering self-confidence in their knowledge of the right way for teen players to approach their careers.

This foregrounding of and overinvestment in Venus's difference emerges again at the next grand slam—the 1997 U.S. Open—on a different network (CBS) and with some different announcers: Ted Robinson, Pam Shriver (by quotation), and Mary Carillo (again). This time the announcers reflect on the novelty of the Williamses' approach, rather than worry about it. Again, it is worth quoting the exchange at length:

TR: A *New York Times* reporter spoke with [Shriver] today and asked her impressions of Venus Williams. She said, "I think she needs to raise her level a little bit in order to make it to the final as I did back in '78." I think more interestingly, she said also, I'm quoting now, "I just think there's been a little too much criticism, particularly about the fact that she hasn't played enough." Fancy that, finally someone criticizes a teenager for *under*playing. We should celebrate that. What are your thoughts on Pam's thoughts, Mary?

MC: Listen, there's been so much divisiveness about Venus Williams on and off the court. Questioning how she was raised, how she was groomed to become a tennis professional, the fact that she bagged all the junior events, the fact that she and her mom and sister stay in such a tight little knot away from the rest of the players in the locker room.

There's an awful lot of what I think is unnecessary tension. I just wish the late great Arthur Ashe were still around, because Ashe would be able to speak to Venus and her family, and speak to the other players in the locker room. And, boy, I miss him. Because this should be better than it is right now.

Here, not only does Carillo support Shriver's (and by extension Robinson's) argument that perhaps limiting junior play is a good thing, but she states—almost explicitly—that the critique of the Williamses for doing things differently racializes the family. She suggests that the "late great Arthur Ashe," known as a mediator in terms of race in tennis, could help the current situation, and she assumes both Venus and the other players could benefit from Ashe's wisdom. She leaves what she means by this vague, but one available interpretation is that she believes Ashe could help the Williams family understand and come to terms with racism on the tour, and he could help the other players recognize that their response to the Williams family is—at least in part—structured by assumptions about race rather than about the people themselves.

The multiple and conflicting perspectives on the importance of the juniors are evident not only through comparisons of different conversations but also in direct disagreements among commentators. For example, at the 1998 Australian Open, Drysdale claims that the fact that Venus and Serena did not play juniors means "it's going to take a while" for them to become number one. Shriver disagrees: "I actually think the fact that they have not played that many junior tournaments . . . is not hurting them at all. I think their progress has been terrific." But Drysdale still insists: "I think it's dangerous to suggest that the way to get great is not to play any junior tournaments." Later in the tournament, Shriver brings the issue up again while calling the third round Venus Williams versus Amélie Mauresmo match. Pointing out that they are both teenagers, she goes on to say, "The one [Venus] with no junior tournament experience currently ranked number sixteen in the world . . . and the one playing all the junior tournaments [Mauresmo] ranked ninety-ninth in the world."

Overall, then, the discussion of the fact that Venus and Serena did not play in the juniors expresses a deep investment in Venus and her particular relationship to the tennis world. This coverage oscillates between almost vitriolic disdain for Richard and equally strongly worded defenses of the family's choices. Either way, though, this difference—limited play—becomes a racialized difference in at least two ways. First, the excessiveness of the rhetoric and the length of the conversations produce a debate-like atmosphere, suggesting that, as a unique player, Venus brings contention with her to the tour. No similarly contentious coverage of the other players emerges, contributing to the more cohesive character of their narratives. In other words, if Kournikova is the sexy one, Hingis is the dominant one, Mauresmo is the lesbian one, and Venus is the African American one, only Venus's difference—but not the other players' differences—is a difference about which commentators express dissent and debate. Here, difference = race = volatility. Yet, second, because several different perspectives emerge during the debate, it is possible to hear at least some critique of racism within the discussion. Specifically, not only does Carillo raise questions about the disapproval of the Williams family, at times defending them, but she also uses a discussion of Ashe to articulate what I read as an only partially veiled condemnation of racism on the tour. While her fantasy seems to be to have Ashe magically teach everyone how to be friendly, nevertheless she makes clear that those who dislike the tight-knit Williams family might have something to learn about why the family might want and need to remain tight knit in the context of the white professional tennis tour. Here, I mean to push an interpretation of the coverage that makes as much space as possible for reading Venus's girlhood—her status as a teen player—as a vehicle for both an articulation of the existence of racism and a critique of that racism.

The Bump

The possibility of reading an explicit critique of racism in the depiction of Venus's behavior emerges even more strongly in two completely unanticipated events that took place on live television, as I explore in this and the next subsection. During the 1997 U.S. Open semifinal match between Venus Williams and Irena Spîrlea, the two players bumped into each other during crossover, just as CBS was going to commercial. This moment of live television produced extended discussion first about the supposed ongoing tensions among players, but then soon after explicitly about racism on the tour. As with the discussion of the Williams family and the juniors, the coverage took multiple positions on that racism.

With only a few minutes to figure out how to react to the collision between Venus and Spîrlea, CBS returned from commercial break and began replaying the bump repeatedly from several different camera angles, along with commentary in which Robinson explicitly claims Spîrlea intentionally caused the collision. Robinson points out that immediately after the bump Spîrlea looked up at the player's box "with a smile," and a relatively long take—which pans from the bump, to Spîrlea sitting, to Spîrlea looking off-screen right while smiling—supports his claim. Robinson and the producer/editor support his interpretation further by showing an image of Venus looking calm and focused during the change-over break while Robinson says, "Venus is all business here," and Carillo follows this comment by saying "Yeah, she just handled that whole stupid incident a lot better."

In a post-match interview O'Brien asks Venus about "the bumping incident," and in her usual fashion, Venus downplays it: "Irena wasn't really looking. She was looking that way, actually. And then we were both walking into each other. And I kind of looked away, and when we both looked back it was too late." Spîrlea, however, is less sanguine about it. At her press conference she says, "I'm not going to move. She's never trying to turn or whatever. She thinks she's the [bleeped: fucking][60] Venus Williams and she's not going to turn, or she just went like this. I want to see if she's turning." During an interview with Venus the next day, Pat O'Brien and Patrick McEnroe ask Venus to respond to the fact that Spîrlea used "a four-letter word," and Venus gasps, saying "I never heard this." They continue talking about it while the camera stays on Venus's face, with her mouth slightly open, showing shock. When they then play the clip for her/us, she gives a half laugh, shakes her head, and says, "I mean, she has her opinion. I can't change it."

The live and immediate post-match television coverage clearly holds Spîrlea responsible for the bump and for offensive commentary about the bump. It also depicts Venus as taking the high road. Things become more complex, however, as discussion about racism on the tour grows in relation to the bump. Late in the match itself, Carillo actually uses the word "race" to discuss the tensions among the players, defining the bump as part of that tension (rather than, for example, considering it a mistake): "This has been building for months, really. The animosity felt between the other players and Venus Williams. Some of it is all the hype, the legend, the publicity that Williams has enjoyed. But also, let's face it: it's a whole new thing, this young black woman. This race issue is the elephant in the room." After the incident, Richard spoke publicly to the press about racism on the tour, and during the final match, Joyce asked Oracene if she agreed with her husband that "the Spîrlea incident was racially motivated." Oracene deflected attention away from the question, saying "I really don't know. I can't say what's in a person's mind. So, only [Spîrlea] knows." Interestingly, while later coverage assumes it was Richard who first brought up race in relation to the incident, in fact Carillo mentions it during the live coverage, almost immediately after it happened. Beyond that, two days later during the final match, Carillo brings up Richard's critique from a sympathetic perspective, making an argument that sounds very much like black feminist standpoint theory:[61] "Richard Williams really felt that the whole moment was weighted with racial meaning and tension. . . . Richard Williams is a product of poverty in Louisiana, Old South. He sees things that not everyone else sees, which is fair enough." In short, during the match and throughout the tournament, Carillo explicitly defines the tension in the locker room as in part a result of other players' discomfort with this "whole new thing, this young black woman"; she assumes Spîrlea bumped into Venus on purpose in this context; and she supports Richard's naming of the tension and players' behavior as racist. And all of this takes place through live/near-live match commentary.

Other coverage, however, is less sympathetic to Richard's perspective. For example, a *New York Times* article reports that Richard claims the bump was racially motivated, but then turns to other players on the tour as if to prove that his claim is inaccurate. The article quotes Gigi Fernández as saying "There's no racism on the women's tour. I can tell you it's more the way she carries herself in the locker room and not so much her appearance or her race. I think she has to show a little respect for her elders"; and it quotes Lindsay Davenport saying "If somebody doesn't want to be friendly, it's not our fault. . . . I can't even get into this; I'm getting upset."[62] Two days later, the *New York Times* returns to the issue, now following Fernández's claim that "there's no racism on the women's tour. . . . I adamantly deny that. We've had Zina [Garrison] and Lori [McNeil],"[63] with a quotation from Zina Garrison herself, who offers a different perspective: "Venus is out there playing for the African American race. . . . It's an all-white sport; you feel it, are made to feel it, like you don't belong. So you protect yourself. And all this criticism for Venus not talking to people—Monica and Steffi didn't talk to people either. Why are the standards different?"[64] Here, the *New York Times* simultaneously offers two different perspectives on race: (1) there is no racism and therefore bad feelings between Venus and other players must be Venus's fault, and (2) there is racism and therefore bad feelings between Venus and other players must be their fault or the fault of racism. The bump itself really is no longer an issue, as it functions instead simply as a vehicle to discuss racism, sometimes in a way that denies it exists and sometimes in a way that illustrates that it does exist.

To end this section, I would like to return to the moment of the bump itself, replayed over and over on television for several days, and offer two possible readings that embrace what one can read as Venus's critique of racism in tennis as a whole: (1) Did Venus bump into Spîrlea, thus standing up to the hostility she faced on tour and insisting on her right to take up space? Or, (2) Did Spîrlea bump into Venus, who responded in a calm and collected manner, unfazed by a physical jab that may or may not have been motivated by racial resentment? Either way, the bump, some of the commentary about it, and available readings of Venus's actions all help to make possible a version of African American girlhood that stands up to racism.

The Beads

As I discuss above, the beads that Venus, and Serena, wore from 1997 through 1999 were a constant topic of discussion. Commentators marvel at the amount of work it takes to make up their hair with the beads, draw attention to the sound they make, and use them to play on words; promotional spots show Venus and Serena together, laughing with pleasure as they shake their heads to make their beads rattle; and editors use pictures that capture Venus and Serena in motion with their beads flying, and sometimes flying off: the beads thereby augmenting their photogenicity. The vast majority of this coverage is affectionate, functioning as a badge for the media to illustrate just how comfortable they are with Venus's and Serena's implicitly black bodies.[65] The beads set them apart; the beads allow the media to love them.

At the 1999 Australian Open, however, the beads took a turn for the worse when Venus lost beads several times during a match against Lindsay Davenport, facing first a warning, then a let (meaning the point will not count and will be replayed), and then a lost point. As she revealed in a post-match interview, she had known since the 1997 Wimbledon that the beads could cause her to lose a point under the involuntary hindrance rule: "Back in 1997, we were at Wimbledon and it kept raining, and it kept raining, and the press had nothing to write about. They started writing about if the beads fell out of my hair. After that, I asked a tour director what the rule was on it. And that was '97, and I think the rule has changed since then."[66]

Yet, because in the two years since that Wimbledon she had never even received a warning for losing beads (even though, as the coverage consistently illustrates, they often did fall out of her hair), she was shocked when she lost the point over the beads at the 1999 Australian Open. As she put it, "I don't think it was a very fair call. . . . I just found it quite odd and it was a little bit disrupting. . . . I was just pretty alarmed by it." When it happened, on live television, she was more than alarmed; she was visibly furious, yelling and arguing with the umpire. She was so angry, her voice cracked during the following exchange:

vw: But I mean she can't even see the beads, no one sees the beads drop.
umpire: [explains the rule]
vw: But wait a minute, the problem is no one is distracted. I am not causing a disturbance here.
u: I can't tell that.
vw: Well, I think the referee should come out because no one is disturbed.
u: If you'd like me to call the referee, I'm happy to do that.
vw: Come on out then!

What I read here as intense anger in Venus's cracking voice and angry words—available only because it happened on live television—works at least implicitly to articulate a critique of an unfair and racist application of a rule that was written without Venus or, potentially, other African American players in mind. Of course, if a hair tie or barrette fell out of Kournikova's hair, for example, she would theoretically be subject to the same rule. In other words, the rule was not written explicitly for Venus's (and Serena's) beads. Yet the specificity of how beads function, and what Venus defines as a two-year tradition of ignoring her beads when they fell out, makes the application of this rule problematic, and Venus's willingness to express a critique—not only in anger during the heat of the moment but also calmly and articulately after the match—makes clear the implicit racism in what happened.

In the post-match interviews, even as Venus argues that the rule was applied to her unfairly, she also responds with her usual aplomb, deflecting the issue of racism and taking the high road. She admits, "It's up to me to keep up on the rules," but goes on to say in response to an implied question about whether she will change her hair, "No, I shouldn't have to change for any other circumstances. I like my hair." When Shriver asks her what she will do in the future, she says, "My best bet is just to tie my beads a little bit tighter and move on." Here, she rearticulates her comfort with her racial identity/body and therefore makes clear that the tour and the media have no choice but to come to terms with it. Thus, both during and immediately after this controversy, one can read Venus as articulating a critique of racism on the tour, while also embracing the method she has used to deal with that racism since she began: refuse to engage in debate, focus on her own game and life, and move on. This in itself can be read as a critique of racism on the tour, since she makes clear that, in the end, racism is the problem of the tennis world; it is not her problem, even as the media and others may work desperately to try to foist onto her the difference they make of her.

Conclusion

The drama of race in Venus's breakthrough teen years begins with the media's ignorance and somewhat stereotypical depictions, but, as Venus competes in more matches, the possibility for a complex drama, emerging in part because of the immediacy of live/near-live coverage, complicates the versions of girlhood available. Certainly, neither the rules of tennis nor the sport's overwhelmingly white history come under direct or sustained scrutiny. Rather than focus on the system and norms of whiteness, the coverage focuses on difference and defines that difference as located in Venus and her family. The coverage then either revels in affection for that difference or blames the Williamses for the difference that racial difference makes—both to tennis and to media coverage. In other words, the coverage favors hyper-visibility of implicitly black difference, but does so by representing it as unconnected to social, cultural, or historical racialized power relations. Nevertheless, in some of the live/near-live coverage, when the announcers (temporarily) lose control of the narrative threads they so carefully build around the players and the matches, there are moments when Venus's presence and actions can be read as challenges to the whiteness that pervades both tennis and most media coverage of the sport. From this perspective, media depictions of Venus acknowledge racism on the tour and in the media, and they make space for several different individuals' critiques of racism: Carillo's, Richard's, Oracene's, as well as Venus's. I do not want to overstate this claim, however, or to imply that there is something inherent in televisual liveness that promises a kind of utopic resistance, particularly because much of the problematic racialized depiction of Venus I discuss in the first section of this chapter also takes place during live/near-live coverage.

In the end, by focusing primarily on live/near-live sports coverage and drawing a comparison between Venus and the other players, my goal is to make particularly visible the process of producing Venus as an African American girl athlete. That process reveals standard narratives that lovingly reduce black girls to their bodies by celebrating their "wingspan" and charming hairstyles and by desexualizing them. It also reveals standard narratives that define a black girl as cocky and her black father as overbearing and unorthodox for refusing to follow the standard path toward tennis success. And it reveals standard narratives about postracism, racial exceptionalism, and assimilation, and the value of the black girl for "her" people—defined as poor black kids. The process also reveals moments, however, when Venus emerges as an independent girl who makes her own decisions and speaks back to and out against racism with both her actions and her words. Certainly, this resistant Venus is a part of the media depiction of her. Nevertheless, and especially when she emerges at unexpected moments of stress and surprise in the live coverage, she can be understood not only to have changed tennis, but also to have changed U.S. media culture's conception of what it can mean to be a girl, to be an African American, and to be an African American girl.

5

Sakia Gunn Is a Girl

Queer African American Girlhood in Local and Alternative Media

In the early morning hours of Mother's Day, May 11, 2003, fifteen-year-old African American gay/lesbian/transgender/AG (aggressive)[1] Sakia Gunn and several of her friends (including her close friend/cousin Valencia Bailey and her girlfriend Jamon Marsh) were returning home to Newark, New Jersey, from Greenwich Village/Christopher Street Piers in New York City via public transportation. While they were waiting for a bus at 3:30 a.m., two men approached them. The men may have invited them to party or simply initiated a conversation. The girls stated that they were not interested and that they were gay/lesbian. At some point, at least one of the men (Richard McCullough) began making homophobic insults (either before or after the girls also "gave lip");[2] he then physically attacked at least two of the girls, including Gunn. Gunn struggled both physically and verbally, until McCullough knifed her and fled. A passing motorist drove Gunn and her friends to the hospital, where Gunn was pronounced dead. Newark was rocked by her death: multiple rallies and vigils were held; 2,500 people, many of whom were African American LGBTQ youth, attended her funeral; Newark's mayor made an ultimately unfulfilled promise to open a community center for LGBTQ youth; and several new LGBTQ activist groups started, including a (now-defunct) Newark chapter of Parents, Family, and Friends of

Lesbians and Gays (PFLAG), and a (now-defunct) PFLAG scholarship named in Gunn's honor.[3] McCullough turned himself in five days after the murder, "just as the rally [outside City Hall] was breaking up,"[4] and was indicted for murder with bias intimidation, which the *Washington Post* calls "one of New Jersey's first bias-crime murder cases."[5] Eventually McCullough negotiated a plea bargain, pleading guilty to aggravated manslaughter with bias intimidation. He was sentenced to twenty years in prison.

In this chapter, I analyze the coverage of Gunn's death in alternative and local media, while also referring occasionally to the mainstream coverage that does exist. There was not a large quantity of national coverage of Gunn, as there is or was of most of the other girls I discuss in this book. Nevertheless, alternative media outlets—including local, African American, LGBTQ, and/or other left-leaning sources—frequently discuss and refer to Gunn. In these contexts, Gunn is highly mediated and highly visible: she is a spectacular girl, and hence an appropriate topic for this book. Thus, I choose Sakia Gunn as a case study for this chapter to challenge myself, as well as girls' studies scholarship generally, to push beyond mainstream, nationwide mass-media representations when thinking about mediated girlhoods. If I were to have looked for Gunn only in the national mass media, I would have found little. She would not have appeared spectacular and there would have been little to say other than to point out that "silences and hesitations, within . . . the dominant American public sphere . . . underscore the social devaluing of the identities that Gunn embodied, or was presumed to embody."[6] While it is crucial to make this critique of mainstream media, to stop there is potentially to reproduce the neglect of Gunn—and of queer, African American, and/or poor girls generally—that mainstream media produce, a neglect that defines some girls as spectacular and other girls as background figures, passing references, or nonexistent. This was not a methodological move I wanted to make in the book. Thus the case study in this chapter insists on including local and alternative media in the book's overall definition of spectacular girls.

By moving away from mainstream coverage, I find a high-profile, explicitly queer African American girl, a type of girl that would never become a national celebrity or appear on the cover of *Time, Newsweek,* or *People* or at the center of a widely viewed and discussed film.

While, of all the mediated girls I discuss in this book, Gunn is likely the least well-known, she nevertheless functioned and in some ways continues to function as a spectacular girl for particular communities. She is well-known to some of us: to queer, African American, feminist, and/or Newark-based journalists, activists, and scholars. This chapter, then, takes seriously the role spectacular girls play in more specific and explicitly defined contexts. If the goal of the book is to look for alternative versions of girlhood, then I pursue that goal here by asking what a queer African American girlhood looks like in the parts of media culture in which it does appear.

One way to answer this question is to point out that while, for example, I have to work to read Jessica Dubroff as queer (chapter 2), and while I have to work to find a critique of heteronormativity in *Mean Girls* (2004) (chapter 3), in the local and alternative press Gunn is already explicitly queer; thus, by looking at this kind of media I do not have to use an interpretive practice that works against more explicit representations to invest her case with queer sensibilities. Similarly, while I have to grab at mere seconds of live television in which I hear Venus Williams's voice crack in anger as she stands up to racism in professional tennis, the press coverage of Gunn's death explicitly and with no resistance accepts and defines it as a bias crime against an LGBTQ youth, thereby taking a specifically politicized position. This does not make Gunn a "better" example of a queer and/or African American girl; rather, it makes her a different kind of example, one only observable through the lens of local and alternative media.

As I illustrate through my analysis in this chapter, however, turning to the alternative press does not mean one will necessarily find a radical critique of dominant girlhoods. As Kent Ono and John Sloop argue, vernacular discourse requires as careful critical attention as does more mainstream discourse,[7] and, as Sarah Banet-Weiser argues, alternative media outlets (such as YouTube) do not necessarily guarantee liberatory representations.[8] In this case, I argue, it is particularly troubling that almost none of the local and alternative coverage addresses the specificity of Gunn as girl. In my analysis and in response to the coverage, then, not only do I point out that Gunn functions as a tragic and/or heroic African American and/or queer figure, but I also insist on pausing over brief and/or passing references to her youth in order to build a picture of Gunn specifically as a queer African American *girl*, even when the coverage, as a whole, deflects such a reading.

In what follows, I move through various types of media coverage of Gunn numerous times in order to build a complex and heterogeneous understanding of Gunn and her relationship to girlhood. In the first section, I lay out as objectively as possible (1) where the coverage appeared and (2) how that coverage defined the facts of the case. When I discuss where coverage appeared, I illustrate that the level of detail and complexity in Gunn's characterization—particularly in terms of LGBTQ and African American issues—increases as one moves from the mainstream press, to the local press, and finally to the alternative press. I then move through these three types of sources again in order to identify the different ways the various types of media reported the facts. In particular, I focus on the emergence of LGBTQ issues as well as issues of power in relation to race, gender, and sexuality, as manifested most strongly in the alternative press and one national *Washington Post* article.

Because all the coverage, regardless of type, downplays Gunn's identity as a girl, in the second section of the chapter I use my analysis to seek an alternative queer African American girlhood. Focusing on (1) the few places where coverage does define Gunn as a girl, as well as two recurrent topics in the coverage—(2) the attention paid to Gunn in relation to pro-LGBTQ and antiracist activism, and (3) comparisons between Gunn and other instances of hate crimes, homophobia, heterosexism, and racism—I challenge the national, local, and alternative press for its use of Gunn as a generic symbol of pathos and/or the need for "activism." And by reading across as many depictions of Gunn in various different types of media as possible, I also bring together scattered details from the coverage that provide a picture of what Gunn's life as a girl in Newark might have been like, thereby finding moments where Gunn as a queer African American girl displaces heteronormative whiteness and drawing attention to the gendered politics of public space. In short, this chapter builds a layered picture of Gunn as a queer African American girl—both acknowledging the ways in which some of the coverage displaces Gunn from the very stories that are about her, and asking what versions of girlhood do emerge when using a critical method that insists on centering her, insists on seeing her as a spectacular girl.

Media Specificity: From National, to Local, to Alternative

As I illustrate below, when moving from national, to local, to alternative media, one finds an increasing quantity of coverage, level of detail, and attention to LGBTQ and power issues beyond the Gunn case in particular, as well as authors who more explicitly support LGBTQ issues, sometimes writing from personal experience. To document this, I first discuss where articles were published and then address how different types of media defined the facts of the case.

Where Was the Media Coverage?

While it is unquestionably true that there was little national coverage of Gunn's death, what little national press, television, and radio coverage there was is worth considering. Fifteen nationally distributed articles or programs either reported on (twelve) or mentioned (three) Gunn, beginning two days after her death and ending more than four years later. On television, only a few weeks after Gunn's death CNN covered the events briefly during *On the Story*[9] and one week later ran a special on "The Death of Sakia Gunn" as part of *Live from the Headlines*,[10] a show the Gay and Lesbian Alliance against Defamation (GLAAD) Media Awards nominated for best TV journalism.[11] The *New York Times* (*NYT*)[12] published four short articles reporting the facts of the case, starting two days after the murder and ending with McCullough's indictment.[13] No *NYT* article covered McCullough's plea bargain or sentencing, but one year after her death the paper ran an article titled "Newark Preaches Tolerance of Gays Year after Killing."[14] Unlike the *NYT*, the *Washington Post* did not cover the murder when it happened, but seventeen months later it published a two-part front-page story about one of Gunn's friends as part of a special series on "Growing Up in an Evolving America," referring to Gunn from time to time throughout the articles.[15] Subsequently, it reported briefly when McCullough pled guilty and again when he was sentenced.[16] More than three years after the murder, NPR broadcast an interview with journalist and public intellectual Kristal Brent Zook, during which she discussed the Gunn case in conjunction with her book *Black Women's Lives: Stories of Pain and Power*.[17] Finally, Gunn appears in passing as a generic example of "crimes against gays" both in a *USA Today* article written by Mat-thew Shepard's mother five months after Gunn's death[18] and in a *NYT* article primarily about gay male experiences in and around New York City, this one published more than four years after Gunn's death.[19] These examples are the totality of the national coverage.

Slightly more material on Gunn appeared in what I call "non–NJ/NY local coverage." I found twenty-six articles in fifteen states other than New Jersey or New York,[20] with the first article appearing when the warrant was issued for McCullough's arrest and the latest appearing in late 2011. While some of these articles are Associated Press (AP) reprints, staff writers and occasionally commentators author many of them. Of these articles, about one-third focus on the Gunn case directly, four focus on the founding of the Newark PFLAG chapter and the PFLAG scholarship in Gunn's name, and the remainder mention Gunn in relation to various forms of local activism or as an example of hate crime more generally. This non–NJ/NY local coverage offers slightly more detail and spends more time on activism against anti-LGBTQ violence than does the national coverage, but this is primarily a difference of degree rather than of kind.

Despite the paucity of coverage at the national and non–NJ/NY local levels, there was a great deal of coverage in the local area[21] in newspapers published in ten different New Jersey cities,[22] and in six different New York[23] papers. This material covered the facts of the case up through McCullough's sentencing and reported on various demonstrations and vigils that took place in Newark at the time of the murder as well as on the anniversary of Gunn's death. In addition, a number of editorials and opinion pieces appeared, as did periodic brief references to Gunn as an example of a victim either of a hate crime against LGBTQ people or of violence in Newark's African American and/or youth communities. These articles address the specificity of the Newark LGBTQ community in one of three ways: (1) they report on LGBTQ activism, (2) they claim a lack of coverage and awareness of LGBTQ issues in the African Amer-ican press and community (sometimes defined as religious), or (3) they claim a lack of coverage and awareness of African American issues in the LGBTQ press and community. These references to Gunn in the NJ/NY press continued up until the present, ten years after Gunn's death.[24]

Overall, the local NJ/NY coverage is more detailed than both the national and the non–NJ/NY local coverage, providing fuller

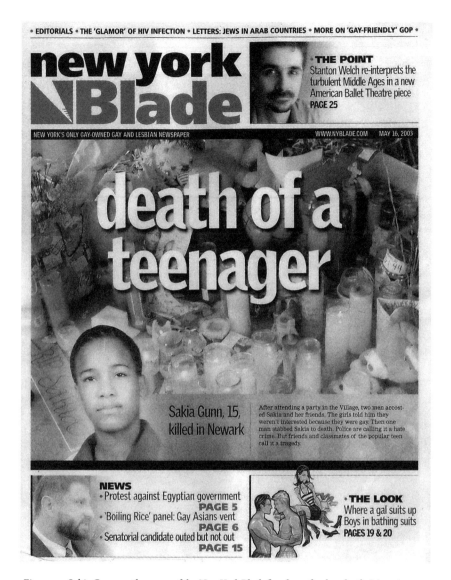

• EDITORIALS • THE 'GLAMOR' OF HIV INFECTION • LETTERS: JEWS IN ARAB COUNTRIES • MORE ON 'GAY-FRIENDLY' GOP •

new york Blade

• THE POINT
Stanton Welch re-interprets the turbulent Middle Ages in a new American Ballet Theatre piece
PAGE 25

NEW YORK'S ONLY GAY-OWNED GAY AND LESBIAN NEWSPAPER   WWW.NYBLADE.COM   MAY 16, 2003

death of a teenager

Sakia Gunn, 15, killed in Newark

After attending a party in the Village, two men accosted Sakia and her friends. The girls told him they weren't interested because they were gay. Then one man stabbed Sakia to death. Police are calling it a hate crime. But friends and classmates of the popular teen call it a tragedy.

NEWS
• Protest against Egyptian government
PAGE 5
• 'Boiling Rice' panel: Gay Asians vent
PAGE 6
• Senatorial candidate outed but not out
PAGE 15

• THE LOOK
Where a gal suits up Boys in bathing suits
PAGES 19 & 20

Figure 5.1. Sakia Gunn on the cover of the *New York Blade* five days after her death, May 16, 2003.

characterizations of Gunn; reporting on many more vigils, rallies, and forms of activism than the other two sets of sources; and spending time addressing a "lack of coverage/outrage" about Gunn's death. In these ways, the NJ/NY coverage represents Gunn much more as an individual who matters than does the national and non–NJ/NY local coverage, while concomitantly using her as a tragic LGBTQ and/or African American symbol of Newark.

There was a great deal of coverage in the alternative press, about equivalent to the NJ/NY local coverage. The first citation I found was a cover story in the LGBTQ paper the *New York Blade*, published five days after the murder.[25] And, as in the NJ/NY press, Gunn continues to appear periodically in alternative media, as of this writing.[26] This coverage includes AP reprints as well as stories based on the facts as drawn from other published sources. Early on, there is little variability from the national and local coverage. Over time, however, the level of detail in the alternative press provides a much fuller and more complex representation of the events, including specific information garnered through interviews with some of the girls who were with Gunn when she was killed. This coverage produces Gunn as a nuanced character through details about her life, such as her relationships with her friends and her experiences as an LGBTQ youth navigating high school in Newark. In addition, frequent comparisons in the alternative press between Gunn's death and others emphasize the pervasiveness and continuation of anti-LGBTQ hate crimes and murders.

Regardless of media type, all the coverage works fairly seamlessly to tell a consistent story about Gunn, and in my analysis below I try to illustrate this consistency. There are also important differences among the types of coverage, however, particularly in terms of how race, gender, and sexuality get worked out in relation to one another. In short, as I show below, moving from the national to the local to the alternative coverage, Gunn becomes more and more a symbol of blackness and/or queerness, while simultaneously becoming a more and more complex character on her own terms.

What Were the Facts?

As portrayed by the national press and the non–NJ/NY local articles, the story had little variability, with mention of LGBTQ issues emerging only occasionally. Gunn is a "15-year-old girl,"[27] "10th grader,"[28] high school "sophomore,"[29] and/or "teenager."[30] None of the national articles and few of the non–NJ/NY local articles[31] mention that she was African American, although all refer to Newark, which arguably functions as code for "black" and "poor." Gunn was traveling home from a "party in Manhattan"[32] or simply "New York City"[33] with friends. While waiting for a bus at "the busiest [intersection] in the city,"[34] two men in a car made "advances."[35] The "girls rebuffed" them.[36] Some articles mention that the girls said "they were not interested in the men because they were gay"[37] or "lesbians."[38] None of the national articles and only one of the non–NJ/NY local articles reports that "the men began spewing homophobic insults,"[39] although one article, published when McCullough pled guilty, reports that "he admitted calling Gunn a 'dyke.'"[40] When reporting the murder, without mentioning McCullough's and/or his companion's inflammatory comments, most articles simply report that a "scuffle"[41] or "shoving match"[42] or "struggle"[43] or "tussle"[44] or "fight"[45] ensued after Gunn/the girls stated they were gay/lesbians. During the fight either McCullough or both men "accosted the girls,"[46] and McCullough stabbed Gunn in the chest.

Admittedly, while not explicitly presented as such, it does not take much for the reader of the national and non–NJ/NY local press to realize this story is about an African American girl killed, at least in part, because of her sexuality and gender presentation. Nevertheless, the NJ/NY local press actually reports the facts in a way that emphasizes this is an LGBTQ rights case: no reading between the lines is required. These details include reports of Gunn and her friends' self-definition as AGs who explicitly performed masculinity through dress and behavior, as well as the fact that they were returning not from a "party" in New York City but from Greenwich Village and/or the Christopher Street Piers, well-known LBGTQ hangouts. An article in one local New York paper even paints an (imagined) picture of the night Gunn spent on the Christopher Street Piers: "Perhaps she roosted on the pier, or feasted at McDonald's, or simply delighted in holding hands with another girl and being part of the undesignated street parade."[47] A *Star-Ledger* article published just two days after the murder is the first of many local articles to include information and quotations from local LGBTQ rights activists.[48] In fact, most NJ/NY articles include LGBTQ information, even when their titles imply that they are simply "fact pieces" about different aspects of the case as they develop (e.g., "Man Charged in Bus Stop Stabbing Arraigned").[49] Often, the articles end with a quotation from a pro-LGBTQ activist, thus closing with a positive and supportive perspective on LGBTQ people.

The alternative press similarly takes a pro-LGBTQ stance when reporting the facts, sometimes using detailed descriptions and quotations that represent people involved in the case as queer-identified. For example, Lt. Derrick Glenn, the Newark Police officer in charge of the case, tells the *New York Blade*, "I tend to have more of a personal issue with this because some of my close friends and family members are gay. . . . It's sad. Their lifestyle didn't interfere with anyone's. . . . It's like racism. It hasn't progressed, even in this case. Bias crime [is] an aspect we're investigating."[50] Here, not only does Lt. Glenn have a personal investment in the case, but the article also presents him in such a way that he offers an anti-racist, pro-LGBTQ intersectional analysis of the crime. The national and non–NJ/NY local coverage frequently mentions Lt. Glenn, but his personal relationship to LGBTQ issues emerges only in the alternative coverage. In short, in the national and non–NJ/NY local coverage this case is about the murder of a gay/lesbian teenager, period. In the NJ/NY local and alternative coverage, however, it is about the murder of an African American lesbian/transgender/AG teenager in the context of a community—Newark—that should be and now is working for LGBTQ rights.

A second difference between the national, local NJ/NY, and alternative coverage concerns how much attention is paid to power differences between McCullough and Gunn and her friends. In general, the national coverage reports on a "fight" or "struggle" between the men and the girls, thus perhaps implying a level of equality between them: a fight escalated and someone unfortunately got hurt. This is, in fact, the position that McCullough took during his trial: he claimed Gunn "fell" on his knife. It is not, however, the position that some of the NJ/NY coverage took. For example, one article quotes the assistant prosecutor as saying "All these girls were very small in stature. . . . They were never any threat to him."[51] Another NJ/NY article reports that McCullough faced charges for "chok[ing] and attempt[ing] to stab"[52] two additional girls in the group, which changes the picture from a fight between Gunn and McCullough to an image of McCullough having completely lost control as he attacked the three girls. Further, comparing Gunn's murder to an event Anne Hull reports in her two-part, front-page *Washington Post* feature on Gunn's friend Felicia makes clear the feminist argument that it is never an equal fight when gendered street harassment and homophobia are involved.[53] While Gunn and her friends chose to respond to McCullough by verbally declaring their sexuality, Felicia reports to Hull that after Gunn's death she and another friend of Gunn's were walking down the street when four men tried to talk to them. Rather than respond, as did Gunn and her friends, they made a different choice: "The girls kept their heads down." This different response made no difference: the men jumped them, "Valencia [got] a bloody nose and mouth, and Felicia [was] thrown to the ground."[54] While Hull does not make this point herself, through comparison a reader might reflect on the fact that there is no safe response once gendered harassment begins. Thus the article implicitly suggests it was beside the point how Gunn and her friends responded: McCullough initiated street harassment and, in this case, carried it through to its most extreme conclusion.[55]

Overall, the national coverage downplays LGBTQ aspects of the case. In contrast, the local NJ/NY coverage acknowledges LGBTQ aspects of the case and the alternative press foregrounds them. Additionally, the national press (except for the *Washington Post* feature) at least initially implies Gunn and McCullough have equivalent power and are equally at fault, while the NJ/NY press, as well as a reading of Gunn's case in relation to the later case on which Hull reports, suggest that the facts illustrate gendered power differences between Gunn and McCullough. Thus, in terms of these two issues, there are significant differences among the national, local NJ/NY, and alternative press.

Consistent across all these sources, however, is lack of attention to Gunn as a girl. While articles sometimes mention her age, as a whole the way they present the facts—a man approached her, she resisted, he stabbed her—suggests she just as well could have been an adult woman. In other words, when thinking specifically about the facts of the case through all this material, this is not a story about a girl. This finding, of course, leads me in the next section, in which I set about reading Gunn as a girl *nevertheless*.

Is Sakia Gunn a Girl at All?

As I discuss below, the various types of media separate specific aspects of Gunn's identity—defining her as a tragic victim, or as a fallen LGBTQ hero, or as an impetus for pro-queer or anti-racism activism. By reading across the substantial media coverage of her death, however, I collect moments in which the representations of her can be put in the service of the alternative girlhoods this book explores. I do this first by examining the few places in which the coverage actually discusses Gunn as a girl, and then by moving on to two ways she becomes an abstract symbol of LGBTQ and/or African American rights. In each subsection, after describing the depictions, I pause over aspects of the coverage that help me to emphasize and reclaim her girlhood, that provide a representation of a girl taking up queer, black, transgendered space.

Gunn as Youth: Innocent and Heroic

Gunn's age is occasionally at issue in aspects of the coverage that describe her as an individual. In these isolated examples, Gunn is an innocent victim: a young girl who had big dreams for the future and yet still enjoyed childish things. In the mainstream press this innocence emphasizes the tragedy of her death. The alternative press also offers pathos, but concomitantly constructs Gunn as a role model and hero. Thus, by reading across all these sources, Gunn can be seen as an innocent, yet also heroic, girl.

The first *NYT* article, which is also the longest national news article, provides a few facts about Gunn's life alongside the facts of the murder. It reports that she was on the basketball team but was cut for low grades. Nevertheless, she was working to pull her grades back up so she could return to the team and hopefully play for the WNBA one day.[56] One of the syndicated non–NJ/NY local articles provides details: Gunn "had a handle on algebra and liked to sit in front of the class." The article also mentions that she played basketball, smoked, and was popular at school. "She was described as self-possessed, assertive, sometimes restless."[57] Together, these two articles construct Gunn as an ambitious and (usually) high-achieving teenager who had only a few minor faults (e.g., smoking, restlessness, low grades), some of which she was working to overcome. But this picture emerges in only these two articles. Other than the fact that she was gay/lesbian, Gunn, as a character, is absent from all the other national and non–NJ/NY local news coverage.

A fuller picture of Gunn appears in the NJ/NY local coverage, which primarily presents her as an innocent girl victim. In addition to details about basketball and school, NJ/NY articles mention that, for example, she "had a talent for braiding hair and doing fashionable hairstyles for friends."[58] The same article reports that Gunn liked to eat, especially "Cap'n Crunch and hot wings." Such food conjures up an especially childlike diet, more so because (the article implies) she enjoyed eating those two foods together. This article ends on a particularly poignant note, pointing out that "Aaliyah, a singer who died in an airplane crash almost two years ago, was her favorite" musical artist.[59] Further, some of the supposed difficulties in Gunn's life the one national article and one non–NJ/NY local article report drop out of the NJ/NY local coverage. For example, one NJ/NY article implies she was still on the basketball team: "A high school basketball player, Gunn dreamed of going to college on a basketball scholarship on her way to becoming a professional ball player."[60] Emphasizing her innocence and value to the community, another article reports that her friends remember Gunn "as a fun-loving teen who didn't like to see anyone sad or in pain. They said she shared what she had, kept a smile on her face, and lived for the moment."[61] As the judge put it in a quotation that ends a NJ/NY article reporting on McCullough's sentencing hearing, "This is a young lady who would have accomplished a lot in her life."[62] In retrospect, then, Gunn was nothing but happy and optimistic, taking great pleasure in the little things in life and looking forward to a bright future. In short, she was an innocent, loveable child.

While the national and non–NJ/NY local coverage define Gunn simply as "a gay/lesbian," the NJ/NY local coverage makes the fact of her sexuality part of the tragedy of the loss. Thus, in the NJ/NY coverage the innocent loveable child is a queer child. For example, local coverage often reports that Gunn "dressed in boyish clothes,"[63] sometimes mentioning that this "marked her as an 'AG,' or aggressive lesbian,"[64] sometimes defined as "aggressive girl."[65] One article acknowledges "transgender" as one way to describe Gunn, reporting on Princeton University's celebration of Transgender Day of Remembrance. It quotes a representative of the Gender Rights Advocacy Association of New Jersey as saying "She may not have identified as a transgendered person but we included her because she exhibited a cross-gender presentation."[66] Many articles suggest not only that Gunn was comfortable with her sexuality,[67] but also that "nobody bothered her about it."[68] Because of her openness about her sexuality, there is a quiet strength in her innocence. David Tseng, PFLAG executive director, observes, "Here is a young woman who was killed for simply being honest."[69] Here, Gunn was innocent—even childishly naive—enough to think it was safe to be honest, making her death all the more tragic.

The alternative coverage depends on the same depiction of explicit honesty about her sexuality and gender, but constructs Gunn as "courageous"[70] and independent, rather than as innocent victim. She is a fallen hero, someone who would have led a honest, open, and brave life that would have contributed significantly to the LGBTQ community. One article claims she "decided [she was] not going to be forced to hide [her] identity."[71] In another article, Gunn becomes a role model, paradoxically, because she is dead. When discussing the scholarship established in Gunn's name a PFLAG spokeswoman says, "We want to [show] she can, by living her life in an honest way, help other kids."[72] In several articles, activist LaQuetta Nelson speaks of Gunn as "brave. Sakia's like our hero."[73] Another article states, "The LGBT and Black communities have lost a viable part of the future."[74] These examples are particularly interpretive, producing Gunn as an activist in a way that does not coincide with the coverage of the facts of the case—it seems Gunn and/or her friends simply declared their sexuality in the hopes that McCullough would leave them alone. Yet, because these articles engage in so much editorializing, they make particularly clear how aggressively this alternative coverage turns Gunn into a young queer hero after her death.

In the national and local press Gunn is an innocent victim—specifically a queer one in the NJ/NY coverage—whereas in the alternative press she is a queer hero. These two kinds of characterization are not necessarily contradictory (and, in fact, the alternative press also constructs her as a victim), but they do potentially lead to somewhat different understandings of the politics of her case and the nature of her queer girlhood. For example, nothing in the national or local coverage assigns blame to Gunn for inviting the violence by dressing inappropriately (in this case, "like a boy"), for being out so late, for challenging McCullough verbally, or even for supposedly fighting with him. She is simply a victim. Occasionally, however, the alternative press does ask, "What was a 15-year-old doing out with friends at 3:30 . . . in the morning?"[75] While this question is asked to discount it (i.e., to insist "We can't blame the victim!"), once it is asked it subtly changes Gunn's characterization, depicting her as independent and risk-taking as much (more than?) as innocent and victimized. Here, the alternative press produces a much more powerful figure than does the mainstream press and suggests that by taking up space she was not "supposed" to be in at 3:30 a.m., Gunn confronted the gendered and sexualized politics of public space.

Importantly, the alternative coverage that produces Gunn as hero does not also emphasize her youth or girlness as do the national and local depictions of her as innocent. Thus, one possible argument is that collectively the coverage situates heroism in a separate sphere from girlhood, and that therefore girlhood remains endangered and in need of protection. Nevertheless, youthful innocence does emerge alongside her heroism in some of these articles. Thus, I would argue that—especially if one reads across multiple types of media and emphasizes the brief comments on Gunn's youth, as I do here—Gunn is a heroic queer girl.

"Sakia Gunn Is the Impetus"

The themes of activism for LGBTQ rights in general, as well as the environment for members of LGBTQ communities, African Americans, and/or youth in Newark in particular, appear frequently throughout the coverage, but with different inflections in the various types of media. In the non–NJ/NY local press, Gunn usually appears not because of her death in particular, but as evidence that the paper takes LGBTQ concerns seriously: her death is thus an impetus for general interest in LGBTQ issues. Similarly, the alternative coverage uses Gunn as evidence, but here the less-optimistic argument is that Gunn's death proves the need for continued vigilance against hate crimes: Gunn is the impetus for further activism. The NJ/NY local coverage is also pessimistic, focusing specifically on the way in which Newark—as a city and a community—may have contributed to and then did or did not respond to Gunn's murder in relation to both LGBTQ and race issues. In fact, all three types of media use Gunn's murder to define Newark as a generic problem, so much so that over time the LGBTQ specificity of her case falls away and her death becomes just one more example of violence in Newark. As I illustrate below, regardless of the inflections in the coverage, the particularity of Gunn as a queer African American girl is not relevant. Nevertheless, I end this section as I do the previous one: by using critical analysis to reconnect Gunn to an (imagined) active and vibrant life as an LGBTQ African American girl prior to her death.

One way the coverage brings attention to LGBTQ issues is by reporting on rallies, vigils, and other forms of activism resulting from Gunn's death. Non-NJ/NY local articles report on vigils taking place around the country, including "Minnesota Briefs," which announces a rally to take place in Duluth, and a *Boston Globe* article, which mentions a rally for Gunn that had been held in Boston the previous month.[76] Non-NJ/NY coverage also reports on a student at Michigan State University (MSU), Lajoya Johnson, who started an online petition to persuade the principal of Gunn's school to have a moment of silence "to bring awareness and discussion to the murder of Gunn," as well as persuaded MSU to establish a scholarship for "LGBT students of color."[77] Collectively, then, non–NJ/NY articles celebrate activism that emerged as a result of Gunn's death, but little if any attention is paid to Gunn herself or to the details of what happened to her as related to the activism.

The alternative press reports on many more vigils, emphasizing that Gunn's LGBTQ death is only one among many like it. For example, a *Bay Windows* article quotes a vigil organizer saying "Sakia Gunn is the impetus, but clearly the violence in our community is overwhelming."[78] Further, articles often end with sad or depressing quotations that emphasize the severity and horrific nature of Gunn's murder as a symbol of general anti-LGBTQ violence. For example, a guest opinion in which the author reflects on the continuity between her experiences as a youth and Gunn's death ends with the following: "In the twenty years since I hung out on the piers off the West Side Highway, the LGBT movement has matured into a powerful force. . . . Despite all this, I can't help but ask: Are we any safer today than we were twenty years ago?"[79] In short, the alternative press is implicitly optimistic about the amount and variety of activism that exists—indirectly related to Gunn—but discouraged about the seemingly inevitable need for continued activism and vigilance. Either way, though, Gunn is just one among many.

NJ/NY local coverage also reports on activism following Gunn's death and draws attention to continued discrimination against, or at least neglect of, the local LGBTQ community. Again, Gunn serves as an abstract justification for activism; the particularities of her case are irrelevant. Within less than a month after Gunn's death, NJ/NY cover-age began critiquing the mayor's office for failing to provide resources for LGBTQ youth. For example, one article reports on a march that took place two and a half weeks after the funeral, "calling on Mayor Sharpe James to follow through on a pledge to meet with [gay rights advocates] about setting up a gay and lesbian counseling center for teens." The article says the city's health director had been assigned to meet with members of the LGBTQ rights community, but that activ-ists "believe the city is moving too slowly."[80] Other articles mention the fact that the city still has not opened a community center for LGBTQ youth[81] and that the new PFLAG chapter plans to continue pressuring the city.[82] In short, the local NJ/NY press uses Gunn to make clear the need for continued attention to LGBTQ issues in Newark.

When reading across multiple types of media, the problem with Newark becomes not only a lack of commitment to LGBTQ issues, but also a question of race. For example, the author of a *NYT* article published on the anniversary of Gunn's death is concerned about "the plight and isolation of a growing number of minority teenagers who are openly gay or lesbian in cities like Newark."[83] A great deal of the coverage is quite direct in its indictment of Newark. An AP commen-tary specifically discusses "anti-gay bias within the predominantly black community" of Newark, and holds the (implicitly African American) local church responsible (in part) for Gunn's murder because of preach-ing "homophobia." The article also criticizes the lack of "mainstream gay-rights" media coverage of the case, blaming the silence on Gunn's race and socioeconomic class. Emphasizing the indictment of both the church and these gay rights groups, the author reports that when he tried to contact these groups "calls were not returned."[84]

Despite all this attention early on to LGBTQ issues in the context of an African American community, as time wore on the NJ/NY local coverage began to report on the case in ways that dissociated Gunn's death from LGBTQ issues entirely, instead linking it to general street and youth violence, particularly in African American communities such as Newark.[85] For example, some articles report on a caravan of cars that moved through Essex County to protest violence in the area. The articles mention Gunn's name as one among the many murders the caravan protests, but they do not mention that her murder was an

LGBTQ bias crime.[86] And, on the one-year anniversary of Gunn's death, the press reported that Newark schools held a moment of silence on the newly instituted "No Name Calling Day," to recognize "student victims of violence," again mentioning Gunn but addressing generic violence rather than specific anti-LGBTQ harassment. One article strategically sets aside LGBTQ issues, quoting the director of student services in the schools saying "It doesn't matter who the individual is that was murdered. They all deserve the same kind of remembrance."[87] These articles, then, imply that things were bad when Gunn was killed, but they are now getting better—so much better, in fact, that they can turn their attention to general violence, rather than to LGBTQ rights and safety. The fact that this progressive model is a fallacy is revealed in a June 2007 article that reports that the Newark schools faced controversy when they decided to "black out a photograph of two men [presumably, actually high school *boys*] kissing in a high school yearbook." The article quotes the school superintendent, who mentions Gunn when admitting that "the district's staff may need more training. 'We had that in the aftermath of Sakia Gunn, . . . but I guess we need more.'"[88]

In short, while the coverage oscillates between depicting Newark as a horrendous place for youth and depicting Newark as hard at work to improve itself, "more" is always needed. In the coverage, Newark—coded as African American, poor, and fraught around LGBTQ issues—was not a safe space for Gunn and, in fact, was a contributing factor in her death, whether that death is understood as an LGBTQ bias crime or as an example of the high rate of violence against African American youth. Through all this, Gunn is just one example of violence, and ultimately not even LGBTQ-specific violence.

That said, the coverage does provide enough information about LGBTQ activism to enable a reading in pursuit of the strength and diversity of LGBTQ youth life in the area. When I pull out passing references to LGBTQ life in Newark prior to the murder from a variety of sources, I can build a picture of a vibrant and active LGBTQ community both in Newark and in Gunn's high school. One article reports, "Whatever the reason, urban girls . . . are openly displaying same-sex sexual behavior." "Gaggles of girls," apparently, gather on what is called "Gay Corner" (the corner where Gunn was killed) to hang out, "chat," and "roughhouse."[89] While the word choice here ("gaggles") suggests a bit of discomfort with and disrespect for these girls' behavior on the part of the author, this is just one of many articles that make clear that many queer youth lived openly prior to Gunn's murder. Collectively, the NJ/NY coverage also mentions as many as ten activist organizations in the Newark area that existed at the time of the murder, including the New York City Gay and Lesbian Anti-violence Program,[90] the Lambda Legal Defense and Education Fund,[91] the Anti-defamation League of New Jersey,[92] the Anti-violence Enough Is Enough Coalition,[93] the New Jersey Stonewall Democrats,[94] the African American Office of Gay Concerns in Newark,[95] the Northern Jersey Community Outreach Initiative,[96] the Lesbian, Gay, Bisexual, and Transgender Student Services at Princeton University,[97] the Gender Rights Advocacy Association of New Jersey,[98] and Queer Watch.[99] Additionally, coverage mentions some religious organizations as sharing the outrage over Gunn's death and supporting LGBTQ rights. For example, one article quotes "Rev. Thomas Ellis, head of the Anti-violence Enough Is Enough Coalition and an outreach minister at Newark's Jehovah Jehri Christian Worship Center."[100] And Rev. Jacquelyn Holland, pastor of Newark's Liberation in Truth Unity Fellowship Church, appears frequently, illustrating that this church openly supports LGBTQ rights and has many LGBTQ members. Several articles report that Reverend Holland hopes "to establish a neighborhood drop-in center where gay teens can come for counseling, employment help, and reassurance." The article quotes her as saying "We want to let [LGBTQ youth] know it's OK to be who they are. . . . [Gunn] didn't do anything wrong by being a lesbian."[101] Further, additional organizations emerged immediately following Gunn's death. For example, the press reports on Newark Pride, defined as "a coalition of gay and lesbian advocates and supporters";[102] the Aggressive'z and Fem'z,[103] also identified as "the Sakia Gunn Aggressive and Fem Organization," founded by Jamon Marsh and Valencia Bailey;[104] and finally the Newark chapter of PFLAG, generally reported as being formed in response to both Gunn's death in May 2003 and the death of Shani Baraka (daughter of poet Amiri Baraka) in August 2003.[105] Many articles also report on the PFLAG scholarship established in Gunn's name.[106]

In ending this section by turning to a reading of the coverage that pulls out snippets of evidence of LGBTQ youth life in Newark prior to and immediately following Gunn's death, my goal is to imagine the life

Gunn might have led as an LGBTQ/AG teen. I emphasize, however, that this is entirely imaginary. Not surprisingly, no media coverage of Gunn exists prior to her death, and the coverage of her death spends little time on her life beyond telling us she was a loved and loveable girl who enjoyed basketball, Cap'n Crunch, hot wings, and dressing like a boy. As time wears on, even these few details about Gunn disappear from the coverage and she becomes only a motivation for LGBTQ activism or a symbol of violence against African American youth. My move here, then, is to use the coverage to produce an alternative picture of Gunn to reconnect her to a specific queer girlhood located squarely in African American Newark, a particular queer girlhood from which the bulk of the coverage, especially over time, disconnects her.

Sakia Gunn Is (Not) Matthew Shepard

Later coverage most often represents Gunn through comparison and association. Here, she becomes a figure or marker—evidence—of continuing or escalating anti-LGBTQ violence and therefore of the need for LGBTQ activism. Although these comparisons refer to Gunn's LGBTQ identity, no other details from her story appear and thus that identity remains generic.

The most obvious comparison, of course, is to Matthew Shepard. For example, two years after the murder, "Even Today, Gays Are Stonewalled" argues that, "despite the carnival atmosphere of today's [gay] pride and festival," same-sex marriage is opposed, and hate crimes like Shepard and Gunn's deaths reveal "hostility and hatred." This, the article argues, is why "'gay pride' is so important." Another example linking Gunn and Shepard is a letter to the editor of the *Bismarck Tribune*, which serves to normalize "same-sex couples" and ends by urging readers to "protect the ones you love. . . . Protect them from becoming Matthew Shepard or Sakia Gunn."[107] The author does not explain who Gunn is, but presumably most readers would know who Shepard was and therefore could assume that Gunn was also killed in an LGBTQ hate crime.

Comparisons between Gunn and Shepard are often about "media coverage." Here, the argument is that Gunn should have received the kind of national media blitz that emerged when Shepard was murdered, but did not. For example, a commentary published in the *Staten Island*

Advance compares the lack of coverage of Gunn to the substantial coverage of Matthew Shepard's and Brandon Teena's deaths, and points to race and class as the reasons for the difference. This article claims, "News of Sakia's murder barely made any newspapers in the tri-state area,"[108] and, despite the fact that this is not true, the comparison to the quantity of national coverage of Shepard and Brandon Teena still stands. In the alternative press, sometimes authors critique the African American community for not paying more attention to Gunn,[109] sometimes they critique the LGBTQ community for implicit racism and classism evidenced by the intense attention paid to Matthew Shepard as compared to Gunn,[110] occasionally they critique "women's groups" such as the Feminist Majority and the National Organization for Women for not taking Gunn's death up as a feminist cause,[111] but most often the authors critique the mainstream corporate press by writing articles with titles such as "Sakia Gunn: Why the Silence?"[112] They argue that, in comparison, Shepard was easy to take on as a fallen son of the nation because "he was the 'All-American' boy": white, middle-class, and educated.[113]

Coverage also compares Gunn to less famous and generic cases. For example, articles sometimes use Gunn to illustrate and confront continuing "violence against gays,"[114] as evidence that "antigay hate crime may be on the rise,"[115] or "as an example of how far anti-gay discrimination can go."[116] These articles mention Gunn only briefly and are primarily about other topics (e.g., the Denver PrideFest, an "antigay" assault on a Boston woman, and the "Blacks Facing AIDS Crisis," respectively). Published in the African American newspaper the *New York Beacon*, Kay Wright's "Bigotry by Any Other Name" is about the intersection of race and sexuality and the importance of fighting bigotry against gays, blacks, and "Black gay people." She writes:

> By banning same-sex couples from legal marriage, our government makes a statement to its gay taxpayers: Your love is not valid. *That is the same statement Sakia Gunn's killer made.* It is the statement made by those who torment the one-third of gay students who report having skipped school in the last month due to fear. And it is the statement too many Black community leaders made as they watched thousands of Black gay men die of AIDS rather than rally to demand our government invest in scientific research and pay for treatments that could have saved those Black lives.[117]

This article, like many others, is not about Gunn; instead, it uses her death to illustrate the existence of "Black gay people," to produce pathos, and to encourage the reader to take LGBTQ rights seriously.

The most poignant comparison for me appeared more than three years after Gunn's death and is the only one to preserve some of the specificity of Gunn's experience. In April 2007, a group of young black lesbians (who came to be known as the "Newark Four")[118] were convicted of "second-degree gang assault" when a scenario very similar to the one in which Gunn found herself ended quite differently. In August 2006, a man approached the women and both propositioned them and used homophobic insults. Unlike McCullough, however, he did not kill any of them; instead, the women physically attacked him, and he ended up in the hospital. In a commentary on the case, Reva McEachern uses the Gunn case to explain why "19-year-old Patreese Johnson . . . a 4-foot-11, 100-pound woman, would carry some instrument of protection—in this case a knife."[119] The court, however, did not take this perspective, convicting the women of assault rather than defining their actions as self-defense. While McEachern's piece is explicitly a commentary, even a news article about the case uses Gunn to make a similar argument. After reporting that "the judge bluntly said he didn't believe testimony by Johnson that she carried a knife because she was 4-foot-11 and 95 pounds and came from a dangerous neighborhood," the article ends by confirming that not only did Johnson live in a dangerous neighborhood, but it was the same neighborhood in which her "high school classmate" Sakia Gunn was murdered "after she spurned a man who tried to pick her up."[120]

In all but one of these comparisons (the Newark Four), Gunn is an abstract symbol of anti-LGBTQ sentiment and/or racism. She functions as evidence of continuing homophobia and the need for continued activism, but her story is not told at any level of specificity. Instead, her death becomes a versatile yet generic symbol. It takes a purposeful analytical move—one dependent on systematic examination of a huge quantity of media material—to find and use the one article about the Newark Four to re-center Gunn as an individual. By understanding these two cases as linked, I seek to reread Gunn as a queer African American girl living as a transgendered AG and drawing on the support of the vibrant LGBTQ Newark community, while likely facing frequent street harassment. Reading across multiple media to construct her thusly, I define her as a spectacular girl taking up public space, one who is available through media representation, despite the fact that I have to work fairly hard with and against media representations to find (this version of) her.

Conclusion: Queer African American Girlhood
Taking Up Social, Creative, and Intellectual Space

The goals of this chapter are (1) to insist Sakia Gunn is a spectacular girl, that there is substantial coverage of her case even if it is not in the national press, and (2) to challenge the way in which Gunn most often functions as a relatively empty signifier in this coverage. I can read the specificity of Gunn's case—her racialized transgender/AG presentation and the fact that she took up space (by going into the Village, using public transportation at 3:30 a.m., and fighting back both verbally and physically)—as long as I turn not only to nonmainstream sources but also to brief moments in all the coverage that at least gesture toward a girlhood other than the tragic dead girl who can become everyone's darling and/or hero. On the one hand, admittedly, lack of sustained mainstream national attention means that "Sakia Gunn" is not a household name as are "Selena Gomez," "Juno," and "Venus Williams." On the other hand, using a feminist media criticism methodology to look beyond the national media can turn our attention to girls such as Gunn who provide an opportunity to imagine a queer black girlhood that unapologetically takes up public space, that participates in a public conversation about girlhood, and that unequivocally is a part of media culture.

A few other scholars and artists have imagined Sakia Gunn in the specificity of her girlhood as well. Three in particular do more than mention Gunn in passing.[121] First, Charles B. Brack's documentary film *Dreams Deferred: The Sakia Gunn Film Project* (2008) follows Gunn's family and friends after the murder and through McCullough's sentencing hearing. By documenting both mundane elements of everyday life and the dramatic trauma of her friends' and family's pain as played out in the courtroom, the film defines Gunn as meaningful as an individual friend/daughter/niece. Journalist/scholar Kristal Brent Zook also draws on interviews with Gunn's family and friends, writing an entire chapter

about Gunn in her book *Black Women's Lives: Stories of Pain and Power.*
Zook includes details that appear nowhere in the massive media coverage, including that Gunn went by "'T,' . . . referring to her male alter ego,
Tyquinne Aleante Gunn," and that "as two aggressives" she and Valencia
Bailey "were players together." Not only does Zook paint a fuller picture
of the specificity of Gunn's gender and sexuality, but she also takes the
story forward. She does not leave Gunn only as a tragedy, but instead
reports that "Jamon Marsh, Sakia's fiancé, . . . enrolled in a local community college" and that Valencia Bailey "was a high school graduate on
her way to Morgan State University in Maryland."[122] Thus, while Gunn
is gone, life did not stop for the LGBTQ/AG girls in her community.
These girls are not Gunn, but they are connected to Gunn, and thus the
nuances of their lives reflect back on how one might imagine Gunn's
life. Finally, performance artist and scholar Ruth Nicole Brown also
imagines Gunn through her friends. In her multimedia performance
piece, *The Rhythm, the Rhyme, and the Reason*, Brown stages the location of Gunn's death (but not the death itself), performing as an African
American queer/AG girl confronting the audience with personal pain

Figure 5.2. Ruth Nicole Brown performing a critique of the death of Sakia Gunn, in *The
Rhythm, the Rhyme, and the Reason*. Photo by Kathy Perkins. Used by permission.

and cogent critique. Gunn is present in the performance not only as a literal image in the background, but also as a queer black girl who matters—to the character in the play, to Brown as playwright and scholar, and (through engagement with the performance) to the audience.

I am influenced and inspired by Brack's, Zook's, and Brown's work on Gunn, I want this chapter to speak with and to this other work, and I, too, strive to imagine Gunn's girlhood in its specificity. Nevertheless, because of my focus on media coverage I also want to draw attention to three limitations in the girlhood I read through Gunn. First, narratives of Gunn as innocent victim and as a symbol of all that is wrong with (African American) Newark and the media (both LGBTQ and mainstream) predominate. Thus, the bulk of the coverage systematically eliminates Gunn's uniqueness as an African American AG girl—(at least part of) the very reason Brack, Zook, Brown, and I take her up as a subject in the first place. Second, this chapter identifies a media-type continuum running from the mainstream national coverage and local non–NJ/NY coverage, through the local NJ/NY coverage, and finally to the alternative press. On the national end of a continuum, Gunn is an innocent girl tragically killed for vaguely sexualized reasons. On the alternative press end of the continuum, Gunn is a hero and a warrior, fighting at the moment of her death and as a symbol after her death for LGBTQ rights. On the one hand, thinking of the analysis in this chapter in this way makes clear the importance of reading across multiple types of sources in order to understand a particular case study in a multidimensional way. On the other hand, like the dominant narratives about Gunn, this continuum is rather predictable, implying a national = bad but alternative/queer = good argument that is all but a given when someone writes from the feminist, antiracist, queer-identified perspective I seek to maintain throughout this book. Finally, and perhaps most importantly, it is important to remember that Gunn is spectacular in any media context only because of her death. Thus, while I insist on understanding Gunn as a spectacular alternative girl, I also want to stress that her spectacularization depends on her death; her presence in this book requires her absence from the world.

Here in the conclusion, I want to acknowledge the predictable narratives and media types, as well as the tragic irony of the necessity of death for Gunn to become spectacular. Nevertheless, I also want to pause over and emphasize the complexity of the girlhood available when reading across the collective coverage, and thereby add that complexity to my understanding of mediated girlhood. In other words, this analysis of media coverage of Gunn illustrates that contemporary media girlhood includes queer AG girlhood, African American girlhood, a girlhood that takes up space, and a girlhood that brings all these issues together. None of the media—national, local, or alternative—ever gets at Gunn's full human complexity in all its variation and dimensions. Of course, neither do I, nor does anyone writing or performing about Gunn. But what I hope to have done is to illustrate how reading across multiple types of media—and doing so with a critical eye in search of the intersections of gender, race, sexuality, and youth—at least moves in the direction of insisting on the multiplicity and complexity of Gunn's girlhood. This kind of girlhood rarely appears in the mainstream press, but when we define media more broadly and explicitly look for and value girlhood, the multiplicity does appear, the complexity does become available as one (among many) versions of spectacular girlhood in turn-of-the-twenty-first-century media culture. In this way, I argue that even if the media coverage rarely addresses Gunn as a girl, we can nevertheless seek her out as a girl—in fact, insist that she is a spectacular African American queer/AG girl who continues to take up public space in our mediascape even many years after her death.

6

"Sometimes I Say Cuss Words in My Head"

The Complexity of Third-Grade Media Analysis

> SARAH: Mina, what would you think if I came into your classroom and did a media criticism project?
> MINA: I'm not critical!
> SARAH: Oh. I mean, a media *analysis* project.
> MINA: What's that?
> SARAH: That means I would talk with you and your friends about television and movies and find out how you analyze them, just like the way your teacher teaches you to analyze poems and literature.
> MINA: I guess that would be fun.

While the bulk of this book offers a critical analysis of media representations of girls, this final chapter is based on research with actual girls. Here, I write about a media project I did in 2009 with my daughter's twenty-one-student third-grade class in a Midwestern, public elementary school. As I describe below, I designed this project to identify children's analytical perspectives on media, and on representations of girls and gender in particular. I wanted to know: How is it that girls (or boys, for that matter) interact with and make sense of media representations of girlhood? How do girls and boys think about the relationship between media and their own lives and selves? And, most important, in what analytical ways do they approach media?

I am not trained as an ethnographer, education scholar, or media effects researcher, nor do I study audiences. Nevertheless, as I researched and wrote this book, this was a project I felt compelled to do for two reasons. First, as I discuss in the book's introduction, not only do innumerable books continue to declare that media are "bad" for girls,[1] but I also encounter many people—at both coffee shops and scholarly conferences—that upon hearing I am writing a book about "girls in U.S. media culture" spontaneously tell me how awful (i.e., antifeminist and/or overly sexualized) media representations of girls are, assuming the purpose of my book is to identify "damaging media effects." I feel fairly confident that this incorrect assumption about my scholarly motivations develops out of the moral panic identified and spurred on by Mary Pipher's 1994 self-help book, *Reviving Ophelia: Saving the Selves of Adolescent Girls*, and thereby articulates what I call the Ophelia Thesis. When I respond with comments such as, "My book is about the fact that other versions of girlhood are available in media culture," or "I think many girls are actually critical of the kinds of representations you are thinking of," I most often encounter blank stares or comments such as, "I know. But, still . . ." This chapter is thus, in part, a response to the Ophelia Thesis and the entrenched "but, still . . ." belief it authorizes. Having spent the first five chapters illustrating a variety of alternatives to the Ophelia Thesis and thereby proving that, indeed, Ophelia and the representations of girls that presumably produce her are not the only girls in media culture, in this chapter I seek to test (and to some degree prove) my claim that "many girls are actually critical" of media representations.

Certainly, scholars have been making the argument that media audiences are "active . . . plural . . . [and] locally resistant"[2] at least since the late 1970s when cultural studies emerged in the Birmingham school,[3] but this large body of research exists alongside a steadfast moral panic about girls and media, as well as some media effects and media literacy scholarship that persists in the belief that media affect girls negatively.[4] As David Buckingham argues, "Against this background, it remains important to assert that children are often highly selective, discriminating, and sophisticated viewers."[5] Thus I reject the Ophelia Thesis by relying on previous cultural studies research to take as a given that girls are not cultural dupes; I then move on to define girls as media critics and ask what kind of criticism they do. In short, this chapter asks "What does girls' media analysis look and sound like?"

Second, I felt compelled to write this chapter because of the book's investment in exploring alternative girlhoods. Most simply, in the context of a book primarily about media representations of girls, "girl as media critic" is an alternative to "girl as media representation." The media critic girl in this chapter is alternative in three specific ways: (1) The ways in which students interpreted media representations of girls by and large did not reduce them to the moral panic about hyper-sexualized girls. In other words, the students found much more complex and nuanced ideas about girls and gender in media. In this way, the students helped me see versions of girlhood that were alternative, even where I had not expected to find them. (2) The girls in the class did not express a "lack of self-esteem" or an overinvestment in a sexualized identity. While this finding undoubtedly is partly evidence that a researcher will find what she is looking for (i.e., in my case, proof the Ophelia Thesis is false), by addressing specific ways that girls articulate an analytical relationship to media representations, I hope to give shape and depth to the alternative versions of girlhood the students presented to me. (3) The girls in the classroom turned out not to be that different from the boys in terms of their analytical relationship to the media, and thus they did not take on the role of a vulnerable or damaged (or empowered, for that matter) class of gendered media consumers. As I discuss more fully below, while there were certainly differences in the shows girls and boys watched and what they had to say about the representation of gender, and while most of them self-segregated along gender lines when they chose small groups, and while they certainly wanted to talk about gender (with little to no prompting from me), girls and boys alike tended to approach media analysis in quite similar ways.

In short, in this chapter, I argue that girls (and boys) offer analytical perspectives on media. Further, I argue that understanding girls as media critics is a useful response to the Ophelia Thesis, one that can not only challenge it but also go some way toward deflating it—a key goal of this book. And, finally, I argue that media scholarship about girls and literacy programs for girls can profitably start with an understanding of girls as media critics in order to better achieve the goal of helping girls maintain and grow a healthy and skeptical relationship to all media.

In the first section, I build my argument for a scholarly understanding of girls as media critics, as related to but distinct from a series of other bodies of literature about girls' relationships to media: (1) popular crossover Ophelia Thesis books about the dangerous impact of media on girls; (2) what I consider a scholarly investigation of this argument in some media effects literature; (3) work on girls as media producers, sometimes in the context of after-school and/or empowerment programs for girls; (4) critical media literacy; and (5) audience studies focused on girls in particular. We have strong literatures on girls as media victims, audiences, producers, and students, but what of girls as media critics? If we value media criticism in our scholarly communities and university class-rooms, shouldn't we also value it for girls? And if we want to understand girls in media culture, isn't their analytical relationship to media part of that picture? In my discussion of each of these areas, I both challenge some of the assumptions and goals of this research and acknowledge the ways my own project is indebted to this work.

After an explanation of the media project's method in the second section of the chapter, in the third section I turn to a discussion of specific aspects of the students' analytical relationship to media, iden-tifying activities such as noticing minute details, asking insistent ques-tions, producing creative work (e.g., fantasy, drawing, performance), and returning again and again to interest in and concern about media depictions of gender and the specific ways girls versus boys think about those depictions. As I discuss below, the students did not describe themselves as critical, nor did they have any interest in my showing them how I understood them to be analytical. Yet, as the third section demonstrates, they did participate in sustained, insightful, and chal-lenging media analysis.

Having built the argument that it is important to understand girls as active media critics and shown ways they are so, in the final section of the chapter I turn to a discussion of the ways the girls' overall ana-lytical approach to media only goes so far, and I acknowledge that at times they directly resisted me as I urged them to articulate analyti-cal perspectives. Here, I argue that even though the students are media critics—even often feminist critics—their analytical activities are some-times fraught and delimited, especially when comparing their detailed analysis of gender to their struggle to articulate an analysis of race.

Before turning to my analysis, I want to mention two issues that complicate what I mean when I say "girl media critics." First, as the epi-graph to this chapter implies, the term "critic" does not necessarily fit eight- to ten-year-olds. My daughter's response to my use of the word "criticism" reminded me that her school works hard to prevent "mean girl" behavior and bullying more generally. The children are constantly told not to be "critical" of one another but rather to be supportive. For my daughter, the word "critical" did not evoke the concept of "critical thinking," but rather implied that she was making a bad choice to use that word, because it would mean she was insulting someone.[6] I shifted, then, to talking with the students about analysis rather than criticism whenever possible, and I use "analysis" rather than "criticism" throughout this chapter, wherever possible. While I do mean "analysis" simply as a synonym for "criticism," I want to acknowledge here that the very word "critical" feels wrong to at least some of the students with whom I worked. This does not mean they do not engage in critical thinking (far from it), but I do think that this regulation of language and thought (they are not allowed to be—or possibly to say—"critical") could influence the ways that the students think about their relationships to the texts they encounter at home, at school, and/or in the media. Regardless, in deference to the students, throughout this chapter I emphasize their analytical abilities as examples of what scholars and educators might call "critical thinking" but that they would likely call "being smart."

Second, while one of my goals was to "include girls' voices" as evidence of their analytical relationship to media, the idea of "giving voice" to girls is problematic. Even if I were to publish girls' written media analyses (as I had hoped to do), that would not mean they did not already have voice, or that what I (as a sanctioned university professor) had to offer (i.e., publishing their writing in a relatively obscure academic book) would somehow benefit or even interest them. In *Black Girlhood Celebration*, Ruth Nicole Brown discusses the fraught process of presenting girls' creative production publicly. She challenges scholars and artists (including herself) not to "pimp" girls' work by using it to serve the interests of the adult in the academic or performance world.[7] She also challenges scholars who reproduce girls' work in a way that implies the work can "speak for itself," without providing the context of production, information about the girls who produced the work, or the scholar's own interpretation and understanding of the work, including why she or he chose to make the work public. Thus, following Brown, I make space for girls' media analysis, but I do so in an attempt to speak to/with, rather than to co-opt, that material. This approach is particularly important because (as I discuss in more detail below) none of the girls wanted to sit down and write a media analysis essay for me anyway. Even when I asked them to do so in a variety of different ways, they both implicitly and explicitly refused. Thus they made it impossible for me simply to "publish" their work, and they asserted the specificity of their (non-writing) voices from day one.

Envisioning the Relationship between Girls and Media

As many scholars argue, the assumptions and arguments Pipher makes in *Reviving Ophelia* have done much to define contemporary girls as victims in need of protection, to perpetuate the cultural obsession with "saving" and protecting white middle-class heterosexual girls, and to define the media as dangerous for girls.[8] Following these previous critiques, I argue that *Reviving Ophelia* and the Ophelia Thesis construct (1) an imaginary pre-media girl child who is innocent, free, and pure; (2) a vulnerable and damaged media-immersed tween/teen; and (3) a monolithic media system that overwhelmingly defines girls as sexualized objects. Not only *Reviving Ophelia*, but also the many moral panic books that followed, the "Report of the APA Task Force on the Sexualization of Girls," and recent documentaries such as *Miss Representation* (2011) and *Sexy Baby* (2012), blame media (usually because for them the dollar is the bottom line), but hold parents (i.e., primarily mothers) responsible for protecting their daughters. The titles of some of the moral panic books, mainly marketed as self-help books, make the vulnerable girl and protective parent/mother explicit (emphasis added):

> *Reviving Ophelia: **Saving the Selves** of Adolescent Girls* (Pipher, 1994)
>
> *Queen Bees and Wannabes: **Helping Your Daughter Survive** Cliques, Gossip, Boyfriends, and the New Realities of the Girl World* (Wiseman, 2002)
>
> *Packaging Girlhood: **Rescuing Our Daughters** from Marketers' Schemes* (Lamb and Brown, 2006)
>
> *The Lolita Effect: The Media Sexualization of Young Girls and What We Can **Do about It*** (Durham, 2008)
>
> *The Triple Bind: **Saving Our Teenage Girls** from Today's Pressures* (Hinshaw, 2009)
>
> *Cinderella **Ate My Daughter**: Dispatches from the Front Lines of the New Girlie-Girl Culture* (Orenstein, 2011)

Further, while these titles may not make Ophelia's racialization clear, the book covers do. Of the six books I list above, every one features a white girl on the cover. All but two of the girls have light or blonde hair and light or blue eyes; and each looks miserable or in trouble.[9]

I should be clear that I am not making a counterargument that it is perfectly all right for girls to strive to achieve the idealized bodies and selves media present. In fact, as Maya Götz illustrates, only approximately 30 percent of the girl bodies that appear in children's television worldwide are physically attainable by an actual human body (compared to approximately 70 percent of boy bodies in children's television). This does not even mean were girls' bodies to look like those 30 percent of attainable media bodies that they would be healthy: many of the 30 percent attainable bodies would be anorexic.[10] Certainly, these kinds of representations of girls' bodies need critique. Neither am I making an argument that the many, many young college women who have told me that they read *Reviving Ophelia* when they were in high school and that it "really helped them" are deluding themselves. In fact, I am delighted these girls found a resource that helped them navigate their ongoing relationships with themselves, their bodies, and the media. Nevertheless, what I am arguing is that both *Reviving Ophelia* and, more important, the way "Ophelia" has become a household word contribute to an ideology of white girl in peril and in need of protection. The more pervasive this ideology, the more it obscures other versions of girlhood.

Of all the Ophelia Thesis books I have managed to read all the way through, M. Gigi Durham's *The Lolita Effect* is the most nuanced and maintains the most systematic intersectional feminist analysis throughout. Yet, even Durham, who is an important girls' studies scholar and has done much to complicate our understand of the relationship between gender and race in her scholarly research on girl audiences[11]— given the genre of the Ophelia Thesis books—was unable to avoid in *The Lolita Effect* reproducing the assumption that "thong underwear for ten-year-olds" are, by definition, bad. Even as she makes the bold feminist move in her book of defining herself as a "pro-sex feminist" and of insisting on the importance of girls' sexuality and the existence of sexuality in tweens and children, even as she repeatedly insists that "sex is a normal and healthy part of life, even of children's lives,"[12] in this crossover book she is unable to imagine how a tween might experience her own sexuality through, for example, micro-minis. I am not making a "postfeminist playground"[13] argument here that objectifying fashion is just plain fun and we (i.e., old-fashioned feminists) should get over it.[14]

Rather, I am arguing that the Ophelia Thesis renders adult protection of girls' sexuality and agency an incontrovertible requirement. Concomitantly, the thesis defines girls as unthinking in relation to the media they consume, other than to think negatively of themselves. Hence, my pursuit of the girl media critic is a turn away from the Ophelia Thesis and toward the thinking girl.

Media effects scholarship tends to conceive of the relationship between girls and media similarly to the Ophelia Thesis. While this is a huge body of literature that deserves more attention than I have space to give it here, overall it begins with the assumption that specific aspects of media (e.g., depictions of violence, smoking, sex) affect children. Most findings generally suggest that media have negative effects. Some research, however, explores ways of using media for positive ends (e.g., public service announcements that teach children the dangers of smoking).[15] And, more specifically, some feminist media effects research looks at the potential impact of body expectations in the media on girls' self-esteem and bodywork, including eating disorders.[16]

Because most of this research begins with the hypothesis that media have negative (or positive) effects, that is what the scholars look for and then find. My point is not that this research is wrong; in fact, I do find some feminist media effects research to be quite persuasive. Rather, my point is that—collectively—this research asks a different set of questions than I do. Rather than assuming that media affect girls in either negative or positive ways, I ask what girls think about the media representations they encounter. In other words, my question is not "How do media make girls feel, and what do they encourage girls to do?" but rather "What do girls think about media and how do they articulate those ideas?"

A second scholarly and policy response that tends to accept the Ophelia Thesis but seeks to transform (rather than describe or critique) the relationship between girls and the media, pursues change by placing the means of production in girls' hands. Many after-school programs and girl-empowerment programs see media production as an important tool for empowering girls to define themselves and "speak back" to media.[17] Relatedly, more and more research is emerging that explores the ways girls actively use media, by producing websites, for example;[18] and a number of programs and projects address the specific experiences and cultural contexts for "Native youth" and "black girls," for example.[19]

These programs and this research flip the Ophelia Thesis in the following way: the girl is figured as powerful, active, and in charge of herself and the production of media. Yet some of the empowerment projects also start from the very same premise as the Ophelia Thesis: that girls need protection from media, and that adults can—indeed, must—provide that protection.[20] The difference is that Ophelia Thesis books and films seek to leave their readers/viewers feeling panicky, guilty, and desperate to shield vulnerable girls from the media; while media production empowerment programs and some scholarship about them hope to leave their readers/observers feeling energized and goal-oriented, ready to take on the world by talking back to media and speaking up by producing media texts themselves.[21]

Despite the invigorating energy generated by media production programs for girls, I found myself relatively uninterested in taking this approach when thinking about how to engage with actual girls. I realized that, while many media production programs exist, to my knowledge there are few if any media criticism programs for girls. As a media critic (as opposed to media maker) I am personally invested in the act of writing and speaking analytically: not by being critical in a third-grade sense, but by understanding, taking apart, and reworking the representations I encounter on a daily basis. Might girls also care about this? Might they, in fact, already engage in this kind of thinking, talking, and writing, given that they already have the means of production (pencil, pen, paint, paper, keyboard, costume, body, and voice) for this kind of response to media? These questions led me to explore additional scholarly literatures that focus on children's interaction with media, starting with media literacy.

There are several approaches to children's media literacy as a field, but all of them have to do with teaching children[22] something about media, and many of them intersect with the Ophelia Thesis's protectionism. One approach starts with the implicit assumption that children know very little about media and "are inherently uncritical[; thus] it is the teacher's job to make them critical."[23] Publications within this area offer suggestions or models for how to teach children about how media work.[24] What is often called "critical media literacy" also seeks to teach children about media, but explicitly articulates a political purpose: to illustrate for students that media reproduce racist and sexist ideas (for example) and to give them the analytical tools they need to deconstruct those representations.[25] Other programs focus on the specificity of media literacy for particular groups, such as "Latina teens."[26]

My project could be considered a critical media literacy project, and in fact when I sought approval from my university's Institutional Review Board (IRB) I did call it "media literacy" as shorthand I assumed scholars outside the field of media studies might recognize. I was working with children in their everyday educational context, and I was collaborating with the classroom teacher to connect some of the material we covered in the media project to many of the things she had been teaching throughout the year (e.g., narrative, identifying evidence, and articulating and supporting one's own opinion). Further, I was working from a feminist perspective and taking a critical perspective on gender representations. In that sense, my project is an example of critical media literacy scholarship.[27] An important difference between my project and media literacy, however, is that I did not want to teach media literacy to the children, or even to teach them how to see the cultural construction of gender, race, and sexuality in the media. Rather, I wanted to identify the ways they were already enacting critical analysis of the media. I was not averse to expanding and building on their existing literacy, but I began with the assumption that they were already highly literate.

In fact, my goal was to learn from them more than to teach them. And in this way my project is like an audience study that seeks to understand how children interact with media. Again, to generalize, many audience studies argue that children negotiate with and derive pleasure from complex engagement with media texts, sometimes even seeming to use them against themselves (e.g., pulling off Barbie's head)[28] or using them to come to terms with their own identities in a mediated world that tells them they should be different from how they are (e.g., girls' engagement with Britney Spears, telenovelas, *Pocahontas* [1995], popular magazines, or girl power).[29] Most audience studies, in fact, draw on both of these arguments, acknowledging that any relationship between audience and text is complex and mediated, and that it would be rare to find anyone who is entirely a cultural dupe or entirely resistant to ideology.

My project is different from audience research, however, because I did not choose a particular text or sets of texts about which to interview, survey, watch, or do participant observations with audiences. Nor did I choose a particular group as an audience, beyond "girls." In other words, my question is not: "How does audience X interact with media product Y?" My goal is not to understand all of the ways students interact with media. Rather, I hone in on students' analytical activities and ask: "What are girls doing, writing, saying, and creating that can be understood to be critical analysis?" This is thus a much more focused question than that of a typical audience study.

In sum, my commitment to girls as media critics is to conceive of thinking girls in contradistinction to the Ophelia Thesis and its impact on various scholarly fields; to imagine—in addition to media production and audience pleasure—media analysis as a powerful experience for girls; and to think about the literacies girls already have rather than the ones I (as an adult scholar) might wish for them. I take girls seriously as media critics with particular strategies, interests, and methods. Can they, in fact, teach trained feminist media scholars, such as myself, a thing or two about how to think analytically about cultural representations of girls?

The Media Project: Methods

For two weeks during spring 2009, I spent one to two hours a day in my daughter's twenty-one-student, third-grade Midwest public school classroom working with students on what they named the "Media Project." After those two weeks, I returned six times over the course of approximately two months to work with students who chose to continue the project in small groups. Finally, I returned to the classroom during the last week of school for one last discussion and to thank the students with a pizza party.

I developed my plan for the project in conjunction with the classroom teacher, who encouraged me both to think of the project in terms of "units" and to link the project to the work she was already doing in class. With her gracious help, I planned four distinct units, which I then adapted in response to students' comments and activities during the project. In effect, I functioned like a student teacher might, working with the students on a topic but also deferring to their teacher as the ultimate classroom authority. That said, the students knew I was a university professor, a parent of a student in class, and an experienced teacher; hence, I was lucky not to have to work very hard to gain their attention or trust.

I covered three of the four units during the two weeks I worked with the entire class. The first unit focused on identifying the students' analytical activities. The classroom teacher had suggested a number of exercises she often used with the class—t-charts (comparisons), webs (identifying relations among ideas), and Venn diagrams (identifying similarities and differences)—all of which I borrowed. During our discussions, I drew the students' attention to the analytical insights they were offering; but I maintained an open agenda, followed their viewing interests as much as possible, and asked questions rather than gave instructions. During this unit we worked together as one large group.

In the second unit, I split the students into small groups and encouraged them to develop creative projects. The purpose of this unit was to expand my understanding of their processes of analysis by exploring creative and performative projects that were not explicitly analytical but could still provide a context for analytical thought. I gave them a series of prompts to choose from that I hoped would encourage analytical activity. The students chose versions of the following four prompts: "Argue that television, movies, or videogames are good for you." "What would your television or videogame say if it could talk?" "Create a scene from a television show." And "Create a conversation with a television/ movie/videogame character."

I began the third unit (again in a large group) by using vocabulary they would recognize from their regular classroom activities to describe for them all the analytical methods I had observed them using during units 1 and 2—observe details; compare, contrast, and connect; evaluate, form an opinion, tell a story; and make an argument—proving (to myself) that they were in fact already analytical and providing (for them) an explicit explanation of how to do media criticism. My plan was then to show examples of television that were specifically about girls and the representation of gender, and to have them apply the analytical methods I had just summarized for them. They were completely uninterested in my presentation, however. Instead, they wanted me to hurry up and show them the television I had been promising but also delaying. After trying briefly to get them interested in my summary (much to the classroom teacher's amusement, I think), I quickly gave up and showed them the television examples I had prepared. First, we watched a series of television advertisements I had selected from those airing during several different contemporary children's programs. Then, we watched an episode of *Wizards of Waverly Place* (2007–2012, hereafter *Wizards*)—the television show that many of them voted we watch, that they had mentioned most often, and that stars Selena Gomez, the girl celebrity they had mentioned most often. After that, we watched an episode of *Sabrina, the Teenage Witch* (1996–2003, hereafter *Sabrina*), which I chose (even though they had not voted for it) because I hoped it would help them think about Alex—Selena Gomez's girl wizard character—in a comparative way. After each screening we discussed what we noticed. I occasionally tried to encourage them to enact the analytical methods I had told them they already knew how to use, but they just wanted to tell their classmates and me what they thought about the material.

The fourth and final unit of the project was designed for students who expressed interest in pursuing media analysis further. I invited all the students to participate in the fourth unit during their lunch hour. While I provided lunch, they had to give up their recess time in order to participate. I was pleased that approximately one-third of the students chose to continue the project. My plan was to work with the students as they wrote short media analysis essays that I could then include in my book. As I discuss in more detail below, none of the students wanted to write an essay, and only a few of them cooperated when, on the second day (with the classroom teacher's encouragement), I actually insisted that they write analyses rather than create their own stories; the first two days were mostly frustrating for them and for me. After the second day, this unit evolved into two small group discussions (one all girls, the other most of those same girls plus one boy) in which we gave up all semblance of trying to write anything and just talked about media.

With the students' and their parents' permission, I audiotaped as much of the project as was technologically feasible—using several different recorders to pick up as many different comments and conversations as possible—including group work when I was not present. I transcribed the approximately twenty hours of audiotaped material myself. The analysis that follows is based on those transcripts, on the notes I took following each day in the classroom, and on my memories of the experience. All quotations are taken from the transcripts.

Looking for and Finding Critical Analysis

Whenever I drew attention to the students' analytical abilities or asked them to reflect more deeply on what they were saying, they either seemed not to understand or found ways to resist me. For example, early on I was frustrated that the students never could/would answer me when I asked, "Why do you think that?" or "What do you think about that?" So, from one perspective, I could argue that they really do not have media analysis skills, that they are not able to achieve a critical distance from media. Yet, to make this argument would be to ignore the premise I started with, which was to ask what analytical skills they already had. When I look at the research from that perspective, I see a variety of forms of critical interaction with media: their ability to notice details, their thoughtful questions, their pleasure in creating their own stories and drawings, and their concern about gender difference. In this section, then, I define media analysis as any activity that reveals a perspective on the structure of or produces an interpretation of a media text.

As I mention above, I did not find significant differences between how girls and boys expressed these kinds of analytical thoughts about media. Hence, in the discussion that follows I do not define girls as different from boys, and I sometimes provide examples of things boys said or did. To put this another way, the version of third-grade girl media critic I discuss here is not gender-specific. Certainly, this could be developmental, given that the children were all between eight and ten years old and had not yet started entering puberty. Nevertheless, they were also by definition "tweens," perhaps the key group of girls about which the Ophelia Thesis is concerned. The lack of gender difference, in and of itself, is significant, then, because it articulates a gender-nonspecific version of girlhood in contrast to the Ophelia Thesis's definition of girls as a distinctly vulnerable group in relation to media. That said, because this book is about the cultural production of girlhood, most of the examples I use below at least implicitly allow me to reflect on girlhood and most often come from girl students.

"But It Was a Big Part!" The Analysis Is in the Details

The students' ability to notice details came through especially clearly in one group performance of a scene from *Wizards*. The group took the prompt "create a scene from a television show" to mean "duplicate," such that their performance was extremely accurate in its reproduction of the original scene. While planning their performance, they thought carefully about how to use costume to portray the characters accurately. After their performance, classmates asked them why they chose to leave out particular parts of the episode, revealing that they also knew the text extremely well. Thus, here I am suggesting that the act of knowing a text in intricate detail is itself a form of analysis.

More specifically, many students implicitly employed genre and/ or narrative analysis when describing details, although they did not label it as such. For example, one student showed she understood how generic conventions produce humor when she said, "Sabrina is funny because she usually gets into trouble [and then] fixes it with magic." And Rachel[30] praised what I would call adventure stories for their narrative structure:

SARAH: Why do you like stories that are so complicated or "wrapped up," as you said it?[31]

RACHEL: Because it gives more tang to the story.

SARAH: Why do you like a story that has tang?

RACHEL: Because if it was a very plaid [sic] story and it didn't have enough interacting then it wouldn't be as good as one with tang.

SARAH: You described tang, but what do you like about it?

RACHEL: It makes me be excited for what's happening in the next part or the next part.

Here, Rachel creates her own analytical vocabulary in order to express her ideas about narrative structure and tone, to make clear her understanding of the fast pace of adventure narratives with "tang."

While their ability to use what I would call close textual analysis to describe structure, genre, and narrative matches a typical definition of media criticism, I would argue that the intensity of their attention to detail is, in and of itself, a form of analysis in that it provided them with unequivocal evidence to support their arguments. At times, I was slow to realize just how analytical their attention to details was. For example, after we watched an episode of *Sabrina* in which Sabrina's class goes on a fieldtrip to Salem, Massachusetts, I asked what themes or "lessons" they saw in the episode. While in Salem, Sabrina's class role-plays as "Puritans," including accusing both Sabrina and her friend Jenny of being witches. Jenny has lost the evidence that she is not a witch: she discards the piece of paper that states her role on the field trip—townsperson—when disposing of a piece of gum (rather than using the gum wrapper). As a result, Jenny must stand trial. While defending both Jenny and herself, Sabrina learns to accept herself as "different" (an actual witch who has to hide her identity because of mortals' prejudice) and even gives a speech to her classmates (i.e., the audience) about stereotyping and why being different is not "bad." When the episode concluded, in response to my question about what "lessons" the episode taught, one girl offered what I (mis)interpreted as an overly literal answer:

> ELLA: [The lesson is that you should] spit your gum in a wrapper.
> SARAH: [good-natured laughter]
> ELLA: [defensively, and probably hurt] But it was a big part!
> SARAH: [apologetically] Right. It was a key narrative element that moved the story forward.

My point here is that Ella's attention to detail meant she noticed the exact moment in the text that set up the entire problem of the episode: she knew that if Jenny had thrown away her gum in the wrapper instead of in the piece of paper that confirmed she was a townsperson (not a witch), the story could not have moved forward. Thus, while I thought the moral of the episode in which Sabrina has to deal with anti-witch hysteria was something like "accept yourself for who you are" or "don't be prejudiced," Ella did not focus on those predictable morals. For her, the "moral" of the story was about the very structure of the text, about how the story was told more than about the story itself. She simply was uninterested in the aspect of the show that the Ophelia Thesis might identify as "good" for her. Instead, she focused on her understanding of the narrative structure, which of course is a key aspect of scholarly media criticism.

"Why Does TV Rot Your Brain?" Questions as a Form of Analysis

I invited the students to ask questions of me about media, and they took to this request with relish (unlike many of the other requests I made), asking question after question. I would argue, then, that not only the questions they ask of media but also the act of questioning are a dimension of their analytical activity. Some of the questions were about media as a global industry:

> Why did they do that thing in February where they make your TVs [digital rather than analog]?
> What's the country with the most TV factories in it?

Other questions were about how media technology works:

> When they make a movie . . . do they . . . film one part and then . . . take a break, because . . . in different movies it's day for thirty minutes and [then] it's night?
> Is there a similarity [in] the build of the television and the radio?

A few students also challenged me by asking me questions about myself:

> Which kind of computer do you like better [Apple or PC]?
> Why do you study media?

Perhaps my favorite question was one that challenged the invisible parents in the room: "Why does TV rot your brain?" While the student who asked this could have meant, "How does it happen?" or "Why do adults think that?" either way, she was reflecting back to the (imagined) speaking parent/teacher, challenging that adult to explain her/himself. Here I want to draw attention to the way this question challenges the idea that media are inherently "bad." Really, why is it that we assume media rot our children's brains? In fact, I would argue that the many, many questions these third graders ask of media are evidence that their brains are not rotten and that, at least at times, media encourage inquisitive thinking. Given that the assumption that "TV rots our brains" is a non-gender-specific version of "media lower girls' self-esteem," by extension I would hypothesize that for some girls media do not necessarily lower their self-esteem but instead provide a context in which to ask questions such as "Why [do adults think] media lower my self-esteem?" or "Why do girls on TV spend so much time thinking about their fashion and bodies?"

In short, through their questions, the students revealed analytical thinking about many aspects of media, from its role in globalization, to details of media technology, to assumptions behind adult opinions about media. And through these questions the students analytically took apart both media and common assumptions about media.

"I Don't Really Get It, Like Are We Writing Stories?" Creativity as Analysis

SOPHIA: I just want to do a comic. I feel like drawing right now.

In response to my prompt to "create a scene from a television show," one group merged characters from two different Disney shows (*Wizards* and *Suite Life of Zack and Cody* [2005–2008]/*Suite Life on Deck* [2008–2011], hereafter *Suite Life*) into an original performance. When I praised them for their ability to create an original story while still maintaining the consistency of the characters, one girl commented, "We just squeezed them in so they would fit," after which a student from the audience commented, "They're like puzzle pieces." Here the students not only put the puzzle together but also created its form. Thus the students' ability to bring creative invention together with meticulous character consistency reveals their analytical understanding of genre, narrative, character, and media culture, including the Disney TV formula.

LeAnn's work during unit 4 best exemplifies this productive tension between creativity and analysis, and also implicitly addresses issues of gendered power in relation to media and the family. When I insisted that she write about media, she repeatedly said she did not want to, before then writing an essay titled "What I Like about TV." Here is her "essay"—which is also a creative fantasy—in full:

I like TV because I don't have to do it by myself. All I do is press the switch with the remote and push in 5 and then 7 [Disney is on channel 57 in her town]. That's all I have to do with the TV, but when someone changes the channel when I'm in the bathroom I get so mad I scream at the person so loud I can almost break a glass that is made of glass. It is so cool when it happens! That's why I like TV.

At first, LeAnn's description feels literal ("I push 5 and then 7"), although already humorous and cheeky (not "I push 57," but "I push 5 and then 7"), and maybe even worrisome: she is happy the remote saves her some labor and she yells at her family. Is she a media-damaged girl, glued to the couch and addicted to the Disney Channel? Yet by the end of the essay it seems clear that she has written a fantasy of empowerment about her relationship to media. One way to understand her fantasy is as resistant to my resolve that she write about media. While she did so, she also created a scene—wrote a screenplay—thereby making media as much as she wrote about it. Further, her story can be understood to be about the power of her voice over and against both the medium and the technology of television. Thus her essay goes from a girl who barely wants to lift a finger (Ophelia?) to a girl who has a voice so powerful it can (almost) break glass. In LeAnn's story, television enables her power. And by writing her story, she addresses the relationship between television and power and how it intersects with her, her place in her family, and her relationship to a school project—writing about media—that she had made very clear she really did not want to do. In all these ways, her creative story works as an analysis of both media and social power.

"I Think It's Kind of Unfair": Gender Analysis

Noticing details, asking questions, and being creative—what I am calling analytical activities—are all powerful tools used by the students to engage with media. While the students used these methods to touch on a variety of topics, they spent a great deal of time talking about the relationship between media and cultural definitions of gender and girlhood, sometimes prompted by me, but often initiated by them. In fact, the very first comment made by a student (a boy) during our first group discussion on the very first day was "I hate *High School Musical* because it's girly," after which several of the boys laughed, seemingly in agreement. Later that same hour, Zoe made a similar comment: "I don't like *Ben 10* because it's boyish." Then, in a side comment, another girl said, "Well, you like a lot of boy shows." Arguably this girl was policing Zoe's relationship to gender in a troubling way by reminding her of her tomboy status (an issue to which I return below), yet at the same time both girls were expressing an analytical attitude toward gender, both in terms

of understanding that it plays a role in media production and marketing ("girls' shows" vs. "boys' shows") and in terms of defining their own
relationship to gender as either somewhat fluid (Zoe as able to cross
between girl and boy shows) or as fixed (the second girl's implied difference between Zoe and herself [and other girls]).

When I began to realize that students were categorizing some shows
as girlish and others as boyish, I asked them to tell me how those shows
define girls and boys. The students answered that girls like "romance"
and "sparkles" and are sensitive; and boys like "aliens," "Spider-Man,"
"monsters," "evil against good," "heavy metal," and "violent [shows]." As
Liz put it, girls did not vote for the class to watch the boy show Poké-
mon, "because it's too violent and there are like aliens, monsters, [and]
thingamabobers that fight each other." Other students offered comparisons, suggesting that "boys like action and girls like calmer shows," and
"we [girls] like musicals and singing and boys like loud rock music."

The students also made the point that the television advertisements
we watched were gender-coded (dolls for girls and dinosaur toys for
boys) and defined girl and boy colors: girls—pink, purple, red, white,
blonde; boys—brown, green, white, indigo. When I asked the students
about this, girls said that "boys have ugly colors" and girls have "pret-
tier" colors, while boys said that boys have "cool" colors and girls have
"ugly" colors. Other students, however, critiqued the binary, with one
girl saying "I think it's kind of unfair that they think girls only would
like pink and boys would only like green."

Beyond the students' skill at easily identifying how television represents gendered categories and their willingness to assert the way their
own pleasures and displeasures aligned or differed from them, at other
times students challenged or even rejected what they understood to be
both television's and their classmates' definitions of girl and boy. For
example, Sophia pointed out that, in fact, Ben 10 has a girl character,
and thus even though "people would think that it's boyish . . . it's not
really." Additionally, when a girl suggested that the Danimals Yogurt
Crush Cup advertisement we watched was for boys because "boys like
to crush," a boy responded with "So do girls!" Similarly, when the class
discussed a PJ Sparkles doll advertisement, a boy said, "I disagree with
sparkles [being for girls] because I like them and I know other people
who are boys who like them."

The challenges the students raised to television's gendering process emerged in particular during our discussion of Selena Gomez in both *Wizards* and as a star more generally. For example, Peter said, "I don't really like her acting." When I asked him why, he said, "Her acting is too girly. . . . She's [over]acting." Many of the girls in the classroom objected to this, drawing attention to how girls and boys evaluate representations of girls differently. Alyssa offered a very specific defense, insisting, "It's not her. It's what she's supposed to be doing." Here, Alyssa leaves an opening for a critique of "girly" acting, but she also insists the fault would lie with the producers of the show, not with the actor, Selena Gomez, of whom she seemed protective. Implicitly, here, Alyssa expresses awareness of a distinction between a media-produced star persona and the human being around whom that persona is built.[32] Thus her critique is of the media's production of gender through Gomez's star persona, and it illustrates at least some understanding of how the celebrity system works.

Importantly, this critical attitude toward media's production of gender emerged regardless of whether an adult was present, illustrating just how important this issue was to the students. For example, during an audiotaped conversation, three girls developed a critique of false and unrealistic media femininity:

SOPHIA: You know, Hannah Montana lip-synchs.
KYRA: If we had a Hannah Montana show right here, and I could teleport right here, I would.
SOPHIA: She records her voice, and then she lip-synchs.
ELLA: She lip-synchs, yeah.
KYRA: Yeah, she lip-synchs, but her voice is still amazing.
ELLA: Yeah, but she lip-synchs.
SOPHIA: Barbie's feet would be about that big.

While I have only a sound recording to work with, my guess is that Sophia gestured to a physically impossible small size when referring to Barbie's feet, revealing a critical attitude toward the cultural production of femininity. That she closed out this debate about Hannah Montana with a comment about Barbie reveals that the critique she was making of a girl phenom lip-synching was a critique not only (or at all?) of "bad" performing but (also) of the media's production of femininity.

While the vast majority of both the girls' and the boys' discussion of gender was critical of media constructions of femininity and masculinity, one girl did write a short essay in which she articulates a pleasurable relationship to a media girl. In response to my prompt to "write about what you like about media," Sophia wrote:

> I like *Spiderwick* because there are so many fantastic undiscovered creatures like fairies, the phooka, elves, trolls, and many other amazing creatures. I also like that the girl Mallory is good at sword fighting, not the boys; because the boys are usually the ones that are good at sword fighting. *Spiderwick* is a cool and amazing book/movie.

I start this section on gender analysis with an example of how a student policed Zoe's relationship to "girls' shows" and "boys' shows," and I end the section with Sophia's pleasure in Mallory's gender-crossing behavior in order to draw attention to the complexity of the students' understanding of and relationship to media depictions of gender. Not only are they aware of the media's production of gendered categories and the way those categories function as marketing tools, but they often critique, reject, or rework those categories, especially in terms of the production of femininity. Further, at times, they seek out alternative versions of gendered identities, with girls sometimes taking pleasure in gender-crossing characters and boys sometimes insisting on their right to enjoy sparkles. And, most importantly for my interest in the girl media critic, all of this illustrates not just their ability but also their commitment to thinking analytically about media.

A Series of Complications

Certainly, the students did do the analytical thinking, talking, performing, creating, and occasionally writing I describe in the previous section. However, there were several aspects of the project that were not as neat and did not appear quite so clearly as "analytical thinking." In particular, (1) when I asked them directly about being "like" televisual girls one student did not entirely reject the Ophelia Thesis; (2) a few of them offered critiques of racism in media but did not also seem to understand race as socially constructed (as they did for gender); and

(3) a few of the students returned repeatedly to resistant and confrontational approaches to my overall goal of defining them as "media critics." In this final section, then, I discuss these three issues in turn in order to complicate my claims about girls' analytical engagement with media.

Being Like Media Girls

During some small-group discussions, I purposefully asked leading questions designed to help me disprove the Ophelia Thesis. For example:

> SARAH: What do you do when [TV] makes you mad or you feel like it's unfair [because of how it represents girls and boys]?
> SOPHIA: I talk to the TV, I say it's stupid, I switch the channel, I turn the TV off. Well, I usually don't turn off the TV.
> KYRA: I say cuss words in my head. Sometimes.
> ELLA: Yeah, me too.
> SARAH: If you yell at [TV] or you talk to someone else about it, what kind of things do you say?
> GIRL: It's stupid.
> SOPHIA: I hate this show. It's really irritating because it's being unfair!

Here, the girls were clear that television offers problematic representations of girls, and they had plenty of strategies for rejecting those depictions. Thus they agreed with the Ophelia Thesis that televisual representations of girls are problematic; but they also challenged the thesis by engaging a powerful voice in response to those depictions, rather than falling into self-doubt and depression.

Not all parts of our conversation were so clear-cut, however. For example, when I pursued the topic further, Zoe reported an unpleasant experience:

> SARAH: What happens to you if you [girls] watch boys' shows or if girls like dinosaurs or boys like sparkles?
> ALYSSA: Sometimes girls make fun of boys who kind of like girls' stuff, and boys make fun of girls who kind of like boys' stuff.
> SARAH: You get made fun of?

ZOE: Somebody said that I'm a tomboy just because I was wearing boys'
     shoes. But those were really just the best shoes that I had for now.
SARAH: What did you do when they called you a tomboy?
ZOE: I didn't do nothing. William said, "Just [because] she's wearing boys'
     shoes doesn't mean she's a tomboy."
SARAH: Do you care if you're a tomboy?
ZOE: No.
SARAH: Do any of you kind of like the feeling if you do something [the
     media tell you] you're not supposed to do?
SEVERAL: Yes.
GIRL: It feels good.
SARAH: How does it feel good? Why does it feel good?
KYRA: You stick out in your own special way.
ALYSSA: Especially for girls, because they kind of feel strong, smart.
ZOE: A girl can really do more stuff than a boy can in the dress-up way
     because girls can dress up as boys but if a boy dressed up as a [girl] it
     would be more weird.
ALYSSA: Girls are more of both.
GIRL: It's harder for boys to break the rules.

In this exchange not only do the girls reveal that they take pleasure
(rather than, as the Ophelia Thesis would have it, pain) in their difference from televisual girls, but they know that pleasure comes from
resistance—for example, from rejecting the media definition of boys as
strong and smart (unlike girls). Further, they understand that "cross-
dressing" is not the same for boys and girls, that girls wearing clothes
understood to be for boys is generally easier than boys wearing clothes
understood to be for girls. And, again, they seem to take pleasure in
the fact that they feel relatively comfortable crossing those gender
boundaries. Yet, Zoe's comment reveals how economic class is also
embedded in the freedom to cross gender lines. For her, "choosing"
to wear boys' shoes is about what she has, not about what she wants.
While she does not seem to mind being associated with boys, she does
understand that this is meant as an insult, one that for her is about
both gender and class. Thus this exchange reveals not just their critique
of problematic gender representations and their engagement in alternative pleasures, but also how media and social expectations intersect

with girls' everyday lives in not only gendered but also classed contexts. As a whole, however, the students did not pick up or expand on Zoe's point about socioeconomic class and its relationship to gendered expectations in her everyday life (nor did I). To put this another way, in this exchange they (we) did not seem capable of intersectional feminist media analysis.

Much to my dismay, at one moment the Ophelia Thesis assumption that media's impossible body standards cause low self-esteem did seem to hold true. Kyra, in the following exchange, gave me pause:

SARAH: Do you ever feel bad if you aren't the way the TV says you're supposed to be?

SOPHIA: No.

KYRA: Sometimes, but . . .

ELLA: Rarely.

SARAH: Kyra, you said sometimes. When you do feel bad, how does it make you feel bad?

KYRA: On some shows they make it like they have perfect hair, and I feel bad because they have perfect hair and not everyone does. But it's not their real hair.

SARAH: So, you know it's not real, and we talked [in an earlier session] about how they make the hair look perfect like that, using lighting and makeup and all that stuff, right? And yet it still makes you feel bad because not everybody has hair like that?

KYRA: Yeah.

SARAH: Do you sometimes think, "Oh, I wish I had hair like that?"

KYRA: Yeah.

SARAH: Do you ever try to change yourself to be like the perfect, not-real hair on TV?

KYRA: Yeah, sometimes. I try to convince my parents to go shopping with me.

During this dialogue, Kyra seems to illustrate the danger of media. She knows it is impossible to look like the girls on television, but she feels bad about herself and tries to copy them anyway. Further, she fulfills her role as a televisually produced consuming citizen in pursuit of the unattainable by pressuring her parents to take her shopping. I went home after this conversation feeling depressed. Despite their myriad analytical skills, despite the fact that they understand the constructed nature of both television and gender, nevertheless at least this one girl was trapped by the pull of glamour and desire. Or so it initially seemed. The next day, I asked her about it again.

> SARAH: Kyra, you were really smart about this. You said that you know that [girls on TV are] made up, but you still kind of feel like you want to be that way. You kind of feel both ways.
> KYRA: Also I do want to be on TV and famous. I want to be like Selena Gomez, but for most other people I just want to be famous like them and on TV.

Here, Kyra still reveals the pull of glamour and desire; she still wants to be "like" Selena Gomez in particular, perhaps to have her hair, body, family, ambiguously ethnic identity, and/or fame. Selena Gomez still represents an idealized (but ultimately unattainable) subject position for Kyra. Yet Kyra does not express this in a passive way, nor does she seem to simply objectify her own body. Rather, her desire to be like Selena Gomez is at least in part linked to an active pursuit of a career goal. My argument here is not, "See, isn't it great that she wants to be on television!" but instead that the way she understands her desire to be (like) a girl on television is not to become an unattainable body but to develop a career that involves actually producing media, participating in the production of famous femininity.

Overall, then, the girls' discussions of their relationships to media reveal a complex and sometimes fraught experience. They may develop career goals that require them to engage in commodity consumption in pursuit of a body they know they will never attain. They may feel the need to distance themselves from the shows they enjoy. They may face ridicule that is embedded in not only gender but also class identity. And they may resort to saying cuss words in their heads. That they somehow know they better keep those particular words in their heads (rather than speaking them aloud) suggests that—despite the critical distance from media I found in most of these girls' comments—it is not entirely safe or acceptable for them to reject feminine versions of media girlhood.

The Racialized Body

While the students discussed gender often and with relish, the same was not the case for race. Instead, when a few students brought up race, other students either did not respond or responded in a way that frustrated the original speaker. Further, none of the students' written or creative work addressed race or racialization. This difficulty in discussing race was not caused by lack of diversity in the classroom. In fact, more than half the girls in the class were of color (five out of nine).[33] And the shows the students discussed the most and drew on for their creative performances illustrate what Angharad Valdivia calls "Disney diversity":[34] *Suite Life* includes London Tipton, an Asian American girl portrayed by Brenda Song, and *Wizards* is about a mixed race Mexican/Italian American family.

There are certainly many possible reasons for the students' not discussing race even when consuming it: for example, the fact that it is culturally acceptable to identify and discuss a person's gender based on appearance but culturally unacceptable to discuss race in the same way could make the students reticent to bring up race; and the fact that kids' television shows return again and again to narrative situations structured around gender but rarely address race in the same direct way might make race more invisible for the students.

More to the point for this project, however, I would argue that the fact that the students seem to understand race to be primarily about skin tone and hair texture makes it more difficult for them to understand it—indeed interferes with them being able to understand it—as culturally constructed in the way they understand gender to be. For example, while planning their creative performance, a group of girls discussed which character each student could play, based on appearance. (No adult was present during this conversation.):

KYRA: Let's just decide [on our characters], and whoever is most like that person will be that person.
ELLA: You should be Maddie [a Caucasian character portrayed by Ashley Tisdale on *Suite Life*].
SOPHIA: I don't look anything like that.

KYRA: I don't look like Alex [the mixed race Mexican American character
she planned to play from *Wizards*].

ELLA: I don't look like London [the character she planned to play from
Suite Life].

KYRA: I could be Max [a boy character from *Wizards*].

ELLA: I don't want to do any boys.

SOPHIA: I'll be one.

KYRA: I want to be Max.

ELLA: Fine.

SOPHIA: I sort of do dress like Alex, though. I usually wear pants with skirts.

KYRA: She doesn't wear pants with skirts.

SOPHIA: You don't think I look like any character, do you?

KYRA: I can think of one.

SOPHIA: What? [with distrust in her voice]

KYRA: Corbin. Corbin Bleu. Chad [an African American character from
High School Musical]. [Also,] the one who sings "What It Takes" [in
the Disney Channel movie *Camp Rock* (2008)]. Not Alyson Stoner.
Alyson Stoner has brownish-blonde hair. [You] look like Alyson
Stoner's friend; the one who sings "What It Takes."[35]

SOPHIA: I don't look anything like her. Just because I have [this kind of
body] doesn't mean I look like every [person of color].[36]

KYRA: But it's not really what you look like. This isn't about what you
look like.

This exchange is complex and contradictory. At first, the girls try
to match themselves to their characters by gender and race, but this
immediately breaks down when Kyra wants to portray a boy[37] and when
they cannot find a girl character that "matches" what they perceive to
be Sophia's race. And the same girl who begins the dialogue by suggesting they match themselves to the characters ends the discussion by
saying that it is not about what they look like. Nevertheless, during the
debate, Sophia becomes upset and offended by the way they racialize
her as "Other," going so far as to suggest she portray any character they
can think of with brown skin or curly dark hair, regardless of gender
or whether they were planning to incorporate that particular character
and show into their skit. There is a tension here, then, between some
girls' essentialized assumption that race is defined by skin and hair

and other girls' critique of the way that definition of race flattens out individualized differences among people. Yet, setting aside Sophia for a moment, the critique Kyra offers is based in a postracial dismissal of the debate when she says, "This isn't about what you look like." In short, while Sophia had as developed an analytical relationship to race as she and nearly all the other students had to gender, she was alone in her ability, willingness, and confidence to understand and critique the constructed nature of race on television and its relationship to the racism she sometimes experienced in her own life. For most students, race was a nonissue, at best articulated as a postracial colorblindness, which is particularly troubling given how analytical students were about so many other aspects of media.

Resistance as Analysis

While most students did their best to answer the questions I asked and to participate in the activities I set up, four girls in particular often seemed to resist me. In this section, I explore the possibility of reading their resistance both as an analytical mode of understanding media and as a way to reveal some of the limitations of this project's investment in proving that girls are media critics.

Zoe spoke often of Freddy (from *A Nightmare on Elm Street*) and Jason (from *Friday the 13th*). While, of course, I do not know her motivation, I had the feeling that she raised this issue (at least in part) to challenge me and the classroom teacher, to push the boundaries not only of what we were defining as "media" but also of what I *really* meant when I said, "You can write about any media you want." Did I mean she could actually write about R-rated, violent films? The classroom teacher, in fact, picked up on Zoe's resistance, stating openly that Zoe's interest in Freddy and Jason made her "uncomfortable because I think you're way more special than to be spending a lot of time dealing with that stuff." But the teacher also went on to validate Zoe's interest and to encourage her to figure out what she wanted to say about these characters: "But if that's something that's very powerful and meaningful to you and you think that it's important to write about and you have important things to say about it, then I think it's worth it because that's part of who you are."

Zoe began several projects related to Freddy and Jason. While trying to accommodate my request for analytical writing, she declared that she would write a comparison of the two characters. When I did not respond by suggesting a more "appropriate" topic (which I think she expected) she got my attention again and said, "When I was talking about Freddy Krueger versus Jason, they're not really alike, so I'm going to do their differences. Because Jason is afraid of water and Freddy Krueger is afraid of fire." I ignored what I thought might be her attempt to shock me and responded with, "OK, great. That's still a comparison, but you're saying how they are different."

While I am portraying Zoe as confrontational, I also want to acknowledge that I think she really was interested in these characters, and that, as her teacher articulated, she had something to say about them. She and LeAnn started working together, in fact, on a story combining Freddy and Jason with characters from *High School Musical* (hereafter *HSM*, one of LeAnn's favorite Disney products). The following dialogue partially took place when they were working on their own, without an adult, and when I did enter the conversation it is clear that at the time I entirely missed the valuable, creative, and analytical work they were doing:

> ZOE: Hey, I've got an idea. You could stick these guys [Freddy, Jason, and characters from *HSM*] together.
>
> LEANN: We could make a book of different people.
>
> ZOE: Yeah, come on! Let's go tell her! Come on!!!!!!
>
> ZOE [TO ME, WITH EXCITEMENT]: We want to put our stories together and make a book about it.
>
> SARAH: Maybe. Let me come talk to the two of you next.
>
> [RETURNING TO THEIR PRIVATE DISCUSSION]
>
> ZOE: And in chapter 6, when those college students [referring to *HSM* characters], we'll just say they're college students in this story. And these people meet those college students and they try to go after them. And at the very end . . .
>
> LEANN: Freddy tries to get in their dreams.
>
> ZOE: Yeah.
>
> SARAH [JOINING THE CONVERSATION]: I don't understand how those two things go together.

ZOE: Because when I was watching *Freddy vs. Jason* there were college
students, and we're gonna say these college students are kids and they
defeat Freddy but not Jason. Jason wins. And some of the kids live.

LEANN: Some of them?

ZOE: Some.

LEANN: Oh.

SARAH: I want to encourage you to work separately. . . . But, if you really
have the same idea, go ahead and work together.

LEANN: *College Students versus Freddy and Jason.*

ZOE: No. *Freddy Krueger versus Jason versus College Students.*

LEANN: Are there going to be pictures?

ZOE: No, because some of the things will be too violent to write about and
draw about.

In retrospect, I notice that through their creative combination of the
teen/adult product of horror films and the tween product of the *HSM*
universe, Zoe and LeAnn were (1) challenging me to live up to my claim
that they could write about anything they wanted (again, Zoe reminded
me that I was not supposed to want her to write about this with her
final comment about violence), (2) really delighting in thinking about
their favorite media, and (3) illustrating that they knew both the horror
genre and the *HSM* universe well enough to play with it, capitalizing
on the aspects of these two seemingly dissimilar genres that actually
do intersect. Thus, for me, this example illustrates both that the girls
were trying to confront me—to push the boundaries of the project in
a way that embraced media they understood to be unequivocally bad
for them—and that they were simply participating in the project with
relish, drawing on their fannish experiences to imagine a new narrative
that both drew and commented on the generic conventions at hand.
In other words, while I was oblivious to it at the time, they revealed
analytical thinking, while also implicitly showing me that they understood—and wanted to test—a cultural narrative that defined them as
vulnerable in relation to at least some media.

Alyssa also stood out as a resistant participant, although, like Zoe and
LeAnn, she was also highly involved in the project. Over two days, the
entire class spent time watching television together: advertisements on
the first day and two different shows on the second day. Both days, Alyssa

expressed interest in watching the advertisements/shows, rather than talking about them. For example, in an aside to a friend while we discussed the advertisements she said, "I just want to watch it." Later in the day, she said, "Are we still going to watch the shows?" When I replied, "Tomorrow," she said, "Can we watch some more [advertisements]?" When we did watch more advertisements, she said, "Can we watch the whole thing?" (i.e., the show surrounding the advertisement I had shown.) Then, the following day, as soon as I turned off the episode of *Wizards*, she said, "Can we watch *Sabrina* now?" Importantly, Alyssa often had analytical and insightful things to say. And while she did not initially choose to participate in unit 4, as did Zoe and LeAnn, she did choose to join the group discussions that emerged at the very end of the project. Thus, Alyssa's desire for more and constant "watching" is in no way evidence of a lack of an analytical relationship to media. Given that she did not elaborate on her desire for more television, however, I can do no more than leave it at this: one of the most consistently analytical students in the class made most explicit her desire to watch rather than talk (or worse yet for her, write). Is there pleasure in taking an analytical perspective while watching, but only in the privacy of her mind? Is there relief in escaping the analytical discussion I was pushing, in escaping her (perhaps exhausting) insights about the shows? What does it mean that my bringing television into the classroom meant for her that she could ask for more, and more, and more? Unfortunately, these are not questions I am able to answer based on the way I designed and carried out the project. And, in fact, because they are about this girl's preference *not* to talk or write about media ultimately they are unanswerable. To ask her these questions would be to ignore her preference for watching over talking/writing.

Lisa was also resistant at times, perhaps the most of anyone. For example, she got frustrated with me when I listed shows that got more than one vote from the students and not a single one of the shows she had suggested was included. With disbelief and what sounded like a bit of irritation in her voice, she said, "Are these all of the choices?" When the class discussed Disney shows such as *Suite Life* and *Wizards* she would ask questions that revealed she had not seen the shows and did not automatically understand what was happening in the other groups' performances. This, itself, is a form of analysis—the questions she asked drew attention to what both the students and I were taking for granted about the worlds created by the shows. And, perhaps in the most resistant move, she never did lend me her notebook, even though she was clearly one of the students in the class who really enjoyed writing. Lisa, for me, is a reminder that no matter how invested I was in discovering and supporting their analytical and critical insights; no matter how careful I was to pay attention to issues of gender, race, and class; no matter how supportive I was of their various interests, the fact that I centered the media texts that were most "popular" meant that I was contributing to the ubiquity of Disney and commercialized tween culture and therefore, at least in part, I was perpetuating the way in which these media exclude. I did not provide a context, however, in which Lisa was able and/or felt comfortable expressing this—or any other—critique of the project itself.

* * *

In short, Sophia, Kyra, Zoe, LeAnn, Alyssa, and Lisa help me to imagine idiosyncratic analytical activities taking place beyond the more typical categories of analysis I found (i.e., details as evidence; understanding of narrative, gender, and the star system as structure; questioning media; creating new media; and challenging gendered representation). But also, in retrospect, they help me to see some of the limitations in the project: the way the structure I set up did not encourage critical attention to mediated racialization or to social and economic class; my lack of attention to the relationship between media and some girls' commodity consumption; the lack of space for the pleasure some girls take in media violence; and, perhaps most challenging to me as an individual, my surprise that even girls who made clear their "analytical abilities" in other contexts at certain points would refuse to engage me and perhaps even disliked the media project. These complications, then, both reveal the depth and complexity of the girls' analytical thinking and remind me that that thinking belongs to them and not to me.

Conclusion

The Ophelia Thesis includes two major anxieties about girls and media: (1) media push a hyper-sexuality that is damaging for girls, and (2) by setting up impossible expectations, media decrease girls' self-esteem.

The first concern about media—hyper-sexualization—I purposefully did not address, in part because it would have made obtaining IRB approval very difficult. Additionally, these students were mostly eight and nine years old and therefore are a bit younger than the endangered Ophelia. Yet many of the Ophelia books emphasize, for example, that sexy adult clothing is marketed to girls "as young as four."[38] Thus, the fact that these students never discussed sexy clothing (although the girls did discuss fashion more generally) suggests they may be somewhat oblivious to the adult reading of sexuality in children's media. In other words, I am not making the more common arguments either that media sexualization of girls is dangerous or that girls can participate in mediated sexuality in a playful and productive way. Rather, I am arguing that the media's sexualization of girls may simply be irrelevant, at least for these particular children at this particular age.

In terms of self-esteem, only Kyra seemed to express decreased self-esteem because of a desire to be like Selena Gomez even though she knew that Gomez's image was constructed and therefore unattainable. Yet, when we returned to the subject she matter-of-factly declared that she wanted to be on television. Hence, at least in part, her desire "to be like" Gomez was a desire to be a celebrity like her, not to be a girl like her. From this perspective, I could argue this reveals an *increased* self-esteem in that she had very ambitious career plans. And, while I could argue that Sophia expressed some decreased self-esteem because of her encounters with racism from both her classmates and media representations, she had such a clear sense of herself and such a strong ability to challenge these ideas that "lack of self-esteem" hardly seems fitting. Certainly, her comments were critical of others' comments and of media representations, but not of herself.

Thus, in part, I have disproved the Ophelia Thesis: these girls were not hyper-sexualized, nor did they have low self-esteem. More important to this chapter than disproving the Ophelia Thesis, however, is emphasizing that things that at first glance might not seem to be analytical in fact are ways for the students to express their ideas; whether that means thinking about the minutia of a gum wrapper, asking questions rather than making statements, creating a performance, or even writing, as LeAnn did, a paragraph about the power of her voice that is resistant to me, to her family, and to school, and yet also profoundly insightful about the addiction of Disney, the strength of emotion, and issues of power and control. Further, I want to highlight the particularly nuanced perspective the students had on media depictions of girls and gender. Based on all these girls' (and boys') analytical activities, I would argue, any media literacy research or program that wants to "work with" or "help" or "empower" girls in relation to media has to start with the assumption that girls are already media critics who can set the terms of the conversation in ways that—rather than necessarily disprove the Ophelia Thesis—make it beside the point.

Finally, most important to this book overall, I would argue that this chapter adds to the many alternative girls in media culture that I discuss in previous chapters. Who are the alternative girls in this chapter? They are non-gender-specific girls who engage in media analysis using the same basic skills and strategies as do non-gender-specific boys. They are girls who have the analytical capacity to grasp the complexity of a text through their attention to detail, insatiable questions, and creative play. They are girls who know television femininity is constructed, and who sometimes use that knowledge to reflect on how they can build a career. They are girls who find racism in the media and among their friends untenable. They are girls who find a variety of ways to resist the demands of their visiting teacher. In short, these girls are media critics who use their specific analytical abilities to articulate persuasive insights about both media structure and gender representation.

Conclusion

Girlhood Rethought

CORBI: So, what, are you, like, alternative now?
BLISS: Alternative to what?
—*Whip It* (2009)

As I sat in the lobby of a Melbourne, Australia, airport hotel, trying to put the finishing touches on this conclusion, news of the horrific shooting in Newtown, Connecticut, played almost continuously on the television over the bar. While I tried to tune out the sound, as well as my own pain about the deaths and my aching desire to see and touch my own children, the image of a beautiful young girl with strawberry blonde hair and freckles flashed across the television screen. She sat with her mother, speaking to an interviewer about having survived. She smiled a bit as her mother looked on with what seemed to be love, pride, and gratitude. I couldn't help but wonder, "Why this girl?" Why do we have to imagine the horror of the shooting through the image of this beautiful little blonde girl who survived? Days later, back home in Salt Lake City, Utah, while trying to enjoy a rare lunch with my father who was on his annual winter-break visit, the photo on the cover of the local newspaper sitting on the table next to us caught my attention: a lovely blonde girl smiled up at the camera (and me). The caption informed me that this was one of the children killed in Newtown. I wondered, "Didn't boys also die in this tragic event?" "Didn't adults die?" Why, again, did the image of a little blonde-white girl have to manage our care about Newtown?[1]

I am certain the media makers who chose these girls as representatives were not seeking to elicit the questions I was asking. Rather, I suspect they were drawing on the long-standing use of young white girlhood—which many scholars have established and which I discuss throughout this book—to produce and deepen pathos, to give audiences a familiar way of processing and coming to terms with the unthinkable, and to simplify the story by distilling it to an image of a pure and vulnerable social subject. My questions were a reaction against media using young girls exploitatively in this way; against the lack of attention to non-blonde girls (and boys and adults) and hence their absence, deferral, and therefore representational meaninglessness in relation to the tragedy; and against the phenomenally reductive analysis of the causes and consequences of mass killings[2] we get when dominant media—the media that have the power to appear on bar televisions and newspapers discarded at cafés—give us only the image of the little blonde-white girl as the social subject who matters.

This book offers a two-pronged response to ubiquitous white girlhood, of which the Newtown girls I discuss here are only the very most recent example: (1) it draws on empirical methods to document the dominance of white heteronormative girls in media and (2) it then turns away from those girlhoods to highlight and center the many other girls who appear within media culture. Building on and contributing to previous girls' studies research that documents and theorizes whiteness, heteronormativity, and adoration/disdain as overarching themes in contemporary representations of girls, this book addresses the can-do/at-risk girl, the mean girl, the hyper-sexualized girl, the vulnerable and in-need-of-protection white middle-class girl (Ophelia), the loved because we are "postrace" black girl, the gamma girl, the crash-and-burn girl, and the girl star/celebrity. These are all girls who are either adored, abhorred, or (paradoxically) both. And they are all girls who are spectacularized: they are spectacles who are available for pleasurable consumption, who offer positive/negative role models that call for commodity consumption and neoliberal self-regulation, and who summon protection, discipline, and regulation by discourse, policy, law, parents, and teachers.

Nevertheless, this is only part of the picture. Other girls populate U.S. media culture—visible when, as this book does, one looks for them. Ambiguously ethnic mixed race girls, antiracist girls, feminist girls, black girls who *are* girls, can-do African American girls, sexual girls, girls who express productive and rational anger, girl media critics, queer girls, girls who take up social space, masculine girls, girls who make choices, girls who fly, girls who know that media construct femininity in ways that are impossible for a human body to achieve, girls who read television shows through minute details rather than focusing on a predictable "don't be a mean girl" morality, girls who fantasize about the power of their voice to break glass, girls who discuss and think about abortion, girls who take pleasure in the movement of their own bodies, girls who cross gender borders, and girls who stand up to violent men (sometimes escaping and sometimes dying). These alternative girls are at the heart of this book, at the center of my definition of spectacular girls, and the basis on which I construct my feminist girls' media studies methodology.

Admittedly, defining certain girls as alternative to a dominant runs the risk of producing a binary that reifies the dominance of the dominant. As Isaac Julien and Kobena Mercer argue, "The explanatory concept of 'otherness' distances and particularises ethnicity as something that happens far away."[3] To claim the status of "alternative" or "other" has the potential to reinscribe both center and periphery—thereby reproducing static, arbitrary, and discrete lines of difference outside time and place—rather than to challenge the logic that produces that philosophical polarization. Nonetheless, I take the risk of identifying "dominant" and "alternative" because I consider it crucial to document empirically the high frequency of white heteronormativity in U.S. media representations of girls. The inescapability of media representations of little blonde-white girls as the girls who matter is a form of dominance. As I show in chapter 2, by cataloging every girl to appear on the cover of *Time, Newsweek,* and *People* since 1990, not only are these girls everywhere in the mediascape, but when they appear in ways we cannot escape—such as on magazine covers at the checkout stand (and hotel bar televisions)—we have no choice but to give them our attention, even if only fleetingly or subconsciously. This is a dominance that requires critique. In other words, if I must give these media girls my attention, I will do so by acknowledging their existence: in fact, by documenting their statistical dominance; but I will also challenge the way gender, race, and sexuality are structured—indeed hardened, habitualized, and made meaningful—through them.

Importantly, however, we do not have to spend all of our analytical energy responding to dominant media girls. If critique includes only acknowledgment and challenge, then it runs the risk of reinforcing the dominant even if resisting it. Therefore, in this book, my primary critical response is to turn away from the dominant. I do this in three key ways. First, I simply look for something other than white heteronormativity in all media girlhoods. I employ a feminist lens and filter that persistently introduces an alternative perspective on the dominant, one that engages an intersectional critique interested—simultaneously and in correlation—in questions of race and sexuality. When looking through this lens, diverse girlhoods appear in the very heart of media culture. I take this approach in chapters 2 and 3 in particular. In chapter 2, I argue that when girls of color do appear on the cover of mass-market magazines they can (sometimes) rework race in the public imagination, and when mass-market magazines occasionally represent girls as making decisions and taking action outside a feminized can-do/at-risk binary, that binary is weakened. In chapter 3, I argue that even many films that are economically and critically successful offer—through their stars, characters, and narratives—versions of girlhood that challenge the can-do/at-risk binary, are queer, enjoy autoeroticism, make choices, and engage black girlish pleasure.

Second, in this book I turn away from dominant U.S. media girlhood by investigating multiple, diverse, and alternative types of media, as well as the relationship between actual girls and the media they encounter and consume. I take this approach in chapters 4, 5, and 6 in particular, turning to live/near-live television, alternative (queer and African American) and local media, and an ethnographic exploration of everyday third graders' analytical interactions with media representations of girls and gender. Importantly, the media I examine in these chapters are not just media that one has to dig for—such as, for example, the queer newspaper the *New York Blade* that I discuss in chapter 5 and that is now defunct. These are also media we encounter as a regular part of everyday life—such as, for example, live/near-live sports coverage that runs almost continually on television and the Internet, local newspapers that respond to events happening in our communities, and

the kinds of things children think and say about the media they continuously encounter. Thus I am not only turning away from dominant
media that have the capacity to invade our everyday lives and demand
our attention, but I am also thinking through the complexity of a variety of media forms (including dominant media), as well as the particularities of how some girls actually interact with media. In order for this
book to make an argument about girls in U.S. media culture, then, I
insist on looking at as large a mediascape as possible in as much detail
and with as much specificity as possible.

Third, having used both a critical feminist lens and multiple media
resources to locate alternative girls, the feminist girls' media studies
methodology I employ in this book insists on centering these other
girls. While acknowledging that they are not empirically the girls who
appear most often in the contemporary U.S. mediascape, nevertheless I
insist that these other (as in, other-than) girls are not "marginal"; they
are not girls hovering at the side. The feminist analytical methods I use
in this book make clear that, in fact, these girls are also spectacular and
spectacularized. Thus, just as I resistantly document the dominance of
white heteronormative girls, I also seek out, substantiate, suggest the
importance of, and give serious analytical attention to the many other
versions of girlhood that exist within media and celebrity culture. In
short, the argument of this book is that feminist girls' media studies—
and by extension all media studies—can and should not only examine
the center but, more important, also reframe what we talk about and
how we do so, thereby redefining the center of U.S. media culture itself.

Of course, many of the alternative girlhoods I discuss in this book
are not ideal from an antiracist, queer, feminist perspective. I am not
in pursuit of "better" representations. Rather, I emphasize that all the
representations I discuss in this book are part of the discursive production and spectacularization of cultural knowledge about and understandings of girlhood. Representations of girls often reinscribe, for
example, long-standing understandings of African Americans as necessarily poor (Gunn, Venus, Precious), unless they have pulled themselves up by their bootstraps (Venus, Sidibe), and race as only skin
deep and therefore easily put on or taken off (Gomez, Precious as universal). They also reinscribe the young white girl as profoundly innocent (Olive) and all girls as inevitably heterosexual (Gomez, Hudgens).

Yet representations of these girls also sometimes include, for example, explicit critiques of racism (Venus), articulations of queer AG identity (Gunn), autoerotic girlhood (Olive), and a third-grade understanding of the discursive production of heteronormative white femininity as an (unreachable) ideal.

Further, while remaining skeptical, we can still ask (as I do in chapter 3): How much of an optimistic feminist reading is possible? Throughout the book, I develop optimistic readings that push the possibilities of both the dominant and the alternatives as far as possible toward girlhoods that challenge racism, that express themselves queerly, that take up public space, and that take action. This move, perhaps, is the most important to me personally because pushing oppressive versions of girlhood out of the way opens up a space for the pleasure of creative analytical media consumption, for me a form of media consumption that is committed to social justice.

Why do these girls matter? Why do the multiplicity, complexity, and contradiction of these representations matter? Why does using a feminist lens to foreground race and sexuality matter? Why does moving beyond the most mass-marketed media matter? In part, all this matters because the empirical dominance of white heteronormativity and the can-do/at-risk binary is so highly regulatory, affecting policy and daily life. While media are not the only arbiters of the social expectations of girls, they are a powerful determinant and they operate regardless of whether every girl or every person takes them seriously or even consumes them; that is, the social expectations they help produce are part and parcel of contemporary U.S. society. We are told over and over that we must think about the girls in our lives as objects of worry, fascination, and concern and that we must expect them to achieve phenomenal success, indeed to succeed at all costs, but only within strict boundaries of white heteronormative femininity. Many parents, doctors, teachers, coaches, legislators, and other authorities who may truly have girls' best interests at heart repeat these media narratives about girls, drawing on them in their interactions with girls (and boys). Think of gendered school dress codes, after-school programs, the HPV vaccine, legal prosecution of girls for sexting or bullying, and zero-tolerance policies: media representations of girls directly influence a great deal of public policy about girls and children.

Further, the most mass-mediated versions of girlhood and the public policies linked to those representations *get in the way* of being able to see other ways of making sense of and imagining girlhood. I am not opposed to creating protective structures for girls or to challenging the marketing of sexualized products and ideas to tweens. What I am opposed to is a simplistic, undifferentiated, and totalizing vision of girl-hood that is limited to a neoliberal protectionist stance that writes out of existence—both in how we see media representations and in how we see the actual girls in our everyday lives—girls who are not white, not heterosexual, not vulnerable, and/or not passive. By writing this book, I hope to illustrate that—while the white, heteronormative, can-do/at-risk girl is everywhere—if we choose both to look at her differently and to look away, we can see alternative girlhoods, we can begin to move dominant mediated girlhoods out of our way and thereby imagine new ways of interacting with girls.

How might seeing these alternative girls lead to different ways of regulating and interacting with girls? How might utilizing the antira-cist, queer, feminist perspective I conceptualize here lead to new ways of conceiving of girls within education, the economy, and legislation? And how might new ways of conceiving of girls in these contexts then lead to new cultural narratives and media representations? Certainly, I would be delighted for this academic book to intervene in and alter these mass-mediated representations of girls—to reach far enough for media makers, parents, doctors, teachers, coaches, and legislators to find it, read it, reflect on it, and then rethink their approaches to girls. Thinking about mediated and spectacular girls in the ways I do in this book could embolden educators to change school reading lists to be intersectional rather than simply inclusive, and to create after-school programs for both girls' media analysis and girls' media production; and it could chal-lenge legislators and social workers to stop using regulation and surveil-lance to protect girls from a version of themselves that for most exists more in the mediascape than in their everyday lives. This book could provide parents with new narratives with which to make sense of their children, and thereby new ways of helping those children navigate their social and interior lives; and it could confront media makers with some of the consequences of their work, encouraging them to think carefully about how they might want to represent and narrate girls in the future.

Of course, my primary audience is other feminist and/or media scholars. In this context, this book speaks directly to the area of thought I call feminist girls' media studies. Although moving at the pace of the academy (rather than corporate media), feminist girls' media studies is growing in step with the simultaneous moral panic about and adoration of girls in U.S. media culture. This book is a part of that growth. The contribution I hope to make in this context is to insist on the complexity and multiplicity of girls in the media and to emphasize the importance of race and sexuality—without simply rehashing an already well-established argument about the hegemony of whiteness and heteronormativity. As I discuss in the introduction, some feminist girls' media studies scholars are already doing this work, and I hope this book contributes to this scholarship, but more is possible as well.

For example, future studies could examine the relationship between mediated girlhood and the transnational neoliberal political economy. What do representations of and narratives about girls do for nations and for industries and corporations? Which versions of girlhood are transnational and which are tied closely to particular national and/or cultural contexts?[4] How could thinking outside U.S. media help address intercultural questions and further complicate feminist girls' media studies' understanding of mediated girlhood? How could placing the girl at the center of political economy research deepen our understanding of how transnational media conglomerates function? How could taking seriously the role girls have played in establishing and maintaining the star/celebrity industry strengthen our overall understanding of celebrity culture? Other future studies could use the feminist girls' media studies methodology I develop and advocate for in this book to look carefully at the process of writing, arguing for, and enacting public policy and legislation built on images of and narratives about girls and—more important from a public policy perspective—having an impact on actual girls in their everyday lives. Further, the commitment to approaching multiple types of media and their relationship to our everyday lives from several critical perspectives within the bounds of one research project that I try to model here could be applied to any number of topics other than spectacular girls. While girls are central to celebrity and media culture, they are not the totality of it. What I am suggesting here as possible future research, then, is a feminist (girls') media studies approach deeply involved in questioning the relationship between media and social life in a way that places gender, age, race, and sexuality at the center.

I suspect that U.S. media fascination with girls is going to continue to grow, at least in the short term. In addition to the ready availability of the little blonde-white girl for media to make sense of the Newtown tragedy, think, for example, of the fact that girls now have the capacity to carry media franchises in a way they have not since the early 1950s when, as Mary Celeste Kearney shows, "meta-properties," such as *Meet Corliss Archer* and *A Date with Judy*, helped shape the structure of the increasingly synergistic media industries.[5] Today (depending on how one counts) girls anchor three of the top twelve film franchises: *Twilight, The Hunger Games*, and Disney animated princess/girl films.[6] As of this writing, all three of these franchises continue to grow: former-actual-girl and current-girlish celebrities Kristen Stewart and Jennifer Lawrence frequently appear on the cover of magazines, as the subjects of blogs, and on television talk shows and celebrity news; three more *Hunger Games* films are scheduled; and Disney continues to grow its princess line, with the Princess Fairytale Hall scheduled to open at Disney World in 2013 and future animated girl films in the planning stages.[7] And more girl franchises are on the rise; for example, filming of *Divergent*, based on the first novel in Veronica Roth's successful trilogy (the third novel of which has not yet even been released), began in April 2013.[8] Girls also continue to anchor celebrity culture. Even as *Newsweek* ceased physical publication in the United States in 2012, celebrity gossip magazines are thriving.[9] While girls are not the only celebrities to appear in these magazines, I was recently reminded of the way girlhood clings to former teen celebrities such as Taylor Swift, Selena Gomez, Jennifer Lawrence, and even thirty-one-year-old Britney Spears when they all appeared on the covers of December 2012 mass-market magazines. As the accompanying figure shows, my local 7-Eleven store displayed all these celebrities together (along with Oprah). While these young women are no longer girls, arguably their current success depends on their former spectacularized girlhood and thereby reminds us of the importance of girlhood to the functioning and continuation of celebrity culture.[10]

Figure C.1. Girlhood clings to former girl celebrities: Taylor Swift (twice), Jennifer Lawrence, Selena Gomez, and Britney Spears (along with non-former-girl-celebrity Oprah) on the covers of December 2012 mass-market magazines. Photo by the author.

Given that it seems clear girls will continue to remain central to and in fact likely will become even more important to celebrity and media culture, as an academic feminist researcher my question is: *How* will girls remain central? Is there a way for scholars, through their research, to affect the bases of girls' centrality—their social and cultural meaningfulness—and thus not simply be observers and consumers of media products but also actively intervene in what girlhood can and should be? In an attempt to at least move in this direction, this book calls for a feminist girls' media studies that takes seriously the centrality of multiple, complex, multilayered, contestatory, and contradictory girlhoods in media history, industry, political economy, policy, celebrity, representation, narrative, and consumption and thereby allows for, sees, and makes possible more expansive and liberatory futures for all girls.

NOTES

NOTES TO THE INTRODUCTION

1. Turner, Bonner, and Marshall, *Fame Games.*
2. Harris, *Future Girl*, 16, 32.
3. Ibid., 33, quoting Pipher, *Reviving Ophelia.*
4. Gonick, "Between Girl Power and Reviving Ophelia," 27.
5. Fisher, "We Love This Trainwreck!"
6. Gorin and Dubied, "Desirable People."
7. See Maplesden, "Keisha Castle-Hughes"; Turner, "Approaching Celebrity Studies"; Williamson, "Female Celebrities and the Media."
8. Bhabha, "Other Question."
9. Harris, *Future Girl.*
10. Szabo, "Little Girls Are Made of Sugar—Not Spice."
11. Orenstein, *Cinderella Ate My Daughter.*
12. Hartstein, *Princess Recovery.*
13. See http://www.sexybabymovie.com (accessed May 23, 2013).
14. McRobbie and Thornton, "Rethinking 'Moral Panic' for Multi-mediated Social Worlds"; Springhall, *Youth, Popular Culture, and Moral Panics.*
15. Foucault, *History of Sexuality, Volume I.*
16. McRobbie and Thornton, "Rethinking 'Moral Panic' for Multi-mediated Social Worlds," 180.
17. Mazzarella and Pecora, "Girls in Crisis," 21.
18. See Katz, "Childhood as Spectacle," for a related argument about childhood in general.
19. See Holmes and Redmond, "Introduction to Section IV," 189.
20. Morgan, "Historicising Celebrity"; Braudy, *Frenzy of Renown.*
21. Negra and Holmes, "Introduction," ¶ 23, ¶ 15.
22. Turner, *Understanding Celebrity*, 15.
23. Dyer, *Heavenly Bodies*; Marshall, *Celebrity and Power.*
24. Holmes and Redmond, "Introduction," 11.
25. Turner, *Understanding Celebrity*, 9.
26. Tapia, "Prodigal (Non)Citizens."
27. Turner, "Disney Does Race."
28. Wanzo, "Era of Lost (White) Girls."
29. Duke, "Black in a Blonde World."
30. Dyer, *White*, 45.
31. Wanzo, *Suffering Will Not Be Televised*, 4.
32. Stockton, *Queer Child*, 1.
33. Ibid., 7, 37.
34. Halberstam, "Oh Bondage Up Yours!"

35. Kathleen Sweeney also emphasizes alternative girls in *Maiden USA*, but she draws her examples primarily from what she calls girl power representations, a key type of can-do girl. Further, she does not center analysis of race and sexuality, as I seek to do here.

36. Stillman, "Missing White Girl Syndrome."

37. Turner, "Disney Does Race."

38. Kenny, *Daughters of Suburbia*.

39. Susan Driver makes a similar critique of girls' media studies scholarship that emphasizes dominant culture in *Queer Girls and Popular Culture*, 30.

40. Feng, "Recuperating Suzie Wong," 42.

41. Ibid.

42. Weiss, *Vampires and Violets*.

43. De Angelis, "Keanu Reeves and the Fantasy of Pansexuality"; Nishime, "Guilty Pleasures."

44. Feng, "Recuperating Suzie Wong," 47.

45. Dyer, *Stars*, 65, quoted in Feng, "Recuperating Suzie Wong," 47.

46. Doty, *Making Things Perfectly Queer*.

47. Geraghty, "Approaching Stars Sideways."

48. Brenda Song portrayed a key character, London Tipton, on *The Suite Life of Zack and Cody* (2005–2008) and *The Suite Life on Deck* (2008–2011). In addition, she made two Disney Channel movies, *Get a Clue* (2002) (in which she was a sidekick) and *Wendy Wu: Homecoming Warrior* (2006) (in which she was the hero).

49. Another Disney girl, Raven-Symoné, starred in *That's So Raven* (2003–2007) and all but the last of the Cheetah Girls movies. She got her start as Olivia on *The Cosby Show* (1989–1992).

50. King, *African American Childhoods*, 134, 123.

51. Odem, *Delinquent Daughters*.

52. Nash, *American Sweethearts*.

53. See Katz, "Childhood as Spectacle," for a related argument about a link between childhood and anxiety about "the political economic future . . . the geopolitical future . . . and the environmental future" (6). Katz does not address anxiety about girls in particular.

54. Projansky, "Mass Magazine Cover Girls."

55. Banet-Weiser, *Kids Rule!*.

56. See, for example, *Girls Inc.*, http://www.girlsinc.org/ (accessed June 24, 2011).

57. For a discussion of the increase overall in marketing to girls (and boys) in the 1990s, see Quart, *Branded*, 51.

58. Currie, Kelly, and Pomerantz, "From 'Women' to 'Girls'"; Driscoll, "Girls Today"; Duits and van Zoonen, "Against Amnesia"; Kearney, "Coalescing"; Kearney, "Girls' Media Studies 2.0": Kearney, "New Directions"; Mazzarella, "How Are Girls' Studies Scholars (and Girls Themselves) Shaking Up the Way We Think about Girls and Media?"; Mazzarella, "Reflecting on Girls' Studies

and the Media"; Mazzarella and Pecora, "Revisiting Girls' Studies"; Mendes and Silva, "Girls, Boys, and 'Girlhood' Studies."

59. Gilligan, *In a Different Voice.*
60. Brown, "'Girls' in Girls' Studies," 2.
61. See Pipher, *Reviving Ophelia*, 35.
62. McRobbie, *Feminism and Youth Culture.*
63. Kearney lists most of the examples I include here in "Coalescing," but I also mention some additional examples that have emerged since she published her essay.
64. *Signs* 23.3 (1998), *Feminist Collections* 28.3 and 28.4 (2007), and *Networking Knowledge* 5.1 (2012).
65. "Global Girls Studies: Media and Pedagogical Approaches," May 26, 2009, University of Illinois; "After Girl Power: What's Next?" February 24–25, 2012, University of York.
66. The International Girls Studies Association, the National Women's Studies Association Girls' Studies Interest Group, and the Midwest Popular Culture Association/American Culture Association Area Chair.
67. The University of Missouri–Kansas City's Undergraduate Certificate, and the Appalachian State University Girls' Studies Undergraduate Minor.
68. Lipkin, *Girls' Studies.*
69. Zaslow, *Feminism, Inc.*
70. For example, see Wilcox and Lavery, *Fighting the Forces.*
71. For example, see Currie, *Girl Talk.*
72. For example, see Kearney, *Girls Make Media.*
73. Durham, "Constructing the 'New Ethnicities.'" See also Chin, *Purchasing Power*; Kenny, *Daughters of Suburbia*; Maira, *Desis in the House*; Pillow, *Unfit Subjects*; Silverstein, *Girls on the Stand.*
74. Valdivia, "Latina Girls and Communication Studies."
75. Bejarano, *¿Qué Onda?*; Beltrán, "Más Macha"; Fregoso, "Homegirls, Cholas, and Pachucas in Cinema"; Mayer, *Producing Dreams, Consuming Youth*; Tapia, "Impregnating Images."
76. Shohat, *Taboo Memories, Diasporic Voices.*
77. For an excellent collection of essays exploring the history of girls, see Forman-Brunell and Paris's two volumes of *The Girls' History and Culture Reader*, one on the nineteenth century and one on the twentieth.
78. Mitchell and Reid-Walsh, "Theorizing Tween Culture within Girlhood Studies," 9. In this introduction to their anthology *Seven Going on Seventeen*, Mitchell and Reid-Walsh offer a concise history of shifts in public understandings of "girl," up through the most recent emergence of the concept of "tween."
79. Savage, *Teenage.*
80. Schrum, *Some Wore Bobby Sox.*
81. See Cook and Kaiser, "Betwixt and Be Tween"; Mitchell and Reid-Walsh, "Theorizing Tween Culture within Girlhood Studies."
82. Faris, "Betwixt and Between."

83. Kaare et al., "In the Borderland between Family Orientation and Peer Culture."
84. Butler, *Bodies That Matter*.
85. See Harris, *Future Girl*.
86. Helford, *Fantasy Girls*; Owens, Vande Berg, and Stein, *Bad Girls*.
87. Negra and Tasker, "Introduction."
88. Brown, *Black Girlhood Celebration*. I think here of Beyoncé's song "Run the World (Girls)."

NOTES TO CHAPTER 1

1. Kearney, "New Directions"; Driscoll, *Girls*.
2. Harris, *Future Girl*; Projansky, "Mass Magazine Cover Girls"; Roberts, "Girl Power."
3. Odem, *Delinquent Daughters*.
4. Forman-Burnell, *Babysitter*.
5. Kearney, "Birds on the Wire."
6. For additional work on the history of girls in media and popular culture, see Forman-Burnell and Paris, *Girls' History and Culture Reader* (two volumes); Cahn, *Sexual Reckonings*; King, *African American Childhoods*; Nash, *American Sweethearts*; Peiss, *Cheap Amusements*; Schrum, *Some Wore Bobby Sox*; Yano, *Crowning the Nice Girl*.
7. In addition to these three film stars, key 1970s television girl stars include Valerie Bertinelli and Mackenzie Phillips (*One Day at a Time* [1975–1984]) and Kristy McNichol (*Family* [1976–1980], three *ABC Afterschool Specials* [1975–1977], and three additional made-for-TV movies [1978–1979], including *Summer of My German Soldier* [1978]).
8. For example, see the 1970s "Star Decades" anthology from Rutgers University Press, which includes a chapter on Foster and Shields but no other girl stars. Morrison, *Hollywood Reborn*; Erb, "Jodie Foster and Brooke Shields." Similarly, Barbara Jane Brickman centers Foster in one chapter of *New American Teenagers*, although she does offer a brief discussion of O'Neal in relation to Foster.
9. See James Bennett's excellent development of this argument in *Television Personalities*.
10. Turner, *Understanding Celebrity*, 17.
11. Bennett and Holmes, "'Place' of Television in Celebrity Studies," 66.
12. Boorstin, *Image*, 58.
13. Turner, *Understanding Celebrity*, 9.
14. Ibid., 8.
15. In her 2013 book *Precocious Charms*, Gaylyn Studlar makes a similar claim, pointing out that prior to her book "no single-authored volume explores the convergence between representations of youthful femininity . . . and the phenomenon of film stardom" (10). While Studlar's excellent analysis begins to fill the gap in feminist film studies regarding the girl star, particularly in relation to the

structure of the Hollywood industry during the studio era, I am unable to draw on her work as much as I would like to here because her book was published after *Spectacular Girls* went to press. I do, however, address an earlier essay by Studlar in my discussion of Mary Pickford, below.

16. deCordova, *Picture Personalities*.
17. See Fischer and Landy, "General Introduction"; Chisholm, "Missing Persons and Bodies of Evidence," 149n1.
18. See also Staiger, "Seeing Stars."
19. Kenaga, "Making the 'Studio Girl.'"
20. Ibid., 132.
21. deCordova mentions in passing that many of the "picture personalities" were girls in their teens, but he does not mention any names (*Picture Personalities*, 51). His evidence does not support this claim, however; thus it is possible that this is an uncharacteristic moment in his book where he accepts the standard historical narrative as fact (i.e., "many movie-struck girls flocked to Hollywood as teenagers in hopes of becoming stars") rather than examine the source and veracity of that narrative. Of the many names of female picture personalities and stars he does mention in the book, based on dates provided at IMDb.com, only Mary Pickford and Blanche Sweet made more than one or two films before the age of twenty. Mignon Anderson made several films when she was eighteen and nineteen. All the other women he mentions were at least twenty when they became picture personalities or stars.
22. Cary, *Whatever Happened to Baby Peggy?*
23. Balio, *Grand Design*, 146.
24. Eckert, "Shirley Temple and the House of Rockefeller," 185.
25. See also Fuller-Seeley, "Shirley Temple," 44.
26. Negra, *Off-White Hollywood*, 19, 20.
27. See Hatch, "Fille Fatale"; Kincaid, "Hannah Montana's Bare, Unprotected Back"; Nash, *American Sweethearts*.
28. Dyer, *Heavenly Bodies*, 159.
29. Ibid., 170.
30. Dyer, *Stars*.
31. Gledhill, "Signs of Melodrama," 220.
32. Tibbetts, "Mary Pickford and the American 'Growing Girl,'" 51, 55.
33. Studlar, "Oh, 'Doll Devine,'" 210, 209.
34. In their introduction to *Stars*, Fischer and Landy also discuss Mae Murray as an early star connected to "childishness," even when she herself was an adult (5). IMDb.com lists Murray's date of birth as 1889 and her first film as 1916, placing her at either twenty-six or twenty-seven years of age when she entered the star system.
35. Scheiner, *Signifying Female Adolescence*, 5.
36. Nash, "Saluting Virgins."
37. Shary, *Teen Movies*.

38. Doherty, *Teenagers and Teenpics*.
39. Whitney, "Gidget Goes Hysterical," 55.
40. Ibid., 68.
41. For more on the patriarchal family of the 1950s, see May, *Homeward Bound*.
42. Hatch, "Little Butches."
43. Hatch, "Fille Fatale."
44. According to IMDb.com, *Taxi Driver* was released in February 1976 and *Freaky Friday* was released in December 1976 in Los Angeles, and then in January 1977 nationwide.
45. Negra, *Off-White Hollywood*, 4.
46. I used various key words to identify girl stars of color in two electronic databases: IMDb.com and the now-defunct Microsoft Cinemania CD-ROM. In addition, I used the biographies in Reyes and Rubie, *Hispanics in Hollywood*, to identity Latina girl stars.
47. Brown is not even listed on IMDb.com, for example. She was born in 1918.
48. Hodges, *Anna May Wong*.
49. Reyes and Rubie, *Hispanics in Hollywood*, 550.
50. See Davis, "Rape, Racism, and the Myth of the Black Rapist"; Tajima, "Lotus Blossoms Don't Bleed."
51. See Brown, *Black Girlhood Celebration*; Collins, *Fighting Words*.
52. On the specificity of cultural anxiety about girls as actually about white girls, see Godfrey, "Sweet Little (White) Girls"; and Wanzo, "Era of Lost (White) Girls."
53. Vered, "White and Black in Black and White." See also Snead, *White Screens, Black Images*.
54. Vered, "White and Black in Black and White," 61.
55. See Hatch, "Discipline and Pleasure," for a persuasive argument that, at least initially, Temple's persona was not sexual, but rather disciplined men into domesticity. As Hatch documents, however, some other 1930s public commentary did read Temple as sexual, an interpretation her studio actively sought to repress.
56. See also Wood, "Lolita Syndrome."
57. Dyer, *Heavenly Bodies*, 43.
58. Ibid., 44.
59. Blum, "Real Love Story"; Davis, "American Woman in the Movies"; Le Blanc, "Tatum O'Neal."
60. Wade, "As Tatum Turns Ten," 28.
61. When discussing Tatum O'Neal and Ryan O'Neal in relation to each other, I use their first names for clarity.
62. Bogdanovich makes these comments in the DVD extras while reminiscing about the production of the film. The DVD was released in August 2003.
63. Fandango.com also lists her as an unnamed character in the 1972 film *Pocket Money*. Movies.nytimes.com lists her in two 1990s television shows, *The Steve Harvey Show* and *In the House*. I could not find any reference to her work in

these shows on IMDb.com or TV.com. Further, she is the only member of the *Paper Moon* cast for which Wikipedia provides no entry (http://en.wikipedia.org/wiki/Paper_Moon_(film), accessed May 23, 2013).

64. For more on the displacement of racism in historical texts, see Ono, "*Mad Men*'s Postracial Figuration of a Racial Past"; Projansky, *Watching Rape*.

65. James Snead briefly develops a similar comparison in his discussion of Shirley Temple and the African American character of Sally Ann in *The Littlest Rebel*. See *White Screens, Black Images*, 60.

66. Mulvey, "Visual Pleasure and Narrative Cinema." Obviously, male stars also signify to-be-looked-at-ness, and much excellent work has complicated and challenged Mulvey's rigid gender binary (e.g., see Dyer, *White*; Tasker *Spectacular Bodies*). That said, the female star (whether child or adult) can still be said to have a more heightened sexualized to-be-looked-at-ness quality than do male stars, in general.

67. For an extended discussion of the child star, albeit one that does not address gender and girl stars in particular, see O'Connor, *Cultural Significance of the Child Star*. At the recent Celebrity Studies Inaugural Conference, Jodi Brooks initiated a provocative discussion of "Performing Children, Ideas of Film Time, and the Untimely Remains of the Child Star."

68. "Ryan's Daughter."

69. Davis, "American Woman in the Movies."

70. For example, see Blum, "The Real Love Story"; Wade, "As Tatum Turns Ten."

71. "Ryan's Daughter."

72. Hatch, "Little Butches."

73. "Ryan's Daughter."

74. Klemesrud, "Tatum and Ryan," 36.

75. "Ryan's Daughter."

76. Klemesrud, "Tatum and Ryan," 36.

77. "Ryan's Daughter."

78. Blum, "Real Love Story," 100.

79. Klemesrud, "Tatum and Ryan," 13.

80. Blum, "Real Love Story," 63.

81. Ibid.

82. Ibid., 100.

83. Wade, "As Tatum Turns Ten," 28.

84. Blum, "Real Love Story," 62.

85. Ibid., 98.

86. Ibid., 100.

87. Hatch, "Fille Fatale."

88. Haskell, "Tatum O'Neal and Jodie Foster," 49.

89. Ibid., 50.

90. Hatch, "Fille Fatale," 170.

91. Arguably, O'Neal's tomboyish appearance in *Paper Moon* could be read as erotic or sexualized (see Halberstam, "Oh Bondage Up Yours!"; Stockton, *Queer Child*). Nevertheless, here I argue that *Paper Moon* does not explicitly eroticize O'Neal for the heterosexual male gaze.

92. Haskell, "Tatum O'Neal and Jodie Foster," 49, 51.

93. This reproduces the pattern Studlar identifies in her analysis of Pickford in the early twentieth century ("Oh, 'Doll Devine'"), which I discuss above.

94. Davis, "The American Woman in the Movies."

95. This is a history that Haskell, a well-schooled film critic who wrote the influential feminist film history *From Reverence to Rape* only three years earlier, would have known.

96. Bogle, *Brown Sugar*; Chung, *Hollywood Asian*; Beltrán, *Latina/o Stars in U.S. Eyes*; Ono and Pham, *Asian Americans and the Media*.

97. Gledhill, "Signs of Melodrama."

98. Mayne, *Cinema and Spectatorship*, quoted in Negra, *Off-White Hollywood*, 9.

99. Dyer, *Heavenly Bodies*, 8.

100. Arbuckle was a well-known silent film star. In 1921, Rappe, a film "extra," died at a party Arbuckle was throwing; he was tried for manslaughter. Though he was acquitted, his career was ruined by the scandal.

101. deCordova, *Picture Personalities*.

NOTES TO CHAPTER 2

1. For a fuller discussion of the history of these magazine covers leading up to 1990, see Projansky, "Mass Magazine Cover Girls." *Newsweek* transitioned from paper to online-only publication at the end of 2012 in the United States, though it continues in hard-copy form in Europe.

2. For a related study of *Time* and *Newsweek* from the 1950s to the 1980s, see Dodd, Foerch, and Anderson, "Content Analysis of Women and Racial Minorities as News Magazine Cover Persons."

3. All of these things have happened to me, at least once.

4. Turner, Bonner, and Marshall, *Fame Games*.

5. Holmes and Redmond, "Introduction," 6. Holmes and Redmond are careful to emphasize the blurred boundaries between "star" and "celebrity" and to point out that the star has always existed across multiple media (even if historically there have been fewer media platforms than we have today).

6. Ibid., 8.

7. Williamson, "Female Celebrities and the Media," 118. See also Holmes and Negra, "Introduction"; Negra and Holmes, "Introduction."

8. Braudy, *Frenzy of Renown*, quoted in Williamson, "Female Celebrities and the Media," 119.

9. Geraghty, "Re-examining Stardom," 100–101.

10. Harris, *Future Girl*.

11. Griffin, "Never, Sometimes, Always," 248.

12. Ibid., 247.

13. July 27, 1992.

14. August 10, 1992.

15. June 3, 2002.

16. October 30, 2000.

17. For a detailed study of recent newspaper coverage of early puberty girls, see Mazzarella, "Coming of Age Too Soon."

18. *Time*, April 29, 1996.

19. *Newsweek*, July 15, 1991.

20. *People*, October 1, 2001.

21. *People*, September 26, 2011.

22. *Newsweek*, December 5, 2005.

23. *Time*, June 21, 1993.

24. *Time*, August 27, 2001.

25. *Time*, June 28, 1993.

26. *Newsweek*, May 8, 2006.

27. *Newsweek*, May 29, 1995.

28. *Time*, June 23, 2003.

29. On white blondeness, see Dyer, *Heavenly Bodies*; Redmond, "Whiteness of Stars"; and chapter 1 of this book.

30. Wanzo, "Era of Lost (White) Girls." See also Walkerdine, *Daddy's Girl*.

31. Rae Lynn Schwartz-DePre argues that "*National Geographic's* 1985 . . . Afghan Girl is a dominant discourse . . . that is produced by, produces, and reproduces colonial narratives of rescue." See "Portraying the Political," 337. Admittedly, this is at least in part a discourse of protection of the girl of color, but here specifically from the supposed evils of Afghan men.

32. I address the issue of generic ethnic girls more fully later in the chapter.

33. For more on this argument, see Projansky, "Mass Magazine Cover Girls."

34. August 31, 1998.

35. July 20, 1992, and February 15, 1999.

36. June 18, 2001.

37. August 4, 2008, and November 24, 2008. The first time the Obama girls appeared on *People* their father was still a presidential candidate.

38. June 1, 2009.

39. June 18, 2001.

40. August 4, 2008.

41. November 24, 2008.

42. Westfall, "The Obamas Get Personal."

43. Smolowe et al., "The Obamas' To-Do List."

44. Westfall, "Obamas Get Personal," 52.

45. Ibid.

46. Ibid.

47. Ibid., 56.

48. Ibid., 57.
49. Smolowe, "The Obamas' To-Do List," 58, 60, 61.
50. Wall, "On Dolls, Presidents, and Little Black Girls," 797.
51. Ono, "Postracism."
52. Wall, " On Dolls, Presidents, and Little Black Girls," 799.
53. September 15, 2001.
54. February 12, 2007.
55. January 29, 1990.
56. March 18, 1991.
57. March 25, 1991.
58. September 9, 1991. Doherty was twenty years old at the time of this cover, but her character is a teen.
59. February 17, 1992. Gold was twenty-two years old at the time of this cover, but her character is a teen.
60. June 1, 1992. An inset shows an image of the *Brady Bunch* cast during the series run.
61. August 17, 1992.
62. April 26, 1993.
63. November 28, 1994.
64. September 2, 1996.
65. March 3, 1997. Campbell was twenty-three years old at the time of the cover, but her character is approximately eighteen years old.
66. March 16, 1998. Winslet was twenty-two at the time of the cover, but her character is seventeen years old.
67. April 13, 1998. While Newton-John was an adult when she played the role, her character in *Grease* is a teen.
68. April 19, 1999. While Sheedy was in her twenties when she played the role, her character in *The Breakfast Club* is a high school student.
69. May 17, 1999.
70. May 24, 1999.
71. December 13, 1999.
72. February 14, 2000.
73. October 22, 2001.
74. July 8, 2002.
75. January 27, 2003.
76. May 3, 2004.
77. July 5, 2004.
78. September 6, 2004.
79. December 20, 2004.
80. June 11, 2007.
81. July 2, 2007.
82. July 23, 2007.

83. July 27, 2007. Ashley Tisdale and Monique Coleman were in their twenties at the time of the cover, but their characters are teens.
84. September 3, 2007.
85. May 5, 2008.
86. August 6, 2008.
87. November 5, 2008.
88. May 20, 2009. Brenda Song was twenty-one years old at the time of the cover, but her character is in high school.
89. July 22, 2009.
90. August 10, 2009.
91. October 14, 2009.
92. November 4, 2009.
93. November 16, 2011. While Stewart was twenty-one years old at the time of the cover, her character is a teen.
94. March 26, 2012. While Lawrence was twenty-one years old at the time of the cover, her character is a teen.
95. March 28, 2012.
96. July 2, 2007. This cover appeared before the public fight that erupted in February 2011 between Miley and her father, country singer Billy Ray Cyrus.
97. May 5, 2008.
98. July 5, 2004.
99. December 20, 2004.
100. March 28, 1991.
101. May 24, 1999.
102. June 11, 2007.
103. I base this claim on reviews of Wikipedia, IMDb.com biographies, and general web searches pairing "ethnicity" with each star's name. The EthniCelebs.com site often popped up, detailing various rumors and attempting to uncover stars' "real" ethnicity.
104. A few additional stars on these covers, such as Demi Lovato, Miranda Cosgrove, and Shannen Doherty, are sometimes rumored to be mixed race Latina or Asian American: in other words, they sometimes function as "ethnically ambiguous," much like actors who are mixed Asian American or Latina but whose characters often are not, such as Kristin Kreuk and Jessica Alba. See Valdivia, "Mixed Race on the Disney Channel."
105. Beltrán, *Latina/o Stars in U.S. Eyes*, 7.
106. Ibid., 273.
107. "From Texas to Hollywood," 17.
108. Gomez, quoted in "The Princess Diary," 38.
109. Lovato, quoted in "Demi and Selena's BFF Handbook."
110. Ironically, within only a few weeks of this magazine's release nude photos of Hudgens appeared on the Internet, and scandal broke. As is typical, she apologized, and Disney kept her in the fold, including her in the cast of *High School Musical 3*.

111. Schneider, "High School Sweethearts," 65, 66, 67, 64, 67.

112. Griffin, "Never, Sometimes, Always," 249.

113. *Time*, July 27, 1992; *Newsweek*, August 10, 1992.

114. *Time*, August 5, 1996; *People*, August 19, 1996.

115. *Newsweek*, May 14, 1990; *People*, May 30, 1994.

116. *Time*, September 3, 2001. Venus Williams was twenty-one years old at the time of this cover. Because Serena Williams was nineteen at the time I include the cover in my discussion here.

117. *Newsweek*, February 16, 1998; *People*, February 23, 1998.

118. *People*, February 23, 1998.

119. *Time*, February 11, 2002.

120. August 5, 1996.

121. August 19, 1996.

122. May 14, 1990.

123. The cover shows Zmeskal in extreme close-up, wiping the sweat off her lip with her sparkly, leotard-clad arm.

124. *People*, May 30, 1994.

125. After I completed this study, gymnast Gabby Douglas appeared on the cover of *Time* when she won gold at the Olympics. Like Hughes and Zmeskal, she appears in a physically impossible leap, suspended in the air with no ground in sight. Like Kwan, however, the nationalistic red, white, and blue theme is missing. See figure I.1 in the introduction.

126. Starr et al., "Festival of Youth," 49.

127. Relatedly, an MSNBC.com headline—declaring "American beats out Kwan"—appeared a week or so later when Tara Lipinski won the gold, which led to public outrage over the implication that Kwan was not an American and then a public apology from MSNBC.com. For more on this headline, as well as Kwan's relationship to earlier Asian American figure skater Kristi Yamaguchi, see Creef, "Another Lesson in 'How to Tell Your Friends apart from the Japs'"; and Tuan, "On Asian American Ice Queens and Multigeneration Asian Ethnics."

128. Tresniowski, Benet, and Fisher, "Triple Threat," 96, 97.

129. September 3, 2001. See chapter 4 for an extended discussion of Venus Williams.

130. Stein, "Power Game," 55. For more on this, see chapter 4.

131. Douglas, "To Be Young, Gifted, Black, and Female," ¶ 8.5.

132. Stein, "Power Game," 57.

133. Ibid., 58.

134. Ibid.

135. Ibid., 57.

136. *Newsweek*, May 3, 1999.

137. *Newsweek*, April 15, 2002.

138. *People*, August 5, 1996.

139. September 14, 2009; October 26, 2009.

140. October 19, 2009. Although Smart was twenty-one years old at the time, the cover refers back to her kidnapping as a child.
141. June 23, 2008.
142. March 31, 2003; November 3, 2003.
143. March 23, 2003.
144. July 18, 2011.
145. I base the claim that Marris is Latina on both her dark hair and olive skin (as it appears on the magazine cover), and her grandmother's name, as reported in *People* (Theresa Monares).
146. August 19, 2002.
147. *People*, December 20, 1993.
148. *People*, May 28, 2007; September 24, 2007; October 15, 2007. She remains unfound as of April 2013.
149. *People*, October 31, 2011.
150. *People*, June 3, 2002.
151. March 29, 1999.
152. When Shah found the girls over a year later and kidnapped them back, *Time* published an article, "He Found His Girls" (Lopez), but did not do another cover.
153. May 11, 1998.
154. January 20, 1997; March 24, 1997; October 6, 1997; December 14, 1998; September 4, 2006.
155. January 20, 1997; February 22, 1999.
156. For an excellent analysis of media coverage of Ramsey, see Conrad, "Lost Innocence and Sacrificial Delegate."
157. August 11, 2008; October 27, 2008; February 9, 2009; June 13, 2011; July 4, 2011. *People* did not run a cover story when Casey Anthony was acquitted.
158. *People*, August 27, 1990.
159. October 21, 1996.
160. April 26, 2010.
161. December 11, 1995.
162. April 22, 1996.
163. April 29, 1996.
164. See Wanzo, "Abduction Will Not Be Televised," for a comparison of the massive media coverage of Elizabeth Smart to the almost complete lack of coverage of Alexis Patterson, an African American girl who disappeared around the same time.
165. I make this claim based on her appearance in the photographs published by *Time*.
166. Van Biema and Epperson, "Elisa Izquierdo," 36.
167. Henry L. Kaiser Family Foundation, "Poverty Rate by Race/Ethnicity."
168. Wanzo, "Abduction Will Not Be Televised," 192.
169. For a development of the idea of lack of pathos for girls of color, see Roberts, *Killing the Black Body*.
170. Lopez, "Hide and Seek," 66.

171. Collins, *Fighting Words*.
172. Projansky, "Girls Who Act Like Women Who Fly."
173. On Amelia Earhart as queer, see Ware, *Still Missing*; Herrmann, *Queering the Moderns;* and Weiss, *Vampires and Violets*. For a reading of the figure of the woman pilot as queer, see WomenFly.com.
174. As of May 2013, Women Fly is still in business. See WomenFly.com.
175. April 22, 1996.
176. April 29, 1996.
177. Renold, "Queering Masculinity," 132.
178. Stengel and Drake, "Fly 'til I Die," 35.
179. Howe, "Final Adventure," 97.

NOTES TO CHAPTER 3

1. Sarah Hentges also discusses "girl films" in *Pictures of Girlhood*, although she focuses only on "coming-of-age" films, a narrower category than I use here. While an exploration of genre theory is beyond the scope of this chapter, by joining Hentges in categorizing and naming "girl films" and thereby implying a genre, I am thinking of Rick Altman's work on the critic-produced genre in *Film/Genre*. For the most recent and thorough discussions of "teen films" as a genre, see Driscoll, *Teen Film*; and Shary, *Teen Movies*.

2. I conducted two types of searches on IMDb.com. First, I did a keyword search for "girl," "teen," "kid," and "child" for all films released between 1990 and 2009. Based on plot descriptions, I added relevant films to my list. Second, for each film on my list, I examined the plot descriptions for those films recommended by the site "if [I] enjoyed this title."

3. I used many books for this purpose, but the four that were most useful to me were Driscoll, *Teen Film*; Hentges, *Pictures of Girlhood*; Shary, *Generation Multiplex*; and Shary, *Teen Movies*.

4. Because there are so many of them, deserving a (different kind of) study of their own, I did not include horror/slasher films focusing on girls unless they were widely distributed and generated significant public discussion of some kind, such as *Scary Movie* (2000) and *Jennifer's Body* (2009). Additionally, I excluded made-for-TV and direct-to-video movies. These types of titles also deserve a (different kind of) study of their own.

5. Garner, "*Mean Girls* Is Funny, Thought Provoking, Light-Hearted Fun."

6. Dicker, "Cliquetastic."

7. *Today Show*, April 23, 2004.

8. Bowles, "Female Fans Give *Mean Girls* a Nice Boost"; Zacharek, "No More Little Miss Nice Girl."

9. Waxman, "Cracks in Hollywood's Glass-Slipper Genre." See also *Kudlow and Cramer*.

10. Ebert, "Add *Mean Girls* to Teen-Movie Honor Roll."

11. List, "Monster Mash, Van Helsing."

12. Powers and Steiker, "On the Bright Side."

13. Brunson, "It's All Relative."

14. Cooper, "Trapped," 22.

15. Dargis, "*Little Miss Sunshine.*"

16. Schechner, "Weekend Adviser."

17. Cooper, "Trapped," 21.

18. Leon, "The Family that Plays Together."

19. Ansen, "A Busload of Losers."

20. Chocano, "*Little Miss Sunshine.*"

21. Stein, "Everybody in the Van."

22. Frey, "*Little Miss Sunshine.*"

23. Olszewski, "Bringing Up Maybe."

24. "Ellen Page: *Juno.*"

25. Green, "*Juno.*"

26. *All Things Considered*, December 7, 2007.

27. "In Theaters This Weekend."

28. *All Things Considered*, November 23, 2007.

29. Green, "*Juno.*"

30. Brunson, "*Juno.*"

31. Valby, "Diablo Cody."

32. Cage, "*Precious* Not a Typical Movie Experience." See also Durbin, "Dazzling Performances to Gild the Resumes."

33. Musto, "A *Precious* Mo'Nique Makes It Big."

34. Roberts, "Lee Daniels's Pursuit of the Perfect 'Precious.'"

35. Daniels makes explicit that he wanted to hire someone eighteen or older so that he would not have to contend with child labor laws and so that the actor would be prepared to deal with the R-rated nature of the film. See Verini and Hofler, "Screen Team Spirit."

36. *Fresh Air.*

37. Lamble, "When Push Comes to Shove"; Williams, "Gabby Sidibe."

38. Roberts, "Lee Daniels's Pursuit of the Perfect 'Precious.'"

39. Ebert, "Fest Winner *Precious* on the Oscar Fast Track." See also Wloszczyna, "Women of *Precious* Movie Undertake Transformational Roles."

40. Hu, "A Dapper, Dynamic Opener."

41. Saleh, "Cinderella Story."

42. Wloszczyna, "Transformational *Precious.*"

43. Ebert, "*Precious* Opportunity."

44. Ebert, "Beaten Down by a Cruel Fate."

45. Irwin, "Gabourey Sidibe Is Sweet but Not *Precious.*"

46. "The Bullseye."

47. Karger, "Gabourey Sidibe."

48. Breznican, "Nominees Get into Good Spirits Early."

49. See NPR's *Tell Me More*, March 5, 2010.

50. Murphy, "Living the Life," 78. See also *The Charlie Rose Show*.

51. Irwin, "Gabourey Sidibe Is Sweet but Not *Precious*."

52. February 24, 2010.

53. Many of the negative reviews also express disgust for both Precious's and Sidibe's body. See Jarman, "Cultural Consumption and Rejection of Precious Jones."

54. Unlike CNN, I choose not to reproduce Stern's words.

55. March 11, 12, and 15, 2010.

56. See also HLN's *The Joy Behar Show*, March 12, 2010; and NPR's *Tell Me More*, March 12, 2010.

57. Feelerath, "Rubber Meets the Road." See also Stein, "Everybody in the Van."

58. Schwartz, "Sunshine Band," 30.

59. Weisman, "*Little Miss Sunshine*."

60. Wloszczyna, "Young Nominees Can Face a Hard Go-Round."

61. April 3, 2008.

62. Robinson and Davies, "She's Kickin' Ass, That's What She's Doing!" 343.

63. Senior, "New Queen of Mean."

64. Ibid.

65. Binelli, "Confessions of a Teenage Drama Queen," 60.

66. October 26, 2004.

67. December 15, 2004.

68. February 24, 2005.

69. May 13, 2005.

70. *American Morning*.

71. *Paula Zahn*. Six months later (January 5, 2006), and periodically after that (July 31, 2006; February 1, 2007; February 5, 2007), MSNBC's *Scarborough Country* returned to Lohan's troubles with drugs, partying, and rehab, mentioning her role in *Mean Girls* each time.

72. I discuss this theme in relation to *Little Miss Sunshine* in the last section of the chapter.

73. April 23, 2004.

74. Rooney, "Sassy Teen Pic Links Life Lessons and Laffs," 52.

75. Berg, "Fun."

76. Ellis, "Girls on Film."

77. For an example of scholarly work that takes up this question, see Resnick, "Life in an Unjust Community."

78. Addiego, "Already, They're Talking Oscar for Ellen Page in Film *Juno*."

79. Spines, "*Juno* Nation."

80. Ibid.

81. Knight, "*Precious*."

82. Rice, "Is a Picture Still Worth 1,000 Words?"

83. Glover, "Gabby the Glorious."

84. November 4, 2009.

85. Daniels: *Fresh Air*; Mo'Nique and Perry: *All Things Considered*, March 8, 2010; Winfrey: Graham, "Sentinel Was on the Red Carpet."

86. February 2, 2010.

87. Cohen, "Oscar Buzz for *Juno*."

88. Schwarzbaum, "Knocked Up."

89. Haines et al., "*Juno*," 70, 71, 72. Also see the letter to the editor in Gage, "From Our Readers," for a scathing critique of the film from a feminist perspective.

90. Klingener, "They Kept It at the Movies."

91. Yabroff, "Special Delivery."

92. Sperling, "*Juno* Has Moviegoers Bringing Up Babies," 11.

93. "Much Anticipated *Precious* Premieres in Hollywood."

94. *Fresh Air*.

95. Hornaday, "How Mo'Nique Created a Monster."

96. Sherman, "Not So Precious Moments."

97. Morris, "*Precious.*"

98. Kiefer and Johanson, "Push Comes to Shove"; "Snoop Wants Oprah's Job."

99. *Sunday Morning*.

100. Lee, "*Precious* Spawns Racial Debate."

101. Bournea, "Will the Movie *Precious* Take Home Oscar Gold?"

102. Geraghty, "Approaching Stars Sideways."

103. Gonick, "'Mean Girl' Crisis," 395.

104. Hoff, "*Mean Girls*."

105. *The Today Show*, April 23, 2004.

106. *The Early Show*, April 26, 2004.

107. Interestingly, even though Cady's friends Janis and Damien are actually also quite mean in the film, reviews never define them as such, although they do sometimes read them as "gay." Thus, again, meanness is heteronormative. See "Queer Kids vs. Mean Girls."

108. Roz Kaveney interprets Regina, the Queen Bee, more literally as queer at the end of the film, where she appears playing lacrosse. See *Teen Dreams*, 101.

109. Springer, "Queering Black Female Heterosexuality."

110. Kennedy, "Nice White Girls in/from Africa," ¶ 5. See also Hentges, *Pictures of Girlhood*, 21–23.

111. Powers and Steiker, "On the Bright Side."

112. Puig, "Six Movies for the Grown-up Palate."

113. Ansen, "Busload of Losers."

114. Puig, "*Sunshine* Beams, but Darkly."

115. Lemire, "*Little Miss Sunshine*," E30.

116. Chocano, "*Little Miss Sunshine*."

117. Wallenberg, "Ray of Light from a Clan of Losers."

118. Ridley, "Ain't No Sunshine."

119. Goldenberg, "Lovable Losers."

120. Brunson, "It's All Relative."
121. Bartlett, "Sex Sells," 106.
122. Kisonak, "*Little Miss Sunshine.*"
123. Steele, "Family Outing."
124. Denby, "Hot and Bothered."
125. Dargis, "*Little Miss Sunshine.*"
126. Lauer does acknowledge the irony of mentioning the "lifelong dream" of a seven-year-old character. *Today Show*, July 26, 2006.
127. Edelstein, "Sea, Sun, and Hungry Sex," 71.
128. Robinson and Davies, "She's Kickin' Ass, That's What She's Doing!"
129. See Latimer, "Popular Culture and Reproductive Politics," for an argument about the repetitiveness of media coverage of pregnancy and abortion in relation to both *Juno* and *Knocked Up*.
130. Thompson, "16, Pregnant, and Famous."
131. Lyons, "Teenage Pregnancy Is Not a Tragedy."
132. *Showbiz Tonight*, June 23, 2008.
133. "A Juno Effect on the Teen Pregnancy Rate?"
134. *Showbiz Tonight*, December 20, 2007.
135. Black and Native American feminists often reject an uncomplicated pro-choice position, given the continuing history of forced-sterilization abuse; and pro-choice is a position that feminist disability scholars often challenge for the way it colludes with laws that define "fetal deformity" as a legitimate reason to choose abortion. See Silliman et al., "Women of Color and Their Struggle for Reproductive Justice"; and Hershey, "Choosing Disability," respectively.
136. Probyn, "Choosing Choice."
137. Willis, "Sexual Subjectivity," 254.
138. Hine, "Shaping Motherhood," 192.
139. See Condit, *Decoding Abortion Rhetoric*, for a discussion of the many ways in which fictional narratives about unplanned pregnancy make abortion the choice that never can (or needs to) be taken.
140. Hoberman, "Gone Baby Gone," 75.
141. One scholarly article, however, has made this connection. See Luttrell, "Where Inequality Lives in the Body."
142. Kaplan, *Not Our Kind of Girl*.
143. Varner, "Filmmaker Shares Inspiration for *Precious*."
144. Other scholars offer persuasive critiques of *Precious* for its relationship to postracism (Baum, "Hollywood on Race in the Age of Obama"), its depiction of Precious's mother as a "welfare queen" (Pimpare, "Welfare Queen and the Great White Hope"), and the race and class politics of teen pregnancy (Luttrell, "Where Inequality Lives in the Body"). These critiques notwithstanding, my approach to the film is more akin to Jarman's ("Cultural Consumption and Rejection of Precious Jones") in that we both ask the film to address issues of concern to us: girlhood and disability, respectively.

NOTES TO CHAPTER 4

1. In order to keep my source material to a manageable size, I focus on the four "grand slams" or "majors": the Australian Open (played in January), the French Open (May/June), Wimbledon (June/July), and the U.S. Open (August/September).

2. September 15, 1997.

3. While there was plenty of discussion in 1996 of Hingis's youth and the fact that she was continually setting "youngest ever" records that year, it was not until 1997 that the press and television coverage began talking about the teen queens of tennis as a group and on a regular basis. Hence, I begin my analysis in 1997.

4. In 2010, Kournikova became a U.S. citizen.

5. Because I discuss four different members of the Williams family in this chapter—Venus, her sister Serena, her father Richard, and her mother Oracene—I refer to them by their first names to avoid confusion.

6. For scholarship that focuses more on these players as adults, see Harris and Clayton, "Femininity, Masculinity, Physicality and the English Tabloid Press" (Kournikova); Giardina, "Global Hingis"; Schultz, "Reading the Catsuit" (Serena); Hills and Kennedy, "Space Invaders at Wimbledon" (Venus); Douglas, "Venus, Serena, and the Women's Tennis Association"; Ifekwunigwe, "Venus and Serena Are 'Doing It' for Themselves"; Spencer, "Sister Act VI."

7. See the ad on YouTube: "Nike ad: If You Let Me Play (1995)," http://www.youtube.com/watch?v=AQ_XSHpIbZE (accessed May 23, 2013).

8. She was also raised and coached by her mother. Media coverage, however, overwhelmingly represents her father as the family orchestrator. I develop a fuller analysis of the representation of the Williams family later in the chapter.

9. Shriver, 1998 Australian Open.

10. Drysdale, 1998 Australian Open.

11. Shriver, 1998 Australian Open.

12. Ibid.

13. Holcomb, "Dream Teens."

14. Holcomb, "Teens Spice of Women's Tennis."

15. Shriver, 1998 Australian Open. In fact, all but Lučić were included in and Hingis was featured on the cover of a book for children published that September: Rachel Routledge's *The Best of the Best in Tennis*.

16. On Mauresmo's media visibility, see Forman and Plymire, "Amélie Mauresmo's Muscles."

17. In addition to these teenage players, several other teenage players, ages fifteen through seventeen, broke through and ended 1999 ranked in the top one hundred: Kim Clijsters, who played the last two majors at age sixteen and ended the year ranked forty-seventh; Elena Dementieva, who played all four majors at age seventeen and ended the year ranked sixty-second; Jelena Dokić, who turned sixteen and ended the year ranked forty-third; and Justine Henin, who turned seventeen and ended the year ranked sixty-ninth.

18. After first denying it, Erving eventually confirmed he is Stevenson's father.
19. Maria Sharapova is an important subsequent teen player, but she did not turn pro until 2001, and she was not part of a large group of teen players.
20. Andrews and Jackson, "Introduction," 8.
21. White, "Attractions of Television," 79, 90. See also Feuer, "Concept of Live Television"; McCarthy, *Ambient Television*.
22. Of course, announcers did have a set of materials, narratives, and points from which to draw. For a discussion of the semi-spontaneity of play-by-play announcing, see Schultz, *Sports Broadcasting*, 102.
23. Bruce, "Marking the Boundaries of 'Normal' in Televised Sports," 875.
24. Mary Carillo is an important exception. More on this below.
25. 1997 U.S. Open.
26. 1997 French Open.
27. Austin, 1997 French Open.
28. Macatee, 1997 U.S. Open.
29. Drysdale, 1999 Australian Open.
30. Douglas, "To Be Young, Gifted, Black, and Female."
31. Spencer, "Sister Act VI," 120.
32. Douglas, "To Be Young, Gifted, Black, and Female."
33. Ibid., ¶ 3.2.
34. Carillo, 1997 Wimbledon.
35. Deford, 1998 Wimbledon.
36. King, 1997 Wimbledon.
37. See Clarey, "'Homosexuality Is Part of My Life,' She Says."
38. Miller, McKay, and Martin, "Courting Lesbianism."
39. Of course, media coverage historically has sexualized girl and women players not just in tennis, but also in most sports women play. See Harris and Clayton, "Femininity, Masculinity, Physicality, and the English Tabloid Press."
40. Evert, 1997 Wimbledon.
41. 1997 French Open.
42. Austin, 1997 U.S. Open.
43. See also Douglas, "To Be Young, Gifted, Black, and Female," ¶ 6.3.
44. 1997 French Open.
45. See also Spencer, "From 'Child's Play' to 'Party Crasher,'" 98.
46. See also Douglas, "To Be Young, Gifted, Black, and Female," ¶ 6.5.
47. 1997 U.S. Open.
48. Drysdale.
49. 1997 U.S. Open.
50. "Reach Out and Touch (Somebody's Hand)," by Nick Ashford and Valerie Simpson.
51. O'Brien. Gibson was the first and only African American woman to win a grand slam (1956 French Open; 1957 and 1958 Wimbledon and U.S. Open) until Serena Williams won the 1999 U.S. Open.

52. 1997 French Open.
53. See Spencer, "Sister Act VI," 122–123, for a reading of commentary on the beads as negative.
54. She does, in fact, end up losing a point at the 1999 Australian Open as a result of her beads. More on this below.
55. Austin, 1997 French Open.
56. 1997 U.S. Open.
57. Deford, 1997 Wimbledon.
58. Drysdale, 1998 Australian Open.
59. Austin, 1997 French Open; Carillo, 1997 Wimbledon.
60. It is clear that she used the word "fucking," based on both the slight "f" sound that one can hear before the bleep and the shape of her lips as she speaks.
61. See Collins, *Black Feminist Thought*.
62. Finn, "Denials of Racism." Spencer also analyses some of this material in "From 'Child's Play' to 'Party Crasher,'" 97–98.
63. Garrison and McNeil were the two most recent high-ranking African American female tennis players prior to Venus and Serena Williams.
64. Araton, "Talking about the Country Club."
65. As I discuss in chapter 3, this is akin to the way in which commentators love to love Sidibe's large black body.
66. I believe Venus is wrong on this point. In fact, the rule that the umpire followed at the 1999 Australian Open was the same as the rule reported by the press during Wimbledon in 1997.

NOTES TO CHAPTER 5

1. I use a slash to combine the various terms the collective coverage used to describe the same thing. All the facts reported in this paragraph are based on the collective media coverage of the case.
2. Rostow, "Thousands Rally for Murdered Lesbian, Sakia Gunn."
3. A search of the PFLAG website returns no results for "Sakia Gunn." The list of PFLAG chapters does not currently include a Newark chapter, and the list of both national and local scholarships does not include the Sakia Gunn scholarship. As far as I can tell based on all my research, the scholarship was awarded only once. See http://community.pflag.org/Page.aspx?pid=194&srcid=-2 (accessed December 15, 2012).
4. Parry, "Suspect Held in Killing of Gay Teen."
5. Hull, "Newark Man Pleads Guilty to Killing Lesbian in 2003."
6. Fogg-Davis, "Theorizing Black Lesbians within Black Feminism," ¶ 2. See also Wanzo, *Suffering Will Not Be Televised*.
7. Ono and Sloop, "Critique of Vernacular Discourse."
8. Banet-Weiser, "Branding the Post-feminist Self."
9. June 6, 2003.
10. June 13, 2003.
11. "The Nominees."

12. The *NYT* could be considered a local paper in this case because Gunn was murdered in nearby Newark. However, I categorize it as an example of national coverage because of its wide distribution.
13. Kelley, "Metro Briefing"; Smothers, "Teenage Girl Fatally Stabbed at Bus Stop in Newark," "Man Arrested in the Killing of a Teenager in Newark," and "Man Charged with Bias Crime for Girl's Killing in Newark."
14. Smothers, "Newark Preaches Tolerance of Gays Year after Killing."
15. Hull, "Young and Gay in Real America," and "Using Her Voice to Rise Above."
16. Hull, "Newark Man Pleads Guilty to Killing Lesbian in 2003"; "Nation in Brief."
17. *News and Notes.* I discuss Zook's book in this chapter's conclusion.
18. Shepard, "Five Years Later."
19. Jacobs, "If You Beat Me Up or Shoot Me, I'm Still Going to Be Me."
20. California, Colorado, Delaware, Florida, Illinois, Massachusetts, Michigan, Minnesota, North Dakota, Pennsylvania, Texas, Vermont, Virginia, Washington, and West Virginia.
21. I found ninety-three articles between May 2003 and December 2011. Most appeared in the Newark *Star-Ledger.*
22. Newark (*Star-Ledger*), along with Atlantic City (*Press of Atlantic City*), Bridgewater (*Courier News*), East Brunswick (*Home News Tribune*), Hackensack (*The Record*), Jersey City (*Jersey Journal*), Passaic County (*Herald News*), Toms River (*Ocean County Observer*), Trenton (*The Times*), and West Paterson (*Herald News*).
23. *City Journal, New York Daily News, New York Examiner, New York Post, Newsday,* and *Staten Island Advance.*
24. Wright, "Remembering the Murder of Sakia Gunn."
25. Spence, "NJ Lesbian, 15, Murdered."
26. Anderson-Minshall, "12 Crimes That Changed the LGBT World.".
27. Smothers, "Man Arrested in the Killing of a Teenager in Newark."
28. Smothers, "Teenage Girl Fatally Stabbed at Bus Stop in Newark."
29. Smothers, "Man Arrested in the Killing of a Teenager in Newark."
30. Smothers, "Man Charged with Bias Crime for Girl's Killing in Newark."
31. Strunsky, "Lesbian's Death Fuels Perception of Bias."
32. Smothers, "Teenage Girl Fatally Stabbed at Bus Stop in Newark."
33. Smothers, "Man Charged with Bias Crime for Girl's Killing in Newark."
34. "Gay Teen's Slaying Raises a Host of Issues, Worries."
35. Kelley, "Metro Briefing."
36. Smothers, "Man Charged with Bias Crime for Girl's Killing in Newark."
37. Smothers, "Man Arrested in the Killing of a Teenager in Newark."
38. Hull, "Newark Man Pleads Guilty to Killing Lesbian in 2003."
39. "Man Gets 20 Years in Lesbian Teen's Killing."
40. Hull, "Newark Man Pleads Guilty to Killing Lesbian in 2003."
41. Smothers, "Teenage Girl Fatally Stabbed at Bus Stop in Newark."
42. Ibid.
43. Smothers, "Man Arrested in the Killing of a Teenager in Newark."

44. Smothers, "Man Charged with Bias Crime for Girl's Killing in Newark."
45. Hull, "Newark Man Pleads Guilty to Killing Lesbian in 2003."
46. Smothers, "Man Arrested in the Killing of a Teenager in Newark."
47. "Gay Teen's Slaying Raises a Host of Issues, Worries."
48. Carter, "Girl's Killing Probed as Anti-gay Crime."
49. El-Ghobashy, "Suspect Surrenders in Slaying of Lesbian, 15."
50. Spence, "NJ Lesbian, 15, Murdered."
51. Kleinknecht, "Man Admits to Reduced Charge in Death of Lesbian Teen."
52. "Accused Killer Waives Court Appearance."
53. See Fogg-Davis, "Theorizing Black Lesbians within Black Feminism."
54. Hull, "Young and Gay in Real America," A10.
55. I return to this issue below in relation to coverage that makes a connection between Gunn and the "Newark Four," a group of lesbians who were convicted of "gang violence" for attacking/defending-themselves-against a man who approached them both sexually and with homophobic comments.
56. Smothers, "Teenage Girl Fatally Stabbed at Bus Stop in Newark."
57. "Gay Teen's Slaying Raises a Host of Issues, Worries."
58. Carter, "Girl's Killing Probed as Anti-gay Crime."
59. Ibid.
60. Heyboer, "Scholarship Established in Slain Lesbian's Name."
61. Carter, "Cries for Justice."
62. Kleinknecht, "Lesbian Teen's Family Confronts Killer."
63. Carter, "Bias Crime Suspect Sought."
64. Strunsky, "Newark Teen's Stabbing Death Spurs Call for Gay, Lesbian Community Center."
65. Johnson, "Gay Life Easier for Teens but Still Risky for Some."
66. Fiore, "Day of Remembrance for Gender-Bias Victims."
67. Strunsky, "Newark Teen's Stabbing Death Spurs Call for Gay, Lesbian Community Center."
68. El-Ghobashy, "Suspect Surrenders in Slaying of Lesbian," 15.
69. Kleinknecht, "Newark Stabbing Spurs Rare Bias Homicide Charges."
70. Hoppe, "Sakia Gunn."
71. Newman-Wagner, "An Unnecessary Loss of Life."
72. Heyboer, "Scholarship Established in Slain Lesbian's Name."
73. DuLong, "A Movement Grows in Newark."
74. Newman-Wagner, "An Unnecessary Loss of Life."
75. Ibid. See also Bishop, "Guest Opinion."
76. Stockman, "July 4th Assault on Woman Eyed as Antigay Hate Crime."
77. Williams, "MSU Activist Turns On-line Petition into LGBT Scholarship."
78. "Local Briefs."
79. Bishop, "Guest Opinion," 21.
80. Carter, "Gay Rights Activists March for Newark Mayor's Attention."
81. Ibid.

82. Wang, "Rights Group Begins Where Life Ended."
83. Smothers, "Newark Preaches Tolerance of Gays Year after Killing."
84. Strunsky, "Lesbian's Death Fuels Perception of Bias."
85. See Addison, "It Was Not Meant for Her"; Saha and Wang, "Marchers Ready to Fight for Their Streets."
86. See Carter, "Caravan to Protest Violent Deaths"; McDermott, "Driving Home the Need to End Violence."
87. Strunsky, "Lesbian, Other Slain Students to Be Remembered."
88. Addison, "Newark Relents on Covered-up Yearbook Photograph."
89. O'Crowley, "Student Orientation."
90. Carter, "Girl's Killing Probed as Anti-gay Crime."
91. Carter, "Bias Crime Suspect Sought."
92. Ibid.
93. Carter, "Cries for Justice."
94. Parry, "Suspect Held in Killing of Gay Teen."
95. Carter, "Newark Man Surrenders in Stabbing of Lesbian Teen."
96. Ibid.
97. Fiore, "Day of Remembrance for Gender-Bias Victims."
98. Ibid.
99. Kleinknecht, "Man Admits to Reduced Charge in Death of Lesbian Teen."
100. Carter, "Cries for Justice."
101. "Law and Order."
102. Carter, "Gay Rights Activists March for Newark Mayor's Attention."
103. Smothers, "Newark Preaches Tolerance of Gays Year after Killing."
104. Strunsky, "Newark Teen's Stabbing Death Spurs Call for Gay, Lesbian Community Center."
105. Strunsky, "Gay, Lesbian Group Starts Newark Chapter."
106. Carter, "Gay Rights Group to Introduce Itself to Newark."
107. King, "Look Beyond 'One Thing.'"
108. Lacy-Pendleton, "Vicious Murders, Bigotry and Not Talking for God."
109. See Boykin, "Where's the Outrage Over the Murder of Michael Sandy?"; "Selective Outrage."
110. See Renna, "Laramie"; Wright, "NGLTF Hosts 16th Annual Creating Change Conference in Miami."
111. Jaffe, "Thoughts on the Murder of Sakia Gunn."
112. Hoppe, "Sakia Gunn."
113. Lee and Bagby, "Shepard's Spotlight."
114. Hey, "PRIDEFEST 2003."
115. Stockman, "July 4th Assault on Woman Eyed as Antigay Hate Crime."
116. McGavin, "Blacks Facing AIDS Crisis."
117. Emphasis added.
118. There were seven women in the group, but only four served jail time.
119. McEachern, "Young, Black, Lesbian . . . and Always on Guard."

120. Peet, "Lesbians in Assault to Appeal their Terms."
121. See also chapter 6 of Isoke, *Urban Black Women and the Politics of Resistance*, which focuses on Sakia Gunn. This book was released in January 2013, too recently for me to include it in my analysis here.
122. Zook, "Lover," 32, 33, 45.

NOTES TO CHAPTER 6

1. Orenstein, *Cinderella Ate My Daughter*; Hartstein, *Princess Recovery*.
2. Livingstone, "Engaging with Media," 51.
3. For discussions of the history and politics of cultural studies, see Nelson and Gaonkar, *Disciplinarity and Dissent*; and McRobbie, *Feminism and Youth Culture*.
4. I discuss some of this work in more detail below. See Livingstone, "Do the Media Harm Children?" 5, for a cogent discussion of the need to think across "media are to blame" and "children enjoy media" arguments. See Bignell, "Writing the Child in Media Theory," for a discussion of the discursive figure of the child and its relationship to media self-regulation and policy.
5. Buckingham, "Going Critical," 144. For discussions of girls' complex interactions with media, see Chin, *Purchasing Power*; Kenny, *Daughters of Suburbia*; and Maira, *Desis in the House*.
6. I want to thank the classroom teacher for clarifying why she encouraged the students to avoid saying or being "critical."
7. Brown, *Black Girlhood Celebration*, 112.
8. Ibid.; Gonick, "Between Girl Power and Reviving Ophelia"; Hasinoff, "No Right to Sext?"; Projansky, "Girls Who Act Like Women Who Fly."
9. The only dark-haired girl appears on *Queen Bees and Wannabes*. She is in the foreground, looking unhappy, while three blonde girls laugh and whisper in the background. For a related discussion of the production of the vulnerable white girl in need of protection, see Godfrey, "Sweet Little (White) Girls?"; Projansky, "Mass Magazine Cover Girls"; and chapter 2 of this book.
10. Götz, "Girls and Boys and Television."
11. Durham, "Adolescents, the Internet, and the Politics of Gender"; "Articulating Adolescent Girls' Resistance"; and "Constructing the 'New Ethnicities.'"
12. Durham, *Lolita Effect*, 23, 22.
13. There used to be a website with the title "Postfeminist Playground"; it is now defunct. See Projansky, *Watching Rape*.
14. Durham critiques Jennifer Baumgardner for making this very argument. See Durham, *Lolita Effect*, 23.
15. For a recent literature review that reports on both positive and negative media effects, see Strasburger, Jordan, and Donnerstein, "Health Effect of Media."
16. Gentles and Harrison, "Television and Perceived Peer Expectations"; Harrison, "Body Electric."
17. See Sweeney, *Maiden USA*.

18. Mazzarella, *Girl Wide Web*; Bae, "Trans-Pacific Popular Mediascape."
19. Taliman, "Native Youth Media Project"; Johnson, "Blackgirl Rules!"
20. For a development of this argument, see Brown, *Black Girlhood Celebration*; and Goodkind, "You Can Be Anything You Want, but You Have to Believe It!"
21. See Kearney, *Girls Make Media*, for a nuanced discussion of issues related to girls' media production.
22. A great deal of media literacy scholarship deals with undergraduate students or adults generally. For the purposes of this project, however, I focus on media literacy scholarship about children.
23. Buckingham, "Going Critical," 143.
24. Bergstrom, Paradise, and Scharrer, "Introducing Second Graders to Media Literacy"; Byrne, "Media Literacy Interventions"; Hobbs, "Media Literacy, General Semantics, and K–12 Education."
25. Holtzman, "Mining the Invisible"; Kellner and Share, "Critical Media Literacy Is Not an Option"; Kellner and Share, "Toward Critical Media Literacy."
26. Vargas, "Transnational Media Literacy."
27. For cogent discussions of the complexity of media literacy as a concept, see Buckingham, "Going Critical"; Vande Berg, Wenner, and Gronbeck, "Media Literacy and Television Criticism"; and Wehmeyer, "Critical Media Studies and the North American Media Literacy Movement."
28. Urla and Swedlund, "Anthropometry of Barbie."
29. Aidman, "Disney's *Pocahontas*"; Currie, *Girl Talk*; Durham, "Constructing the 'New Ethnicities'"; Lowe, "Colliding Feminisms"; Mayer, "Living Telenovelas"; Zaslow, *Feminism, Inc.*
30. I have changed names to protect anonymity. Because this was a relatively small group (twenty-one students) and because the racial and ethnic makeup of the class is such that maintaining racial and ethnic clues in names could reveal the identity of the student to some readers, I have not matched pseudonyms to the racial, ethnic, and/or cultural markers in the students' actual names. I return to the issue of race in the classroom below.
31. All dialogue is based on my transcription of the audio recordings. If I do not identify the name of the student to whom I refer it is because the audio quality was not good enough for me to identify who was speaking.
32. Richard Dyer's brilliant analysis of the photo of Joan Crawford that appears on the cover of his book, *Heavenly Bodies*, comes to mind.
33. I make this claim based on my observations, assumptions, and personal knowledge about the girls, but not on their comments during the media project. None of them identified what they considered to be their racial or ethnic identity during the media project, although a few did identify their religion.
34. Valdivia, "Mixed Race on the Disney Channel."
35. This student is thinking of Lola Scott, portrayed in *Camp Rock* by Aaryn Élan Doyle, who, according to Wikipedia, is a Canadian of "Irish/Jewish and West Indian descent."

36. In order to protect anonymity, I have replaced some of the students' specific comments about race and skin tone with more generic terms such as "body" or "people of color."
37. Note that this is Kyra who wants to portray a boy, the same girl who expressed a desire to be like media girls (such as Selena Gomez). Clearly, Kyra's relationship to gender is fluid and complex.
38. Levin and Kilbourne, *So Sexy, So Soon*, 4.

NOTES TO THE CONCLUSION

1. The cover of the December 2012 issue of *People* shows all the victims. As I suspected, there were many people who were not blonde girls among the dead.
2. For a provocative analysis of the link between capitalism and the rise of mass killings in the United States, see Felipe, "Left's Failure." This Internet article is not the kind of media that appears on hotel bar televisions, but it does complicate the discussion.
3. Julien and Mercer, "Introduction," 7.
4. At the recent Celebrity Studies Conference, Christine Holmlund used her analysis of Arnold Schwarzenegger in the context of Sweden to illustrate how crucial it is for media scholars to take seriously the specificity of different national and regional contexts. See Holmlund, "'Brand Arnold' in Transition, in Place."
5. Kearney, "Recycling Judy and Corliss," 272.
6. I make this claim based on figures provided by BoxOfficeMojo.com for the highest-grossing film franchises and highest-grossing film average within particular film franchises. As of December 2012, the Disney animated girl films are the fifth-highest total grossing film franchise, *Twilight* is the ninth-highest grossing film franchise, and *The Hunger Games* has the highest grossing film average (based on just one film) in a film franchise. See http://www.boxofficemojo.com/franchise s/?view=Franchise&sort=sumgross&order=DESC&p=.htm (accessed December 11, 2012). I should note that BoxOfficeMojo.com does not define the "Disney animated girl films" as a franchise; however, because I do, I used the gross income of each individual film to identify what would be the overall ranking of the franchise. For more on contemporary franchises, see Johnson, *Media Franchising*.
7. See http://en.wikipedia.org/wiki/Disney_animated_films#Animated_films_ produced_by_Disney-owned_studios (accessed December 24, 2012).
8. See http://divergent.wikia.com/wiki/Divergent_(film) (accessed May 23, 2013).
9. McDonnell, "Just Like Us."
10. As I write this sentence while sitting in my local coffee chop, Selena Gomez and the Scene's hit single "Love You Like a Love Song" (which was first released when Gomez was eighteen years old) plays in the background.

BIBLIOGRAPHY

Primary Sources, by Chapter

Introduction

Brashares, Ann. *The Sisterhood of the Traveling Pants*. New York: Delacorte, 2001.

Collins, Suzanne. *The Hunger Games*. New York: Scholastic, 2009.

Hartstein, Jennifer L. *Princess Recovery: A How-To Guide to Raising Strong, Empowered Girls Who Can Create Their Own Happily Ever Afters*. Avon, MA: Adams Media, 2011.

Orenstein, Peggy. *Cinderella Ate My Daughter: Dispatches from the Front Lines of the New Girlie-Girl Culture*. New York: HarperCollins, 2011.

Pipher, Mary. *Reviving Ophelia: Saving the Selves of Adolescent Girls*. New York: Putnam, 1994.

Szabo, Liz. "Little Girls Are Made of Sugar—Not Spice: Parents Decry Marketers Who Push Sexuality." *USA Today*, April 12, 2011. 3D.

Wiseman, Rosalind. *Queen Bees and Wannabes: Helping Your Daughter Survive Cliques, Gossip, Boyfriends, and the New Realities of the Girl World*. New York: Three Rivers Press, 2002.

Chapter 1

Blum, Sam. "The Real Love Story: Ryan and Tatum O'Neal." *Redbook*, August 1973. 62+.

Davis, Lorraine. "The American Woman in the Movies: Tatum O'Neal." *Vogue*, June 1973. 112.

Haskell, Molly. "Tatum O'Neal and Jodie Foster: Their Combined Age Is 27—What Is Hollywood Trying to Tell Us?" *Ms.*, April 1977. 49–51.

Klemesrud, Judy. "Tatum and Ryan: Look Closely, It's the Same Jaw." *New York Times*, May 20, 1973. 13+.

Le Blanc, Rena Dictor. "Tatum O'Neal: A Child Once Again." *Good Housekeeping*, June 1977. 56+.

"Ryan's Daughter." *Time*, May 21, 1973. 94.

"Tatum Takes Off." *Vogue*, December 1973. 192–195.

Wade, Valerie. "As Tatum Turns Ten Ryan's Daughter Is Ready for Her Body to Catch Up with Her Mind." *Rolling Stone*, July 1973. 28–30.

Chapter 2

"Demi and Selena's BFF Handbook." *People*, July 22, 2009. 45.

"From Texas to Hollywood: They've Come a Long Way from *Barney*! How Selena and Demi Made It from a Little Kiddie Show to Stardom." *People*, July 22, 2009. 17–18.

Henry L. Kaiser Family Foundation. "Poverty Rate by Race/Ethnicity." *State Health Facts*. http://www.statehealthfacts.org:/comparebar.jsp?typ=1&ind=14&cat=1&sub=2 (accessed June 17, 2011).

Howe, Rob. "Final Adventure." *People*, April 29, 1996. 88+.

Lopez, Steve. "He Found His Girls." *Time*, April 26, 1999. 8.

———. "Hide and Seek." *Time*, May 11, 1998. 56+.

"The Princess Diary." *People*, July 22, 2009. 37+.

Schneider, Karen S., with Rennie Dyball. "High School Sweethearts." *People*, September 3, 2007. 62+.

Smolowe, Jill, et al. "The Obamas' To-Do List." *People*, November 24, 2008. 58+.

Starr, Mark, Jeffrey Batholet, Debra Rosenberg, and Larry Reibstein. "Festival of Youth: Nagano Is Aiming at a Simpler, Gentler, Less Commercial Olympics." *Newsweek*, February 16, 1998. 46+.

Stein, Joel. "The Power Game." *Time*, September 3, 2001. 54+.

Stengel, Richard, and Kerry A. Drake. "Fly 'til I Die." *Time*, April 22, 1996. 34+.

Tresniowski, Alex, Lorenzo Benet, and Luchina Fisher. "Triple Threat." *People*, February 23, 1998. 94+.

"Two of a Kind! From Their Texas Childhoods to Their TV Success Stories, a Look at Disney's Double Whammy—Selena and Demi." *People*, July 22, 2009. 4–5.

Van Biema, David, and Sharon E. Epperson. "Elisa Izquierdo: Abandoned to Her Fate." *Time*, December 11, 1995. 32+.

Westfall, Sandra Sobieraj. "The Obamas Get Personal." *People*, August 4, 2008. 50+.

Chapter 3

MEAN GIRLS

American Morning. CNN, June 6, 2005.

Berg, Laura. "Fun." *Girls' Life*, February/March 2005. 38.

Binelli, Mark. "Confessions of a Teenage Drama Queen." *Rolling Stone*, August 19, 2004. 60–64.

Bowles, Scott. "Female Fans Give *Mean Girls* a Nice Boost." *USA Today*, May 3, 2004. D1.

Dicker, John. "Cliquetastic: *Mean Girls*." *Colorado Springs Independent*, May 6, 2004. 30.

The Early Show. CBS, April 26, 2004.

Ebert, Roger. "Add *Mean Girls* to Teen-Movie Honor Roll." *Chicago Sun-Times*, April 30, 2004. 44.

Ellis, Susan. "Girls on Film." *Memphis Flyer*, March 22, 2007. 24.

Garner, Jack. "*Mean Girls* Is Funny, Thought-Provoking, Light-Hearted Fun." *USA Today*, April 27, 2004.

Good Morning America. ABC, May 13, 2005.

Hoff, Al. "*Mean Girls*: Pretty (Mean) in Pink." *Pittsburgh City Paper*, April 28, 2004. 41.

Kudlow and Cramer. CNBC, April 28, 2004.

List, Bo. "Monster Mash, Van Helsing: Silly but Fun." *Memphis Flyer*, May 13, 2004. 52.

Live From . . . . CNN, October 26, 2004.

Paula Zahn. CNN, June 24, 2005.

Primetime Live. ABC, February 24, 2005.

"Queer Kids vs. Mean Girls." *Advocate*, April 13, 2004. 24.

Rooney, David. "Sassy Teen Pic Links Life Lessons and Laffs." *Variety*, April 26, 2004. 45+.

Scarborough Country. MSNBC, January 5, 2006.

———. MSNBC, July 31, 2006.

———. MSNBC, February 1, 2007.

———. MSNBC, February 5, 2007.

Senior, Jennifer. "The New Queen of Mean." *New York Times*, April 25, 2004. 11.

The Today Show. NBC, April 23, 2004.

———. NBC, December 15, 2004.

Waxman, Sharon. "Cracks in Hollywood's Glass-Slipper Genre." *New York Times*, April 26, 2004. E1.

Wiseman, Rosalind. *Queen Bees and Wannabes: Helping Your Daughter Survive Cliques, Gossip, Boyfriends, and the New Realities of the Girl World*. New York: Three Rivers Press, 2002.

Zacharek, Stephanie. "No More Little Miss Nice Girl." *New York Times*, May 9, 2004. 1+.

LITTLE MISS SUNSHINE

Ansen, David. "A Busload of Losers." *Newsweek*, July 24, 2006. 52.

Brunson, Matt. "It's All Relative." *Creative Loafing*, August 16, 2006. 32.

Chocano, Carina. "*Little Miss Sunshine*." *Los Angeles Times*, July 26, 2006. http://www.latimes.com/cl-et-little26jul26,0,3911043.story (accessed December 15, 2012).

Cooper, Rand Richards. "Trapped." *Commonweal*, September 8, 2006. 20–22.

Dargis, Manohla. "*Little Miss Sunshine*: You're Either on the Family Bus, or You're Off." *New York Times*, July 26, 2006. http://movies.nytimes.com/2006/07/26/movies/26suns.html?_r=0 (accessed May 23, 2013).

Denby, David. "Hot and Bothered." *New Yorker*, July 31, 2006. 13.

Edelstein, David. "Sea, Sun, and Hungry Sex." *New York Times*, July 31, 2006. 70–71.

Feelerath, David. "The Rubber Meets the Road." *Independent Weekly*, August 16, 2006. 54.

Frey, Jennifer. *Little Miss Sunshine*: A Busload of Belly Laughs." *Washington Post*, August 4, 2006. C1.

Goldenberg, Lance. "Lovable Losers." *Weekly Planet*, August 16, 2009. 59.

Good Morning America. ABC, April 3, 2008.

Kisonak, Rick. "*Little Miss Sunshine*." *Seven Days*, August 16, 2006. A59.

Lemire, Christy. "*Little Miss Sunshine*." *Philadelphia Tribune*, August 4, 2006. E29–30.

Leon, Laura. "The Family That Plays Together." *Metroland*, August 24, 2006. http://metroland.net/back_issues/vol29_no34/movie_reviews.html (accessed May 23, 2013).

Powers, John, and Valerie Steiker. "On the Bright Side." *Vogue*, July 2006. 74.

Puig, Claudia. "Six Movies for the Grown-Up Palate." *USA Today*, July 21, 2006. D12.

——. "*Sunshine* Beams, but Darkly." *USA Today*, July 26, 2006. D4.

Ridley, Jim. "Ain't No Sunshine." *Village Voice*, July 26, 2006. 70.

Schechner, Sam. "Weekend Adviser." *Wall Street Journal*, July 21, 2006. W2.

Schwartz, Missy. "The Sunshine Band." *Entertainment Weekly*, August 11, 2006. 28–31.

Steele, Bruce C. "Family Outing." *Advocate*, July 18, 2006. 55.

Stein, Ruthe. "Everybody in the Van—and Don't Forget to Bring Your Emotional Baggage." *Talk of the Nation*. NPR, August 17, 2006.

The Today Show. NBC, July 26, 2006.

Wallenberg, Christopher. "Ray of Light from a Clan of Losers." *New York Blade*, July 24, 2006. 18.

Weisman, Jon. "*Little Miss Sunshine*." *V Plus*, November 17, 2006. A17.

Wloszczyna, Susan. "Young Nominees Can Face a Hard Go-Round." *USA Today*, February 21, 2007. D1.

JUNO

Addiego, Walter. "Already, They're Talking Oscar for Ellen Page in Film *Juno*." *San Francisco Chronicle*, December 13, 2007. E1.

All Things Considered. NPR, November 23, 2007.

——. NPR, December 7, 2007.

Brunson, Matt. "*Juno*." *Creative Loafing*, December 19–25, 2007. 35.

Cohen, Curly. "Oscar Buzz for *Juno*." *People's Weekly World*, January 26, 2008. 9.

Dateline. NBC, January 13, 2008.

"Ellen Page: *Juno*." *New York Times*, November 4, 2007. A16.

Gage, Carolyn. "*Juno*: Reproductively Commodified." *off our backs*, July 2008. 81–82.

Green, Susan. "*Juno*." *Boxoffice*, December 2007. 57.

Haines, Megan, Jennie Ruby, Dawn McCaslin, Karla Mantilla, and Melissa Rodgers. "*Juno*: Feminist or Not?" *off our backs*, April 1, 2008. 70–73.

Hoberman, J. "Gone Baby Gone." *Village Voice*, January 23–29, 2008. 75–76.

"In Theaters This Weekend." *USA Today*, January 4, 2008. D9.

"A Juno Effect on the Teen Pregnancy Rate?" *San Francisco Chronicle*, May 23, 2008. B12.

Klingener, Nancy. "They Kept It at the Movies." *Solares Hill*, January 11, 2008. 2.

Lyons, Scott R. "Teenage Pregnancy Is Not a Tragedy." *Indian Country Today*, February 20, 2008. 3.

Olszewski, Tricia. "Bringing Up Maybe." *Washington City Paper*, December 14, 2007. 48.

Schwarzbaum, Lisa. "Knocked Up." *Entertainment Weekly*, December 7, 2007. 59.

Showbiz Tonight. CNN, December 20, 2007.

————. CNN, June 23, 2008.

Sperling, Nicole. "*Juno* Has Moviegoers Bringing Up Babies." *Entertainment Weekly*, January 25, 2008. 11–12.

Spines, Christine. "*Juno* Nation." *Entertainment Weekly*, February 8, 2008. 24.

Thompson, Arienne. "16, Pregnant . . . and Famous: MTV Series and Their Stars' Celeb Status Run the Risk of Glamorizing Teen Motherhood." *USA Today*, November 23, 3010. D1.

Valby, Karen. "Diablo Cody." *Entertainment Weekly*, November 9, 2007. 44.

Yabroff, Jennie. "A Special Delivery." *Newsweek*, December 1, 2007. 98.

PRECIOUS

All Things Considered. NPR, March 8, 2010.

Bournea, Chris. "Will the Movie *Precious* Take Home Oscar Gold?" *Call and Post*, March 3, 2010. 4.

Breznican, Anthony. "Nominees Get into Good Spirits Early." *USA Today*, March 8, 2010. D3.

"The Bullseye." *Entertainment Weekly*, November 27, 2009. 78.

Cage, Tameka L. "*Precious* Not a Typical Movie Experience." *New Pittsburgh Courier*, December 9, 2009. B6.

The Charlie Rose Show. MSNBC, January 21, 2010.

Durbin, Karen. "Dazzling Performances to Gild the Resumes." *New York Times*, September 13, 2009. AR40.

Ebert, Roger. "Beaten Down by a Cruel Fate: But Hope Beckons in a Landscape of Despair." *Chicago Sun-Times*, November 6, 2009. B1.

————. "Fest Winner *Precious* on the Oscar Fast Track." *Chicago Sun-Times*, September 21, 2009. 39.

————. "*Precious* Opportunity." *Chicago Sun Times*, November 5, 2009. 27.

Fresh Air. NPR, November 5, 2009.

Glover, Terry. "Gabby the Glorious." *Ebony*, March 2010. 110.

Good Morning America. ABC, February 2, 2010.

Graham, Mitchell. "The Sentinel Was on the Red Carpet This Past Sunday at the Premiere of *Precious: Based on the Novel 'Push,' by Sapphire." *Sentinel*, November 5, 2009. B7.

Hornaday, Ann. "How Mo'Nique Created a Monster: In *Precious*, the Comedienne Takes a Serious Turn." *Washington Post*, November 8, 2009. E1.

Hu, Janny. "A Dapper, Dynamic Opener." *San Francisco Chronicle*, October 10, 2009. E1.

Irwin, Demetria. "Gabourey Sidibe Is Sweet but Not *Precious*." *New York Amsterdam News*, November 12–18, 2009. 18.

Issues with Jane Velez-Mitchell. CNN, March 24, 2010.

The Joy Behar Show. HLN, March 12, 2010.

Karger, Dave. "Gabourey Sidibe." *Entertainment Weekly*, February 12, 2010. 43.

Kiefer, Jonathan, and MaryAnn Johanson. "Push Comes to Shove." *Colorado Springs Independent*, December 17, 2009. 57.

Knight, Richard, Jr. "*Precious*." *Windy City Times*, November 4, 2009. 14.

Lamble, David. "When Push Comes to Shove." *Bay Area Reporter*, November 12, 2009. http://www.ebar.com/arts/art_article.php?sec=film&article=693 (accessed May 23, 2013).

Larry King Live. CNN, November 4, 2009.

Lee, Felicia. "*Precious* Spawns Racial Debate: She's Demeaned or Angelic." *New York Times*, November 21, 2009. C1.

Morris, Neil. "*Precious: Based on the Novel 'Push' by Sapphire*." *Independent Weekly*, January 6, 2010. 45.

"Much Anticipated *Precious* Premieres in Hollywood." *Jacksonville Free Press*, November 5, 2009. 11.

Murphy, Tim. "Living the Life: Gabby Sidibe's Astonishing Debut in *Precious*." *New York*, October 5, 2009. 77–78.

Musto, Michael. "A *Precious* Mo'Nique Makes It Big." *Village Voice*, October 7, 2009. 8.

Rice, Linda Johnson. "Is a Picture Still Worth 1,000 Words?" *Ebony*, March 2010. 14.

Roberts, Kimberly. "Lee Daniels's Pursuit of the Perfect 'Precious.'" *Philadelphia Tribune*, November 13, 2009. E7.

Saleh, Erica. "Cinderella Story." *Dramatics*, November 2009. 5.

Sapphire. *Push: A Novel*. New York: Knopf, 1996.

Sherman, Shantella. "Not So Precious Moments." *Washington Informer*, November 19, 2009. 22.

Showbiz Tonight. CNN, March 11, 2010.

———. CNN, March 12, 2010.

———. CNN, March 15, 2010.

"Snoop Wants Oprah's Job: Blacks Split on *Precious*." *Speakin' Out News*, December 2, 2009. 8.

Sunday Morning. CBS, November 1, 2009.

Tell Me More. NPR, March 5, 2010.

———. NPR, March 12, 2010.

Varner, Sandra. "Filmmaker Shares Inspiration for *Precious*." *Sacramento Observer*, November 5, 2009. E2.

Verini, Bob, and Robert Hofler. "Screen Team Spirit." *Daily Variety*, November 30, 2009. A1+.

Williams, Kam. "Gabby Sidibe: The *Precious* Interview." *Skanner*, November 11, 2009. 12.

Wloszczyna, Susan. "Transformational *Precious*." *USA Today*, November 4, 2009. D1.

———. "Women of *Precious* Movie Undertake Transformational Roles." *Miami Times*, November 11, 2009. C3.

Chapter 4

Araton, Harvey. "Talking about the Country Club." *New York Times*, September 9, 1997. 7.

Clarey, Christopher. "'Homosexuality Is Part of My Life,' She Says: A Tranquil Mauresmo Is Hoping for 'Respect.'" *New York Times*, February 1, 1999. http://www.nytimes.com/1999/02/01/sports/01iht-mauresmo.t.html (accessed May 23, 2013).

Finn, Robin. "Denials of Racism." *New York Times*, September 7, 1997. S8.

Fry, Darrell. "At 12, Capriati Too Young for Pros." *St. Petersburg Times*, February 28, 1989. C7.

Holcomb, Todd. "The Dream Teens." *Atlanta Journal and Constitution*, March 29, 1998. E9.

———. "Teens Spice of Women's Tennis: New Flavor: Cocky and Coquettish, Upstarts Making Waves on, off Court." *Atlanta Journal*, August 30, 1998. H1.

Routledge, Rachel. *The Best of the Best in Tennis*. Minneapolis: Millbrook, 1998.

Chapter 5

"Accused Killer Waives Court Appearance." *Times*, December 11, 2003. A12.

Addison, Kasi. "'It Was Not Meant for Her': Mourners Remember Newark Mother Caught in Shootout." *Star-Ledger*, August 28, 2003. 23.

———. "Newark Relents on Covered-Up Yearbook Photograph: Schools Chief Apologizes for Actions over Gay Student's Page." *Star-Ledger*, June 26, 2007. 1.

Anderson-Minshall, Diane. "12 Crimes That Changed the LGBT World." *Advocate*, May 7, 2012. http://www.advocate.com/arts-entertainment/advocate-45/2012/05/07/12-crimes-changed-lgbt-world-0 (accessed December 15, 2012).

Bishop, Jacquie. "Guest Opinion." *Bay Windows*, May 5, 2005. 6+.

Boykin, Keith. "Where's the Outrage over the Murder of Michael Sandy?" *Bay Windows*, October 19, 2006. 6.

Carter, Barry. "Bias Crime Suspect Sought." *Star-Ledger*, May 14, 2003. 23.

———. "Caravan to Protest Violent Deaths: It Will Pass Scenes of Newark, Irvington, and East Orange Killings." *Star-Ledger*, November 26, 2003. 39.

———. "Cries for Justice." *Star-Ledger*, May 15, 2003. 23.

———. "Gay Rights Activists March for Newark Mayor's Attention." *Star-Ledger*, June 4, 2003. 42.

———. "Gay Rights Group to Introduce Itself to Newark: Support Organization Plans a Rally at Intersection Where Girl Was Killed." *Star-Ledger*, October 3, 2003. 39.

———. "Girl's Killing Probed as Anti-gay Crime." *Star-Ledger*, May 13, 2003. 31.

———. "Newark Man Surrenders in Stabbing of Lesbian Teen." *Star-Ledger*, May 16, 2003. 32.

Dulong, Jessica. "A Movement Grows in Newark: The Murder of Lesbian Teen Sakia Gunn Spurred Activist LaQuetta Nelson out of Retirement to Fight for New Jersey's Gay Youth." *Advocate*, October 14, 2003. 22.

El-Ghobashy, Tamer. "Suspect Surrenders in Slaying of Lesbian, 15." *New York Daily News*, May 16, 2003. 3.

"Even Today, Gays Are Stonewalled." *Herald News*, June 16, 2005. B6.

Fiore, Kristina. "Day of Remembrance for Gender-Bias Victims." *Times*, November 29, 2003. A4.

"Gay Teen's Slaying Raises a Host of Issues, Worries." *Daily Press* (Hampton Roads, VA), June 23, 2003. A6.

Hey, Barbara. "PRIDEFEST 2003: Nearly 30 Years Later, Gay Fete a Different Event." *Denver Post*, June 20, 2003. FF1.

Heyboer, Kelly. "Scholarship Established in Slain Lesbian's Name." *Star-Ledger*, January 22, 2004. 15.

Hoppe, Trevor. "Sakia Gunn: Why the Silence?" *Bay Windows*, May 29, 2003. 6–7. http://www.baywindows.com/smallieditorial-small-i-sakia-gunn-why-the-silence-66011 (accessed May 23, 2013).

Hull, Anne. "Newark Man Pleads Guilty to Killing Lesbian in 2003." *Washington Post*, March 5, 2005. A5.

———. "Using Her Voice to Rise Above." *Washington Post*, October 4, 2004. A1+.

———. "Young and Gay in Real America: Braving the Streets Her Way." *Washington Post*, October 3, 2004. A1+.

Jacobs, Andrew. "If You Beat Me Up or Shoot Me, I'm Still Going to Be Me." *New York Times*, December 2, 2007. A39.

Jaffe, J. K. "Thoughts on the Murder of Sakia Gunn." *The Indypendent*, July 23, 2003. 2.

Johnson, Paul. "Gay Life Easier for Teens but Still Risky for Some." *Record*, February 15, 2004. A1.

Kelley, Tina. "Metro Briefing: New Jersey: Newark: Warrant Issued for Arrest in Stabbing." *New York Times*, May 14, 2003. 5.

King, Jean. "Look Beyond 'One Thing.'" *Bismarck Tribune*, July 26, 2004. A4.

Kleinknecht, William. "Lesbian Teen's Family Confronts Killer: Newark Man Sentenced to 20 Years." *Star-Ledger*, April 22, 2005. 19.

———. "Man Admits to Reduced Charge in Death of Lesbian Teen." *Star-Ledger*, March 4, 2005. 27.

———. "Newark Stabbing Spurs Rare Bias Homicide Charges: Teen Allegedly Killed after Rebuffing Man." *Star-Ledger*, November 25, 2003. 13.

Lacy-Pendleton, Stevie. "Vicious Murders, Bigotry, and Not Talking for God." *Staten Island Advance*, August 15, 2003. B2.

"Law and Order: Man Arraigned in Gay Teen's Slaying." *Record*, May 17, 2003. A6.

Lee, Ryan, and Dyana Bagby. "Shepard's Spotlight." *Washington Blade*, October 17, 2008. 41.

"Local Briefs: Boston Activists Plan Vigil to Honor Sakia Gunn." *Bay Windows*, June 19, 2003. http://www.baywindows.com/local-briefs-57417 (accessed May 23, 2013).

"Man Charged in Bus Stop Stabbing Arraigned." *Times*, May 17, 2003. A11.

"Man Gets 20 Years in Lesbian Teen's Killing." *Bucks County Courier Times* (Levittown, PA), April 22, 2005. C6.

McDermott, Maura. "Driving Home the Need to End Violence: Motorcade Pays Tribute to Lives Lost on Streets." *Star-Ledger*, November 30, 2003. 25.

McEachern, Reva. "Young, Black, Lesbian . . . and Always on Guard." *Star-Ledger*, May 14, 2007. 15.

McGavin, Gregor. "Blacks Facing AIDS Crisis." *Press Enterprise*, February 6, 2005. A1.

"Minnesota Briefs." *Duluth News Tribune*, May 22, 2003. B2.

"Nation in Brief." *Washington Post*, April 22, 2005. A10.

Newman-Wagner, Valerie. "An Unnecessary Loss of Life." *Lesbian News*, July 2003. 30.

News and Notes. NPR, November 20, 2006.

"The Nominees." *Daily Variety*, March 26, 2004. A12.

O'Crowley, Peggy. "Student Orientation: More Teenage Girls Are Testing Gender Boundaries." *Star-Ledger*, May 23, 2004. 1.

Parry, Wayne. "Suspect Held in Killing of Gay Teen." *Record*, May 16, 2003. A3.

Peet, Judy. "Lesbians in Assault to Appeal Their Terms." *Star-Ledger*, June 16, 2007. 17.

Renna, Cathy. "Laramie: Five Years Later." *Bay Windows*, October 9, 2003. 10–11.

Rostow, Ann. "Thousands Rally for Murdered Lesbian, Sakia Gunn." *San Francisco Bay Times*, May 29, 2003. 5.

Saha, Paula, and Katie Wang. "Marchers Ready to Fight for Their Streets: 'Stop the Violence' Activists Take Message to Newark, East Orange." *Star-Ledger*, August 31, 2003. 23.

Shepard, Judy. "Five Years Later, Progress against Gay Hatred Lags." *USA Today*, October 13, 2003. A15.

Smothers, Ronald. "Man Arrested in the Killing of a Teenager in Newark." *New York Times*, May 16, 2003. B4.

———. "Man Charged with Bias Crime for Girl's Killing in Newark." *New York Times*, November 25, 2003. 8.

———. "Newark Preaches Tolerance of Gays Year after Killing." *New York Times*, May 12, 2004. B5.

———. "Teenage Girl Fatally Stabbed at Bus Stop in Newark." *New York Times*, May 13, 2003. 8.

Spence, Kevin. "N.J. Lesbian, 15, Murdered: Newark Police Call It a Gay-Related Bias Crime." *New York Blade*, May 16, 2003. 3.

Stockman, Farah. "July Fourth Assault on Woman Eyed as Antigay Hate Crime." *Boston Globe*, July 12, 2003. B1.

Strunsky, Steve. "Gay, Lesbian Group Starts Newark Chapter." *Record*, September 20, 2003. A5.

———. "Lesbian, Other Slain Students to Be Remembered." *Times*, May 3, 2004. 3.

———. "Lesbian's Death Fuels Perception of Bias: Gay-Rights Advocates Say There Is an Anti-gay Bias in the Predominately Black Community of Newark." *Grand Rapids Press*, August 14, 2003. A16.

———. "Newark Teen's Stabbing Death Spurs Call for Gay, Lesbian Community Center." *Press of Atlantic City*, August 10, 2003. E7.

Wang, Katie. "Rights Group Begins Where Life Ended." *Star-Ledger*, October 5, 2003. 16.

Williams, Imani. "MSU Activist Turns Online Petition into LGBT Scholarship." *Michigan Citizen*, July 18, 2004. B5.

Wright, Ellen. "NGLTF Hosts Sixteenth Annual Creating Change Conference in Miami." *Lesbian News*, December 2003. 17.

Wright, Gary Paul. "Remembering the Murder of Sakia Gunn, and Newark's Lost Opportunity: Opinion." May 20, 2013. http://blog.nj.com/njv_guest_blog/2013/05/remembering_the_murder_of_saki.html (accessed May 21, 2013).

Wright, Kay. "Bigotry by Any Other Name." *New York Beacon*, January 21, 2004.

Chapter 6

Durham, M Gigi. *The Lolita Effect: The Media Sexualization of Young Girls and What We Can Do about It*. Woodstock, NY: Overlook Press, 2008.

Hartstein, Jennifer L. *Princess Recovery: A How-To Guide to Raising Strong, Empowered Girls Who Can Create Their Own Happily Ever Afters*. Avon, MA: Adams Media, 2011.

Hinshaw, Stephen, with Rachel Kranz. *The Triple Bind: Saving Our Teenage Girls from Today's Pressures*. New York: Ballantine, 2009.

Lamb, Sharon, and Lyn Mickel Brown. *Packaging Girlhood: Rescuing Our Daughters from Marketers' Schemes*. New York: St. Martin's, 2006.

Levin, Diane E., and Jean Kilbourne. *So Sexy So Soon: The New Sexualized Childhood and What Parents Can Do to Protect Their Kids*. New York: Ballantine, 2008.

Orenstein, Peggy. *Cinderella Ate My Daughter: Dispatches from the Front Lines of the New Girlie-Girl Culture*. New York: HarperCollins, 2011.

Pipher, Mary. *Reviving Ophelia: Saving the Selves of Adolescent Girls*. New York: Putnam, 1994.

Scholarly Sources

Aidman, Amy. "Disney's *Pocahontas*: Conversations with Native American and Euro-American Girls." In *Growing Up Girls: Popular Culture and the Construction of Identity*, edited by Sharon R. Mazzarella and Norma Odom Pecora, 133–158. New York: Peter Lang, 1999.

Altman, Rick. *Film/Genre*. London: British Film Institute, 1999.

American Association of University Women. "How Schools Shortchange Girls." 1995. http://www.aauw.org/learn/research/upload/hssg.pdf (accessed December 25, 2012).

American Psychological Association. "Report of the APA Task Force on the Sexualization of Girls." 2007. http://www.apa.org/pi/women/programs/girls/report.aspx (accessed November 15, 2012).

Andrews, David L., and Steven J. Jackson. "Introduction: Sport Celebrities, Public Culture, and Private Experience." In *Sports Stars: The Cultural Politics of Sporting Celebrity*, edited by David L. Andrews and Steven J. Jackson, 1–19. London: Routledge, 2001.

Ariès, Philippe. *Centuries of Childhood: A Social History of Family Life*, trans. Robert Baldick. New York: Random House, 1960, 1962.

Bae, Michelle. "Trans-Pacific Popular Mediascape: In Search of Girlhood through Korean Immigrant Teenage Girls' Image-Production and Webculture." PhD diss., University of Illinois, 2009.

Balio, Tino. *Grand Design: Hollywood as a Modern Business Enterprise*. Berkeley: University of California Press, 1993.

Banet-Weiser, Sarah. "Branding the Post-feminist Self: Girls' Video Production and YouTube." In *Mediated Girlhoods: New Explorations of Girls' Media Culture*, edited by Mary Celeste Kearney, 277–294. New York: Peter Lang, 2011.

———.*Kids Rule! Nickelodeon and Consumer Citizenship*. Durham: Duke University Press, 2007.

Bartlett, Myke. "Sex Sells: Child Sexualization and the Media." *Screen Education* 51 (2008): 106–112.

Baum, Bruce. "Hollywood on Race in the Age of Obama: *Invictus, Precious*, and *Avatar*." *New Political Science* 32.4 (2010): 627–636.

Bejarano, Cynthia L. *¿Qué Onda? Urban and Youth Cultures and Border Identity*. Tucson: University of Arizona Press, 2005.

Beltrán, Mary. *Latina/o Stars in U.S. Eyes: The Making and Meanings of Film and TV Stardom*. Urbana: University of Illinois Press, 2009.

———."Más Macha: The New Latina Action Hero." In *Action and Adventure Cinema*, edited by Yvonne Tasker, 186–200. New York: Routledge, 2004.

Bennett, James. *Television Personalities: Stardom and the Small Screen*. London: Routledge, 2011.

Bennett, James, and Su Holmes. "The 'Place' of Television in Celebrity Studies." *Celebrity Studies* 1.1 (2010): 65–80.

Bergstrom, Andrea, Angela Paradise, and Erica Scharrer. "Introducing Second Graders to Media Literacy." *Academic Exchange* 8.1 (2004): 294–298.

Bhabha, Homi K. "The Other Question: Stereotype, Discrimination, and the Discourse of Colonialism." In *The Location of Culture*, 66–84. New York: Routledge, 1994.

Bignell, Jonathan. "Writing the Child in Media Theory." *Yearbook of English Studies* 32 (2002): 127–139.

Bogle, Donald. *Brown Sugar: Over 100 Years of America's Black Female Superstars*. Rev. ed. New York: Continuum, 2007.

Boorstin, Daniel. *The Image: A Guide to Pseudo-Events in America*. New York: Atheneum, 1971.

Braudy, Leo. *The Frenzy of Renown: Fame and Its History*. New York: Vintage, 1997.

Brickman, Barbara Jane. *New American Teenagers: The Lost Generation of Youth in 1970s Film*. New York: Continuum, 2012.

Brooks, Jodi. "Performing Children, Ideas of Film Time, and the Untimely Remains of the Child Star." Celebrity Studies Inaugural Conference. Deakin University, Burwood, Australia. December 14, 2012.

Brown, Lyn Mikel. "The 'Girls' in Girls' Studies." *Girlhood Studies* 1.1 (2008): 1–12.

Brown, Ruth Nicole. *Black Girlhood Celebration: Toward a Hip-Hop Feminist Pedagogy*. New York: Peter Lang, 2008.

Bruce, Toni. "Marking the Boundaries of the 'Normal' in Televised Sports: The Play-by-Play of Race." *Media, Culture, and Society* 26.6 (2004): 861–879.

Buckingham, David. "Going Critical: The Limits of Media Literacy." *Australian Journal of Education* 37.2 (1993): 142–152.

Butler, Judith. *Bodies That Matter: On the Discursive Limits of "Sex."* New York: Routledge, 1993.

Byrne, Sahara. "Media Literacy Interventions: What Makes Them Boom or Boomerang?" *Communication Education* 58.1 (2009): 1–14.

Cahn, Susan K. *Sexual Reckonings: Southern Girls in a Troubling Age.* Cambridge: Harvard University Press, 2007.

Cary, Diana Serra. *Whatever Happened to Baby Peggy? The Autobiography of Hollywood's Pioneer Child Star.* New York: St. Martin's Press, 1996.

Chesney-Lind, Meda, and Katherine Irwin. *Beyond Bad Girls: Gender, Violence, and Hype.* New York: Routledge, 2008.

Chin, Elizabeth. *Purchasing Power: Black Kids and American Consumer Culture.* Minneapolis: University of Minnesota Press, 2001.

Chisholm, Ann. "Missing Persons and Bodies of Evidence." *Camera Obscura* 43 (2000): 123–161.

Chung, Hye Seung. *Hollywood Asian: Philip Ahn and the Politics of Cross-Ethnic Performance.* Philadelphia: Temple University Press, 2006.

Collins, Patricia Hill. *Black Feminist Thought: Knowledge, Consciousness, and the Politics of Empowerment.* New York: Routledge, 1990.

———.*Fighting Words: Black Women and the Search for Justice.* Minneapolis: University of Minnesota Press, 1998.

Condit, Celeste. *Decoding Abortion Rhetoric: Communicating Social Change.* Urbana: University of Illinois Press, 1994.

Conrad, Jo Ann. "Lost Innocent and Sacrificial Delegate: The JonBenét Ramsey Murder." *Childhood* 6.4 (1999): 313–351.

Cook, Daniel Thomas, and Susan B. Kaiser. "Betwixt and Be Tween: Age Ambiguity and the Sexualization of the Female Consuming Subject." *Journal of Consumer Culture* 4.2 (2004): 203–227.

Creef, Elena Tajima. "Another Lesson in 'How to Tell Your Friends apart from the Japs.'" In *Imagining Japanese America: The Visual Construction of Citizenship, Nation, and the Body,* 145–171. New York: New York University Press, 2004.

Currie, Dawn H. *Girl Talk: Adolescent Magazines and Their Readers.* Toronto: University of Toronto Press, 1999.

Currie, Dawn H., Deirdre M. Kelly, and Shauna Pomerantz. "From 'Women' to 'Girls': The Emergence of Girls' Studies." In *"Girl Power": Girls Reinventing Girlhood,* 4–9. New York: Peter Lang, 2009.

Davis, Angela Y. "Rape, Racism, and the Myth of the Black Rapist." In *Women, Race, and Class,* 172–201. New York: Vintage, 1981.

De Angelis, Michael. "Keanu Reeves and the Fantasy of Pansexuality." In *Gay Fandom and Crossover Stardom: James Dean, Mel Gibson, and Keanu Reeves,* 179–234. Durham: Duke University Press, 2001.

deCordova, Richard. *Picture Personalities: The Emergence of the Star System in America.* Urbana: University of Illinois Press, 1990.

Doherty, Thomas. *Teenagers and Teenpics: The Juvenilization of American Movies in the 1950s.* Boston: Unwin Hyman, 1988.

Dodd, David K., Barbara J. Foerch, and Heather T. Anderson. "Content Analysis of Women and Racial Minorities as News Magazine Cover Persons." *Journal of Social Behavior and Personality* 3.3 (1988): 231–236.

Doty, Alexander. *Making Things Perfectly Queer: Interpreting Mass Culture.* Minneapolis: University of Minnesota Press, 1993.

Douglas, Delia D. "To Be Young, Gifted, Black, and Female: A Meditation on the Cultural Politics at Play in Representations of Venus and Serena Williams." *Sociology of Sport Online* 5.2 (2002). http://physed.otago.ac.nz/sosol/v5i2/v5i2_3.html (accessed May 23, 2013).

———. "Venus, Serena, and the Women's Tennis Association: When and Where Race Enters." *Sociology of Sport Journal* 22.3 (2005): 256–282.

Driscoll, Catherine. *Girls: Feminine Adolescence in Popular Culture and Cultural Theory.* New York: Columbia University Press, 2002.

———. "Girls Today: Girls, Girl Culture, and Girl Studies." *Girlhood Studies* 1.1 (2008): 13–32.

———. *Teen Film: A Critical Introduction.* New York: Berg, 2011.

Driver, Susan. *Queer Girls and Popular Culture: Reading, Resisting, and Creating Media.* New York: Peter Lang, 2007.

Duits, Linda, and Pauline van Romondt Vis. "Girls Make Sense: Girls, Celebrities, and Identities." *European Journal of Cultural Studies* 12.1 (2009): 41–58.

Duits, Linda, and Liesbet van Zoonen. "Against Amnesia: 30+ Years of Girls' Studies." *Feminist Media Studies* 9.1 (2009): 111–115.

Duke, Lisa. "Black in a Blonde World: Race and Girls' Interpretations of the Feminine Ideal in Teen Magazines." *Journalism and Mass Communication Quarterly* 77.2 (2000): 367–392.

Durham, Meenakshi Gigi. "Adolescents, the Internet, and the Politics of Gender: A Feminist Case Analysis." *Race, Gender, and Class* 8.4 (2001): 20–41.

———. "Articulating Adolescent Girls' Resistance to Patriarchal Discourse in Popular Media." *Women's Studies in Communication* 22.2 (1999): 210–229.

———. "Constructing the 'New Ethnicities': Media, Sexuality, and Diaspora Identity in the Lives of South Asian Immigrant Girls." *Critical Studies in Media Communication* 21.2 (2004): 140–161.

Dyer, Richard. *Heavenly Bodies: Film Stars and Society.* New York: St. Martin's Press, 1986.

———. *Stars.* New ed. London: British Film Institute, 1998.

———. *White.* New York: Routledge, 1997.

Eckert, Charles. "Shirley Temple and the House of Rockefeller." *Jump Cut* 2 (1974): 1, 17–20. Reprinted in *Star Texts: Image and Performance in Film and Television,* edited by Jeremy G. Butler, 184–202. Detroit: Wayne State University Press, 1991.

Erb, Cynthia. "Jodie Foster and Brooke Shields: 'New Ways to Look at the Young.'" In *Hollywood Reborn: Movie Stars of the 1970s*, edited by James Morrison, 82–100. New Brunswick: Rutgers University Press, 2010.

Faris, Crystal. "Betwixt and Between: Tweens in the Library." *Children and Libraries: The Journal of the Association for Library Service to Children* 7.1 (2009): 43–45.

Felipe, Alex. "The Left's Failure: Post–Newtown, Connecticut." *Alex Felipe: Ramblings*, December 22, 2012. http://alexfelipe.wordpress.com/2012/12/22/the-lefts-failure-post-newtown-connecticut/ (accessed December 24, 2012).

Feng, Peter. "Recuperating Suzie Wong: A Fan's Nancy Kwan-dary." In *Countervisions: Asian American Film Criticism*, edited by Darrell Y. Hamamoto and Sandra Liu, 40–56. Philadelphia: Temple University Press, 2000.

Feuer, Jane. "The Concept of Live Television: Ontology as Ideology." In *Regarding Television: Critical Approaches—An Anthology*, edited by E. Ann Kaplan, 12–21. Los Angeles: American Film Institute, 1983.

Fischer, Lucy, and Marcia Landy. "General Introduction: Back Story." In *Stars: The Film Reader*, edited by Lucy Fischer and Marcia Landy, 1–9. New York: Routledge, 2004.

Fisher, Anna Watkins. "We Love This Trainwreck! Sacrificing Britney to Save America." In *In the Limelight and under the Microscope*, edited by Su Holmes and Diane Negra, 303–332. New York: Continuum, 2011.

Fogg-Davis, Hawley G. "Theorizing Black Lesbians with Black Feminism: A Critique of Same-Race Street Harassment." *Politics and Gender* 2.1 (2006): 57–76.

Forman, Pamela J., and Darcy C. Plymire. "Amélie Mauresmo's Muscles: The Lesbian Heroic in Women's Professional Tennis." *Women's Studies Quarterly* 33.1/2 (2005): 120–132.

Forman-Brunell, Miriam. *Babysitter: An American History*. New York: New York University Press, 2009.

Forman-Brunell, Miriam, and Leslie Paris, eds. *The Girls' History and Culture Reader: The Nineteenth Century*. Urbana: University of Illinois Press, 2010.

———, eds. *The Girls' History and Culture Reader: The Twentieth Century*. Urbana: University of Illinois Press, 2011.

Foucault, Michel. *The History of Sexuality, Volume I: An Introduction*. Translated by Robert Hurley. New York: Vintage, 1978.

Fregoso, Rosa Linda. "Homegirls, Cholas, and Pachucas in Cinema: Taking over the Public Sphere." *California History* 74.3 (1995): 316–327.

Fuller-Seeley, Kathryn. "Shirley Temple: Making Dreams Come True." In *Glamour in a Golden Age: Movie Stars of the 1930s*, edited by Adrienne L. McLean, 44–65. New Brunswick: Rutgers University Press, 2011.

Gentles, Kamille A., and Kristen Harrison. "Television and Perceived Peer Expectations of Body Size among African American Adolescent Girls." *Howard Journal of Communication* 17.1 (2006): 39–55.

Geraghty, Christine. "Approaching Stars Sideways." Celebrity Studies Inaugural Conference. Deakin University, Burwood, Australia. December 13, 2012.

———."Re-examining Stardom: Questions of Bodies, Texts and Performance." In *Reinventing Film Studies*, edited by Christine Gledhill and Linda Williams, 183–201. New York: Bloomsbury, 2000. Reprinted in *Stardom and Celebrity: A Reader*, edited by Sean Redmond and Su Holmes, 98–110. Thousand Oaks, CA: Sage, 2007.

Giardina, Michael. "Global Hingis: Flexible Citizenship and the Transnational Celebrity." In *Sports Stars: The Cultural Politics of Sporting Celebrity*, edited by David L. Andrews and Steven J. Jackson, 201–217. London: Routledge, 2001.

Gilligan, Carol. *In a Different Voice: Psychological Theory and Women's Development.* Cambridge: Harvard University Press, 1982.

Gledhill, Christine. "Signs of Melodrama." In *Stardom: Industry of Desire*, edited by Christine Gledhill, 207–229. New York: Routledge, 1991.

Godfrey, Phoebe. "'Sweet Little (White) Girls'? Sex and Fantasy across the Color Line and the Contestation of Patriarchal White Supremacy." *Equity and Excellence in Education* 37.3 (2004): 204–218.

Gonick, Marnina. "Between Girl Power and Reviving Ophelia: Constituting the Neo-liberal Girl Subject." *National Women's Studies Association Journal* 18.2 (2006): 1–23.

———. "The 'Mean Girl' Crisis: Problematizing Representations of Girls' Friendships." *Feminism and Psychology* 14.3 (2004): 395–400.

Goodkind, Sara. "'You Can Be Anything You Want, but You Have to Believe It': Commercialized Feminism in Gender-Specific Programs for Girls." *Signs* 34.2 (2009): 397–422.

Gorin, Valérie, and Annik Dubied. "Desirable People: Identifying Social Values through Celebrity News." *Media, Culture, and Society* 33.4 (2011): 599–618.

Götz, Maya. "Girls and Boys and Television: A Few Reminders for More Gender Sensitivity in Children's TV." *Internationales Zentralinsitut fur das Jugend-und Bildungsfernsehen* (2008).

Griffin, Hollis. "Never, Sometimes, Always: The Multiple Temporalities of 'Post-Race' Discourse in Convergence Television Narrative." *Popular Communication* 9.4 (2011): 235–250.

Halberstam, Judith. "Oh Bondage Up Yours! Female Masculinity and the Tomboy." In *Sissies and Tomboys: Gender Nonconformity and Homosexual Childhood*, edited by Matthew Rottnek, 153–179. New York: New York University Press, 1999. Reprinted in *Curiouser: On the Queerness of Children*, edited by Steven Bruhm and Natasha Hurley, 191–214. Minneapolis: University of Minnesota Press, 2004.

Harris, Anita. *Future Girl: Young Women in the Twenty-First Century*. New York: Routledge, 2004.

Harris, John, and Ben Clayton, "Femininity, Masculinity, Physicality, and the English Tabloid Press: The Case of Anna Kournikova." *International Review for the Sociology of Sport* 37.3/4 (2002): 397–413.

Harrison, Kristen. "The Body Electric: Thin-Ideal Media and Eating Disorders in Adolescents." *Journal of Communication* 50.3 (2000): 119–143.

Hasinoff, Amy. "No Right to Sext? A Critical Examination of Media and Legal Debates about Teenage Girls' Sexual Agency in the Digital Age." PhD diss., University of Illinois, 2010.

Haskell, Molly. *From Reverence to Rape: The Treatment of Women in the Movies*. Chicago: University of Chicago Press, 1974.

Hatch, Kristen. "Discipline and Pleasure: Shirley Temple and the Spectacle of Child Loving." *Camera Obscura* 27.1 (2012): 127–155.

———."Fille Fatale: Regulating Images of Adolescent Girls, 1962–1996." In *Sugar, Spice, and Everything Nice*, edited by Frances Gateward and Murray Pomerance, 163–181. Detroit: Wayne State University Press, 2002.

———."Little Butches: Tomboys in Hollywood Film." In *Mediated Girlhoods: New Explorations of Girls' Media Culture*, edited by Mary Celeste Kearney, 75–92. New York: Peter Lang, 2011.

Helford, Elyce Rae. *Fantasy Girls: Gender in the New Universe of Science Fiction and Fantasy Television*. Lanham, MD: Rowman and Littlefield, 2000.

Hentges, Sarah. *Pictures of Girlhood: Modern Female Adolescence on Film*. Jefferson, NC: McFarland, 2006.

Herrmann, Anne. *Queering the Moderns: Poses/Portraits/Performances*. New York: Palgrave, 2000.

Hershey, Laura. "Choosing Disability." *Ms.*, 1994. 26–32. Reprinted in *Reconstructing Gender: A Multicultural Anthology*, edited by Estelle Disch, 546–554. Mountain View, CA: Mayfield Publishing, 1997.

Hills, Laura and Eileen Kennedy. "Space Invaders at Wimbledon: Televised Sport and Deterritorialization." *Sociology of Sport Journal* 23.4 (2006): 419–437.

Hine, Gabrielle Joanna. "Shaping Motherhood: Representations of Pregnancy in Popular Media." PhD diss., University of Otago, 2011.

Hobbs, Renee. "Media Literacy, General Semantics, and K–12 Education." *ETC: A Review of General Semantics* 61.1 (2004): 24–28.

Hodges, Graham Russell Gao. *Anna May Wong: From Laundryman's Daughter to Hollywood Legend*. New York: Palgrave, 2004.

Holmes, Su, and Diane Negra. "Introduction." In *In the Limelight and under the Microscope: Forms and Function of Female Celebrity*, edited by Su Holmes and Diane Negra, 1–16. New York: Continuum, 2011.

Holmes, Su, and Sean Redmond. "Introduction." In *Framing Celebrity: New Directions in Celebrity Culture*, edited by Su Holmes and Sean Redmond, 1–16. New York: Routledge, 2006.

———."Introduction to Section IV: Producing Fame: 'Because *I'm* Worth It.'" In *Framing Celebrity: New Directions in Celebrity Culture*, edited by Su Holmes and Sean Redmond, 189–192. New York: Routledge, 2006.

Holmlund, Christine. "'Brand Arnold' in Transition, in Place." Celebrity Studies Conference. Deakin University, Burwood, Australia. December 14, 2012.

Holtzman, Linda. "Mining the Invisible: Teaching and Learning Media Literacy." *American Behavioral Scientist* 48.1 (2004): 108–118.

Ifekwunigwe, Jayne O. "Venus and Serena Are 'Doing It' for Themselves: Theorizing Sporting Celebrity, Class, and Black Feminism for the Hip-Hop Generation." In *Marxism, Cultural Studies, and Sport*, edited by Ben Carrington and Ian McDonald, 130–153. New York: Routledge, 2009.

Isoke, Zenzele. *Urban Black Women and the Politics of Resistance*. New York: Palgrave Macmillan, 2013.

Jarman, Michelle. "Cultural Consumption and Rejection of Precious Jones: Pushing Disability into the Discussion of Sapphire's *Push* and Lee Daniels's *Precious*." *Feminist Formations* 24.2 (2012): 163–185.

Johnson, Derek. *Media Franchising: Creative License and Collaboration in the Culture Industries*. New York: New York University Press, 2013.

Johnson, Raelyn C. "Blackgirl Rules! Publisher Kenya James Wins Our 2003 Tennpreneur of the Year Award." *Black Enterprise* (September 2003): T4–5.

Julien, Isaac, and Kobena Mercer. "Introduction: De Margin and De Centre." *Screen* 29.4 (1988): 2–10.

Kaare, Birgit Hertzberg, Petter Bae, Jan Heim, and Tor Endestad. "In the Borderland between Family Orientation and Peer Culture: The Use of Communication Technologies among Norwegian Tweens." *New Media and Society* 9.4 (2007): 603–624.

Kaplan, Elaine Bell. *Not Our Kind of Girl: Unraveling the Myths of Black Teenage Motherhood*. Berkeley: University of California Press, 1997.

Katz, Cindi. "Childhood as Spectacle: Relays of Anxiety and the Reconfiguration of the Child." *Cultural Geographies* 15.1 (2008): 5–17.

Kaveney, Roz. *Teen Dreams: Reading Teen Film and Television from "Heathers" to "Veronica Mars."* London: I. B. Tauris, 2006.

Kearney, Mary Celeste. "Birds on the Wire: Troping Teenage Girlhood through Telephony in Mid-Twentieth-Century U.S. Media Culture." *Cultural Studies* 19.5 (2005): 568–601.

———. "Coalescing: The Development of Girls' Studies." *NWSA Journal* 21.9 (2009): 1–28.

———. *Girls Make Media*. New York: Routledge, 2006.

———. "Girls' Media Studies 2.0." In *Mediated Girlhoods: New Explorations of Girls' Media Culture*, edited by Mary Celeste Kearney, 1–14. New York: Peter Lang, 2011.

———. "New Directions: Girl-Centered Media Studies for the Twenty-First Century." *Journal of Children and the Media* 2.1 (2008): 82–83.

———. "Recycling Judy and Corliss: Transmedia Exploitation and the First Teen-Girl Exploitation Trend." *Feminist Media Studies* 4.3 (2004): 265–295.

Kellner, Douglas, and Jeff Share. "Critical Media Literacy Is Not an Option." *Learning Inquiry* 1.1 (2007): 59–69.

———. "Toward Critical Media Literacy: Core Concepts, Debates, Organizations, and Policy." *Discourse: Studies in the Cultural Politics of Education* 26.3 (2005): 369–386.

Kenaga, Heidi. "Making the 'Studio Girl': The Hollywood Studio Club and Industry Regulation of Female Labour." *Film History* 18.2 (2006): 129–139.

Kennedy, Tanya Ann. "Nice White Girls in/from Africa: The Visibility of Culture and Invisibility of Globalization." *New Global Studies* 6.1 (2012): n.p.

Kenny, Lorraine Delia. *Daughters of Suburbia: Growing Up White, Middle Class, and Female*. New Brunswick: Rutgers University Press, 2000.

Kincaid, James. "Hannah Montana's Bare, Unprotected Back: Miley Cyrus's *Vanity Fair* Outing." *Velvet Light Trap* 65 (2010): 5–6.

King, Wilma. *African American Childhoods: Historical Perspectives from Slavery to Civil Rights*. New York: Palgrave, 2005.

Latimer, Heather. "Popular Culture and Reproductive Politics: *Juno, Knocked Up*, and the Enduring Legacy of *The Handmaid's Tale*." *Feminist Theory* 10.2 (2009): 211–226.

Lipkin, Elline. *Girls' Studies*. Berkeley: Seal Press, 2009.

Livingstone, Sonia. "Do the Media Harm Children? Reflections on New Approaches to an Old Problem." *Journal of Children and Media* 1.1 (2007): 5–14.

———. "Engaging with Media: A Matter of Literacy?" *Communication, Culture, and Critique* 1.1 (2008): 51–62.

Lowe, Melanie. "Colliding Feminisms: Britney Spears, 'Tweens,' and the Politics of Reception." *Popular Music and Society* 26.2 (2003): 123–140.

Luttrell, Wendy. "Where Inequality Lives in the Body: Teenage Pregnancy, Public Pedagogies, and Individual Lives." *Sport, Education, and Society* 16.3 (2011): 295–308.

Maira, Sunaina Marr. *Desis in the House: Indian American Youth Culture in New York City*. Philadelphia: Temple University Press, 2002.

Maplesden, Allison. "Keisha Castle-Hughes: A Case Study of Contemporary Celebrity in Aotearoa, New Zealand." *Celebrity Studies* 1.4 (2010): 351–357.

Marshall, P. David. *Celebrity and Power: Fame in Contemporary Culture*. Minneapolis: University of Minnesota Press, 1997.

May, Elaine Tyler. *Homeward Bound: American Families in the Cold War Era*. Rev. ed. New York: Basic Books, 2008.

Mayer, Vicki. "Living Telenovelas/Telenovelizing Life: Mexican American Girls' Identities and Transnational Telenovelas." *Journal of Communication* 53.3 (2003): 479–495.

———. *Producing Dreams, Consuming Youth: Mexican Americans and Mass Media*. New Brunswick: Rutgers University Press, 2003.

Mayne, Judith. *Cinema and Spectatorship*. New York: Routledge, 1993.

Mazzarella, Sharon R. "Coming of Age Too Soon: Journalistic Practice in U.S. Newspaper Coverage of 'Early Puberty' in Girls." *Communication Quarterly* 58.1 (2010): 36–58.

———, ed. *Girl Wide Web: Girls, the Internet, and the Negotiation of Identity*. New York: Peter Lang, 2005.

———. "How Are Girls' Studies Scholars (and Girls Themselves) Shaking Up the Way We Think about Girls and Media?" In *Twenty Questions about Youth and the Media*, edited by Sharon R. Mazzarella, 253–266. New York: Peter Lang, 2007.

———. "Reflecting on Girls' Studies and the Media: Current Trends and Future Directions." *Journal of Children and the Media* 2.1 (2008): 75–87.

Mazzarella, Sharon R., and Norma Pecora. "Girls in Crisis: Newspaper Coverage of Adolescent Girls." *Journal of Communication Inquiry* 31.1 (2007): 6–27.

———. "Revisiting Girls' Studies: Girls Creating Sites for Connection and Action." *Journal of Children and the Media* 1.2 (2007): 105–125.

McCarthy, Anna. *Ambient Television: Visual Culture and Public Space.* Durham: Duke University Press, 2001.

McDonnell, Andrea Marie. "Just Like Us: Celebrity Gossip Magazines in American Popular Culture." PhD diss., University of Michigan, 2012.

McRobbie, Angela. *Feminism and Youth Culture.* 2nd ed. New York: Routledge, 2000.

McRobbie, Angela, and Sarah L. Thornton. "Rethinking 'Moral Panic' for Multi-mediated Social Worlds." *British Journal of Sociology* 46.4 (1995). Reprinted in Angela McRobbie, *Feminism and Youth Culture,* 2nd ed., 180–197. New York: Routledge, 2000.

Mendes, Kaitlynn, and Kumarini Silva. "Girls, Boys, and 'Girlhood' Studies." *Feminist Media Studies* 9.1 (2009): 109–111.

Miller, Toby, Jim McKay, and Randy Martin. "Courting Lesbianism." *Women and Performance* 21.11 (1999): 211–234.

Mitchell, Claudia, and Jacqueline Reid-Walsh. "Theorizing Tween Culture within Girlhood Studies." In *Seven Going on Seventeen: Tween Studies in the Culture of Girlhood,* edited by Claudia Mitchell and Jacqueline Reid-Walsh, 1–21. New York: Peter Lang, 2005.

Morgan, Simon. "Historicising Celebrity." *Celebrity Studies* 1.3 (2010): 366–368.

Morrison, James, ed. *Hollywood Reborn: Movie Stars of the 1970s.* New Brunswick: Rutgers University Press, 2010.

Mulvey, Laura. "Visual Pleasure and Narrative Pleasure." *Screen* 16.3 (1975): 6–18.

Nash, Ilana. *American Sweethearts: Teenage Girls in Twentieth-Century Popular Culture.* Bloomington: Indiana University Press, 2006.

———. "Saluting Virgins: Teenage Girls and Patriotism in World War II Films." Paper presented at the Society for Cinema and Media Studies Annual Conference. Atlanta, Georgia. March 2004.

Negra, Diane. 2001 *Off-White Hollywood: American Culture and Ethnic Female Stardom.* New York: Routledge.

Negra, Diane, and Su Holmes. "Introduction." Special issue: "Going Cheap? Female Celebrity in Reality, Tabloid, and Scandal Genres." *Genders* 48 (2008). http://www.genders.org/g48/g48_negraholmes.html (accessed May 23, 2013).

Negra, Diane, and Yvonne Tasker. "Introduction: Feminist Politics and Postfeminist Culture." In *Interrogating Postfeminism: Gender and the Politics of Popular Culture,* edited by Diane Negra and Yvonne Tasker, 1–26. Durham, NC: Duke University Press, 2007.

Nelson, Cary, and Dilip Parameshwar Gaonkar, eds. *Disciplinarity and Dissent in Cultural Studies.* New York: Routledge, 1996.

Nishime, LeiLani. "Guilty Pleasures: Keanu Reeves, Superman, and Racial Outing." *East Main Street: Asian American Popular Culture,* edited by Shilpa Davé, LeiLani Nishime, and Tasha Oren, 273–291. New York: New York University Press, 2005.

O'Connor, Jane. *The Cultural Significance of the Child Star.* New York: Routledge, 2008.

Odem, Mary E. *Delinquent Daughters: Protecting and Policing Adolescent Female Sexuality in the United States, 1885–1920.* Chapel Hill: University of North Carolina Press, 1995.

Ono, Kent A. "*Mad Men*'s Postracial Figuration of a Racial Past." In *Mad Men, Mad World: Sex, Politics, and Style in the 1960s*, edited by Lauren M. E. Goodlad, Lilya Kaganovsky, and Robert A. Rushing, 300–319. Durham: Duke University Press, 2013.

———. "Postracism: A Theory of the 'Post-' as Political Strategy." *Journal of Communication Inquiry* 34.2 (2010): 227–233.

Ono, Kent A., and Vincent N. Pham. *Asian Americans and the Media*. Cambridge: Polity, 2009.

Ono, Kent A., and John M. Sloop. "The Critique of Vernacular Discourse." *Communication Monographs* 62.1 (1995): 19–46.

Owens, Susan A., Leah R. Vande Berg, and Sarah R. Stein. *Bad Girls: Cultural Politics and Media Representations of Transgressive Women*. New York: Peter Lang, 2007.

Peiss, Kathy. *Cheap Amusements: Working Women and Leisure in Turn-of-the-Century New York*. Philadelphia: Temple University Press, 1986.

Pillow, Wanda. *Unfit Subjects: Educational Policy and the Teen Mother*. New York: Routledge, 2004.

Pimpare, Stephen. "The Welfare Queen and the Great White Hope." *New Political Science* 32.3 (2010): 453–457.

Probyn, Elspeth. "Choosing Choice: Images of Sexuality and 'Choiceoisie' in Popular Culture." In *Negotiating at the Margins: The Gendered Discourses of Power and Resistance*, edited by Sue Fisher and Kathy Davis, 278–294. New Brunswick: Rutgers University Press, 1993.

Projansky, Sarah. "Girls Who Act Like Women Who Fly: Jessica Dubroff as Cultural Troublemaker." *Signs: Journal of Women in Culture and Society* 23.3 (1998): 771–807.

———. "Mass Magazine Cover Girls: Some Reflections on Postfeminist Girls and Postfeminism's Daughters." In *Interrogating Postfeminism: Gender and the Politics of Popular Culture*, edited by Yvonne Tasker and Diane Negra, 40–72. Durham: Duke University Press, 2007.

———. *Watching Rape: Film and Television in Postfeminist Culture*. New York: New York University Press, 2001.

Quart, Alissa. *Branded: The Buying and Selling of Teenagers*. New York: Basic Books, 2003.

Redmond, Sean. "The Whiteness of Stars: Looking at Kate Winslet's Unruly White Body." In *Stardom and Celebrity: A Reader*, edited by Sean Redmond and Su Holmes, 263–274. Thousand Oaks, CA: Sage, 2007.

Renold, Emma. "Queering Masculinity: Re-theorizing Contemporary Tomboyism in the Schizoid Space of Innocent/Heterosexualized Young Femininities." *Girlhood Studies* 1.2 (2008): 129–151.

Resnick, David. "Life in an Unjust Community: A Hollywood View of High School Moral Life." *Journal of Moral Education* 37.1 (2008): 99–113.

Reyes, Luis, and Peter Rubie. *Hispanics in Hollywood: A Celebration of 100 Years in Film and Television*. Hollywood: Lone Eagle, 2000.

Roberts, Dorothy. *Killing the Black Body: Race, Reproduction, and the Meaning of Liberty*. New York: Vintage, 1998.

Roberts, Kimberly. "Girl Power." In *Girlhood in America: An Encyclopedia*, edited by Miriam Forman-Brunell, 312–316. Santa Barbara, CA: ABC-CLIO, 2001.

Robinson, Kerry H., and Cristyn Davies. "'She's Kickin' Ass, That's What She's Doing!': Deconstructing Childhood 'Innocence' in Media Representations." *Australian Feminist Studies* 23.57 (2008): 343–357.

Savage, Jon. *Teenage: The Creation of Youth Culture*. New York: Viking, 2007.

Scheiner, Georganne. *Signifying Female Adolescence: Film Representations and Fans, 1920–1950*. Westport, CT: Praeger, 2000.

Schrum, Kelly. *Some Wore Bobby Sox: The Emergence of Teenage Girls' Culture, 1920–1945*. New York: Palgrave, 2004.

Schultz, Brad. *Sports Broadcasting*. Boston: Focal Press, 2002.

Schultz, Jaime. "Reading the Catsuit: Serena Williams and the Production of Blackness at the 2002 U.S. Open." *Journal of Sport and Social Issues* 29.3 (2005): 338–357.

Schwartz-DuPre, Rae Lynn. "Portraying the Political: *National Geographic*'s 1985 Afghan Girl and the U.S. Alibi for Aid." *Critical Studies in Media Communication* 27.4 (2010): 336–356.

Shary, Timothy. *Generation Multiplex: The Image of Youth in Contemporary American Cinema*. Austin: University of Texas Press, 2002.

———. *Teen Movies: American Youth on Screen*. London: Wallflower, 2005.

Shohat, Ella. *Taboo Memories, Diasporic Voices*. Durham: Duke University Press, 2006.

Silliman, Jael, Marlene Gerber Fried, Loretta Ross, and Elena R. Gutiérrez. "Women of Color and Their Struggle for Reproductive Justice." In *Undivided Rights*. Boston: South End Press, 2004. Reprinted in *Women's Voices: Feminist Visions: Classic and Contemporary Readings*, 5th ed., edited by Susan M. Shaw and Janet Lee, 340–347. New York: McGraw-Hill, 2012.

Silverstein, Helena. *Girls on the Stand: How Courts Fail Pregnant Minors*. New York: New York University Press, 2009.

Snead, James A. *White Screens, Black Images: Hollywood from the Dark Side*. New York: Routledge, 1994.

Spencer, Nancy E. "From 'Child's Play' to 'Party Crasher': Venus Williams, Racism, and Professional Women's Tennis." In *Sport Stars: The Cultural Politics of Sporting Celebrity*, edited by David L. Andrews and Steven J. Jackson, 87–101. New York: Routledge, 2001.

———. "Sister Act VI: Venus and Serena Williams at Indian Wells: 'Sincere Fictions' and White Racism." *Journal of Sport and Social Issues* 28.2 (2004): 115–135.

Springer, Kimberly. "Queering Black Female Heterosexuality." In *Yes Means Yes: Visions of Female Sexual Power and a World without Rape*, edited by Jaclyn Friedman and Jessica Valenti, 77–92. Jackson, TN: Seal Press, 2008. Reprinted in *Women's Voices: Feminist Visions: Classic and Contemporary Readings*, 5th ed., edited by Susan M. Shaw and Janet Lee, 207–212. New York: McGraw-Hill, 2012.

Springhall, John. *Youth, Popular Culture, and Moral Panics: Penny Gaffs to Gangsta Rap, 1830–1996*. New York: St. Martin's Press, 1998.

Staiger, Janet. "Seeing Stars." *Velvet Light Trap* 20 (1983): 10–14. Reprinted in *Stardom: Industry of Desire*, edited by Christine Gledhill, 3–16. New York: Routledge, 1991.

Stillman, Sarah. "'The Missing White Girl Syndrome': Disappeared Women and Media Activism." *Gender and Development* 15.3 (2007): 491–502.

Stockton, Kathryn Bond. *The Queer Child; or, Growing Sideways in the Twentieth Century*. Durham: Duke University Press, 2009.

Strasburger, Victor C., Amy B. Jordan, and Ed Donnerstein. "Health Effects of Media on Children and Adolescents." *Pediatrics* 125.4 (2010): 756–767.

Studlar, Gaylyn. "Oh, 'Doll Divine': Mary Pickford, Masquerade, and the Pedophilic Gaze." *Camera Obscura* 48 (2001): 197–227.

———. *Precocious Charms: Stars Performing Girlhood in Classical Hollywood Cinema*. Berkeley: University of California Press, 2013.

Sweeney, Kathleen. *Maiden USA: Girl Icons Come of Age*. New York: Peter Lang, 2008.

Tajima, Renee. "Lotus Blossoms Don't Bleed: Images of Asian Women." In *Making Waves: An Anthology of Writings by and about Asian American Women*, edited by Asian Women United of California, 308–317. Boston: Beacon Press, 1989.

Taliman, Valerie. "Native Youth Media Project." *Native Peoples* 17.4 (2004): 34–35.

Tapia, Ruby C. "Impregnating Images: Visions of Race, Sex, and Citizenship in California's Teen Pregnancy Prevention Campaigns." *Feminist Media Studies* 5.1 (2005): 7–22.

———. "Prodigal (Non)Citizens: Teen Pregnancy and Public Health at the Border." In *American Pietàs: Visions of Race, Death, and the Maternal*, 91–108. Minneapolis: University of Minnesota Press, 2011.

Tasker, Yvonne. *Spectacular Bodies: Gender, Genre, and the Action Cinema*. New York: Routledge, 1993.

Tibbetts, John C. "Mary Pickford and the American 'Growing Girl.'" *Journal of Popular Film and Television* 29.2 (2001): 50–62.

Tuan, Mia. "On Asian American Ice Queens and Multigeneration Asian Ethnics." *Amerasia Journal* 25.1 (2000): 181–186.

Turner, Graeme. "Approaching Celebrity Studies." *Celebrity Studies* 1.1 (2010): 11–20.

———. *Understanding Celebrity*. London: Sage, 2004.

Turner, Graeme, Frances Bonner, and P. David Marshall. *Fame Games: The Production of Celebrity in Australia*. Melbourne: Cambridge University Press, 2000.

Turner, Sarah E. "Disney Does Race: Black BFFs in the New Racial Moment." *Networking Knowledge* 5.1 (2012). http://ojs.meccsa.org.uk/index.php/netknow/article/view/250 (accessed May 23, 2013).

Urla, Jacqueline, and Alan C. Swedlund. "The Anthropometry of Barbie: Unsettling Ideals of the Feminine Body in Popular Culture." In *Deviant Bodies: Critical Perspectives on Difference in Science and Popular Culture*, edited by Jennifer Terry and Jacqueline Urla, 277–313. Bloomington: Indiana University Press, 1995.

Valdivia, Angharad N. "Latina Girls and Communication Studies." *Journal of Children and Media* 2.1 (2008): 86–87.

————."Mixed Race on the Disney Channel: From *Johnny Tsunami* through *Lizzie McGuire* and Ending with *The Cheetah Girls.* In *Mixed Race Hollywood,* edited by Mary Beltrán and Camilla Fojas, 269–289. New York: New York University Press, 2008.

Vande Berg, Leah R., Lawrence A. Wenner, and Bruce E. Gronbeck. "Media Literacy and Television Criticism: Enabling an Informed and Engaged Citizenry." *American Behavioral Scientist* 48.2 (2004): 219–228.

Vargas, Lucila. "Transnational Media Literacy: Analytic Reflections on a Program with Latina Teens." *Hispanic Journal of Behavioral Sciences* 28.2 (2006): 267–285.

Vered, Karen Orr. "White and Black in Black and White: Management of Race and Sexuality in the Coupling of Child-Star Shirley Temple and Bill Robinson." *Velvet Light Trap* 39 (1997): 52–65.

Walkerdine, Valerie. *Daddy's Girl: Young Girls and Popular Culture.* Cambridge: Harvard University Press, 1997.

Wall, Cheryl. "On Dolls, Presidents, and Little Black Girls." *Signs* 35.4 (2010): 796–801.

Wanzo, Rebecca. "The Era of Lost (White) Girls: On Body and Event." *Differences: A Journal of Feminist Cultural Studies* 19.2 (2008): 99–126.

————. *The Suffering Will Not Be Televised: African American Women and Sentimental Political Storytelling.* Albany: State University of New York Press, 2009.

Ware, Susan. *Still Missing: Amelia Earhart and the Search for Modern Feminism.* New York: Norton, 1993.

Wehmeyer, Jim. "Critical Media Studies and the North American Media Literacy Movement." *Cinema Journal* 39.4 (2000): 94–101.

Weiss, Andrea. *Vampires and Violets: Lesbians in Film.* New York: Penguin, 1993.

White, Mimi. "The Attractions of Television: Reconsidering Liveness." In *Mediaspace: Place, Scale, and Culture in a Media Age,* edited by Nick Couldry and Anna McCarthy, 75–91. New York: Routledge, 2004.

Whitney, Allison. "Gidget Goes Hysterical." In *Sugar, Spice, and Everything Nice,* edited by Frances Gateward and Murray Pomerance, 55–71. Detroit: Wayne State University Press, 2002.

Wilcox, Rhonda V., and David Lavery, eds. *Fighting the Forces: What's at Stake in "Buffy the Vampire Slayer."* Lanham, MD: Rowman and Littlefield, 2002.

Williamson, Milly. "Female Celebrities and the Media: The Gendered Denigration of the 'Ordinary' Celebrity." *Celebrity Studies* 1.1 (2010): 118–120.

Willis, Jessica L. "Sexual Subjectivity: A Semiotic Analysis of Girlhood, Sex, and Sexuality in the Film *Juno.*" *Sexuality and Culture* 12.4 (2008): 240–256.

Wood, Bret. "Lolita Syndrome." *Sight and Sound* 4.6 (1994): 32–34.

Yano, Christine. *Crowning the Nice Girl: Gender, Ethnicity, and Culture in Hawai'i's Cherry Blossom Festival.* Honolulu: University of Hawaii Press, 2006.

Zaslow, Emilie. *Feminism, Inc.: Coming of Age in Girl Power Media Culture.* New York: Palgrave Macmillan, 2009.

Zook, Kristal Brent. "Lover." In *Black Women's Lives: Stories of Pain and Power,* 29–48. New York: Nation Books, 2006.

Italicized page numbers refer to an illustration or caption on the page.

are/what they do (athletes, celebrities, etc.), 61, 65; girls functioning as social symbols (often nameless), 61–62, 65; girls in peril, 83–92; girls of color, 63, 87, 220; Ophelia Thesis, 64; out-of-focus photos, 87–88; pathos, 87–88; personal challenges, 71; postracial girls, 69–70, 77, 131, 140, 144, 154, 209, 218; race, 86–87; racialized teen celebrities, 73; social issues, 63; social successes, 63; spectacularization of girls, 58–59; sports stars, 65, 78–83; stars of color, 72–77; teen celebrities, 70–77; transformative politics, 60–61; white girls, 61, 63, 64, 78, 92, 219–220

magazines aimed at teen girls, 13

Maiden USA (Sweeney), 228n35

Majoli, Iva, 128, 145

Mallory (*Spiderwick Chronicles* character), 202

Mark (*Juno* character), 121–122

Marris, Jacqueline, 84, 85, 88–90, 93

Marsh, Jamon, 155, 173, 178

masculinity, 47, 53

Mauresmo, Amélie: Davenport, Lindsay, 135–136; defined as a girl, 20; junior competitions, 147; lesbianism, 135–136; media visibility, 130; 1998, 129; 1999 Australian Open, 135–136; celebrity status, 2, 21; physicality, 135; queer girls, 8; stereotype of, 148

Mayer, Vicki, 16

Mayne, Judith, 54, 55

McCann, Madeleine, 84

McClain, China Anne, 2, 7

McCullough, Richard: Gunn, Sakia, killing of, 155–156, 162–165, 168; plea bargain, 156, 159; trial testimony, 164–165; warrant for arrest, 160

McDaniel, Hattie, 53

McEachern, Reva, 176

McEnroe, Patrick, 149

McGuire, Lizzie (*Lizzie McGuire* character), 2, 16

McNeil, Lori, 151

McNichol, Kristy, 230n7

McRobbie, Angela, 5, 13–14

mean girls, 2, 8, 15–16, 85, 114

Mean Girls (film): Cady (character), 113–115, 243n107; Damien (character), 114–116, 243n107; exceptionalism of, 107; femininity, 115; genre-defying girl film, 106; Gonick, Marnina, 113; heteronormativity, 21, 157; hyper-sexualization in, 104–105;

Janis (character), 114–116, 243n107; Kevin (character), 114–115; Lohan, Lindsay, 9, 98, 103, 104, 113–114, 242n71; loss of innocence for the child actor, 103; meanness, 114, 126; pedagogical nature, 107; protectionist discourse, 103; public discussion about, 95, 97, 113; queer girls, 114–116, 126, 243n108; racialized heterosexuality, 114–115; Regina (character), 114; response of girl audiences, 113; teen girl film genre, 99; themes, 125

meanness: heteronormativity, 114–115, 126, 243n107; *Mean Girls* (film), 126

media: alternative (*See* Gunn, Sakia); alternative girls' presence in, 17, 94, 130; antiracism on live television, 144–154; "blonde world" presented by, 8; celebrity culture, 6–7, 20, 59; deregulation, 12, 18; dominant, 10, 17, 218, 220–221, 223; femininity, 59; girl films, 25–56; girlhood, diverse, 220; girls, damage to, 22; girls, representations of (1990–2012), 11–13, 26, 58, 222; girls' capacity to carry media franchises, 225; girls' relationship to, 186–191, 194, 197; live/near-live sports television, 132; local (*see* Gunn, Sakia); mainstream, 10, 15, 22, 37, 43, 57, 64, 110–111 (*see also* Gunn, Sakia); marketing, 4, 5, 6, 8, 13, 17, 18, 29, 30, 53, 73, 95, 186, 200, 202, 214, 223, 228n57; moral panic, 22; national, 62, 92, 224 (*see also* Gunn, Sakia); racism in, 202–203; scholarship, effect on, 188; sexualization of girls, 213–214; spectacularization of girls, 5–6, 6–7; television's representation of girls, 203–204

media audiences research, 182, 187, 190–191

media culture: adoration and denigration of girls, 15; queer girls, 1, 99

media effects, 182, 188

media literacy, children's, 189–190

media literacy scholarship, 215, 222

media production by girls, 15, 188–189, 223

Media Project, 191–193

media studies: Asian American media studies, 10; feminist girls' media studies, 13–17, 221, 224, 226; resistant audiences, 182, 190; resistant readings, 10, 14, 21, 65, 132

Meet Corliss Archer ("meta-property"), 225

Mercer, Kobena, 219

methodology: alternative representations of girls, 21; Asian American media studies, 10; critical method, 158; empirical methods, 218; ethnography, 16; feminist film studies methodology, 98–99, 219, 221, 224;

Sarah Projansky is Professor of Film and Media Arts and of Gender Studies at the University of Utah. She is the author of *Watching Rape: Film and Television in Postfeminist Culture* (2001, New York University Press) and coeditor of *Enterprise Zones: Critical Positions on Star Trek* (1995, Westview).